The Quest for the Fictional Jesus

The Quest for the Fictional Jesus

Gospel Rewrites, Gospel (Re)Interpretation,
and Christological Portraits within Jesus Novels

MARGARET E. RAMEY

PICKWICK *Publications* · Eugene, Oregon

THE QUEST FOR THE FICTIONAL JESUS
Gospel Rewrites, Gospel (Re)Interpretation, and Christological Portraits within
Jesus Novels

Pickwick Publications
An Imprint of Wipf and Stock Publishers
199 W. 8th Ave., Suite 3
Eugene, OR 97401

www.wipfandstock.com

ISBN 13: 978-1-61097-738-8

Cataloguing-in-Publication data:

Ramey, Margaret E.

The quest for the fictional Jesus : gospel rewrites, gospel (re)interpretation, and christological portraits within Jesus novels / Margaret E. Ramey.

xvi + 186 pp. ; 23 cm. Includes bibliographical references.

ISBN 13: 978-1-61097-738-8

1. Jesus Christ—Fiction. 2. Bible. New Testament—History of Biblical events—Fiction. 3. Jesus Christ—Person and offices. I. Title.

BT203 R28 2013

Manufactured in the U.S.A.

Dedicated to Tommy and Betty Ramey,
my loving and supportive parents
who shared with me both the love of reading and the love of Jesus

And there are also many other things which Jesus did,
which if they were written in detail,
I suppose that even the world itself
would not contain the books that would be written.

John 21:25

Contents

Preface

JESUS' STORY HAS BEEN retold in various forms and fashions for centuries. Jesus novels, a subset of the historical fiction genre, are one of the latest means of not only re-imagining the man from Galilee but also of rewriting the canonical Gospels. This work explores the Christological portraits constructed in four of those novels while also using the novels to examine the intertextual play of these Gospel rewrites with their Gospel progenitors.

Chapter 1 offers a prolegomenon to the act of fictionalizing Jesus that discusses the relationship between the person and his portraits and the hermeneutical circle created by these texts as they both rewrite the Gospels and stimulate a rereading of them. It also establishes the "preposterous" methodology that will be used when reexamining the Gospels "post" reading the novels. Chapters 2 to 5 offer four case studies of "complementing" and "competing" novels and the techniques they use to achieve these aims: Anne Rice's *Christ the Lord: Out of Egypt*; Neil Boyd's *The Hidden Years*; Nino Ricci's *Testament*; and José Saramago's *The Gospel according to Jesus Christ*. Chapter 6 begins an examination of a specific interpretive circle based upon Jesus' temptation in the wilderness. Beginning with the synoptic accounts of that event, the chapter then turns to how Jesus' testing has been reinterpreted and presented in two of the novels. Returning to the Gospel of Matthew's version of the Temptation, chapter 7 offers a "preposterous" examination of that pericope, which asks novel questions of the text and its role with Matthew's narrative context based on issues raised by the Gospel rewrites. This monograph concludes by suggesting that Jesus novels, already important examples of the reception history of the Gospels, can also play a helpful role in re-interpreting the Gospels themselves.

Acknowledgments

THIS BOOK IS THE result of the efforts and encouragement of many. I wish first to thank Bruce Longenecker, who served as the primary supervisor for this project from its conception to its conclusion. He offered swift and insightful responses to my work and gave guidance and support through some of the more trying times. Even after being appointed to the W. W. Melton Chair at Baylor University, he faithfully continued on in an unofficial, but certainly not unappreciated, supervisorial capacity. Whatever is good and successful about this work can be contributed largely to him and to Dr. Gavin Hopps, who took over as my supervisor upon Prof. Longenecker's departure from St. Andrews. I will always be grateful for Dr. Hopps' willingness to take me on and for his repeated challenges to produce the best thesis possible. His insights have greatly improved what follows, and any flaws that remain are mine alone.

I wish to thank the University of St. Andrews for providing fine work accommodations at the Roundel, where my experience was greatly enhanced by my Black Room colleagues: Aaron Kuecker, Justin Smith, Kelly Liebengood, Kathleen Burt, and Matt Farlow.

The congregation of St. Andrews Episcopal Church holds a special place in my heart. I found a home among them and am most grateful for the opportunity to serve as their youth director. Charlotte, Naomi, Rory, Samuel, Peter, David, Andy, Penny, and John kept me grounded and reminded me of the vital importance of practical application of biblical studies.

I also must thank my extended "urban" family, some of whom were gracious enough to live with me: Mariam Kamell, Dimali Amarasinghe, Annick Vidonne, Jen Kilps, Alissa Jones Nelson, Jo Ann Sharkey, and Melanie, Drew, and Elaine Lewis. Others, such as John Boothby, Kathleen Burt, Whitney Drury, Matt Nelson, Amber and Paul Warhurst, Paul and Eileen Scaringi, and the Chandler family, who never shared a flat with me nevertheless shared their lives and many adventures with me. Many of you have reminded me of what it means to take literally Paul's words of being broth-ers and sisters in Christ.

Thank you to the University of St. Andrews for awarding me the Overseas Research Students award, which provided partial funding for my second and third years of study. Thank you to Rotary International, whose Ambassadorial Scholars program funded my first year of study. The Flor-ence Rotary Club and District 7770 sponsored me for this program, and in particular I would like to thank Joe Stukes and David Michaux. Through Rotary, I met my surrogate parents, Alan and Irene Constable, and also Jerry, Linda-anne, and Claire Beaulier. They have housed me, fed me, driven me around, introduced me to Scottish culture, and offered their untiring support. My experience in Scotland was richer because of them.

My final year of writing was done while teaching at Messiah College. I am privileged to be a part of such a fine institution whose vision for educat-ing and mentoring students coincides so well with my own. My colleagues and the administration have been unfailingly affirmative as I tried to bal-ance my first year of teaching with the final stages of thesis writing.

I am also grateful for the continued support that I have received from those at Truett Seminary. Thank you especially to Todd Still for his encour-agement to begin postgraduate work and for his continued mentorship throughout this process. Thank you also to Scott Baker for helping me access resources at Baylor's library whenever they were not available elsewhere.

Most importantly, I wish to thank my entire family including John, Stephen, Mikki, Brandy, J.T., Will, and Kaitlin but in particular my parents, Betty and Tommy Ramey. I credit my parents with instilling in me a love for learning and the discipline to study and persevere. I cannot thank them enough for all they have given me: countless hours of their time proofread-ing this work, the management of my affairs while I lived overseas, financial aid, phone calls, and their love and belief in me. I would not be where I am nor the person who I am today without them. This book is dedicated to them with much love and gratitude.

Introduction: Jesus and Jesus Stories

WHEN THE EVANGELIST OF the Gospel of John penned the last words of what would become the last canonical gospel, he most likely did not realize how truly prophetic his words were. At that point, the landslide of writings detailing and often inventing those "other things which Jesus did" was just beginning.[1] Starting as a trickle with the non-canonical gospels, they developed over time to include the present deluge of Jesus novels.

In the last century alone, more than four hundred novels and novellas have been written about the life and deeds of Jesus.[2] The list of authors who have tried their hands at creating a literary Lord include such notable names as D. H. Lawrence, Norman Mailer, José Saramago, Gore Vidal, Jeffrey Archer, Anne Rice, and most recently Philip Pullman. Although their writing styles and philosophical agendas vary drastically, they all share a fascination with the man from Galilee, and they are not unique in this interest either. The modern world cannot seem to get enough of stories about Jesus, and if the current publishing trajectory remains steady, then soon it may not be able to contain all of the books being written.

In this book, we will examine the Jesus novel phenomenon and encounter some of the fictional Jesuses that inhabit their narrative worlds. While we will discuss some of the motivations propelling authors to compose Jesus novels, central to our discussion will be the interpretative relationship between the first biographies of Jesus' life—the canonical Gospels—and these modern rewritten tales. In essence, this work will be an examination of the hermeneutical circle created by those intertextual relationships. Our interest

1. In Bruce Metzger's work on canonization, he suggests that the encouragement to write subsequent gospels may have come from John's ending statement (*The Canon of the New Testament*, 166). Marjorie Holmes in the foreword to her novel *Three From Galilee* also includes this verse as legitimation for her fictionalization of Jesus' life.

2. This number comes from the combined efforts of Zeba Crook and myself. Crook maintains a list of the novels on his website: http://http-server.carleton.ca/~zcrook/JesusNovels.htm.

in the novels, however, pertains not only to how modern authors have taken the canonical Gospel material and supplemented and transformed it within these new tales of Jesus' life but also to how interaction with those stories has the potential to alter readers' perspectives of the canonical Gospels once they return to them. This duality of purpose is reflected in the structure of this monograph that after the initial prolegomenon divides into two distinctive halves.

The first half will explore the practice of rewriting as seen in four representative Jesus novels.[3] These texts serve as case studies for two major categories of Jesus novels—those that offer rewrites intent on competing with the Gospels in some manner and those that hope to complement the canonized versions of Jesus' life. By examining individual novels, we will be able to see some standard techniques as well as some unique devices used by authors to either "complement" or "compete" with the canonical Gospels, and through analyzing the novels' overall Christological portraits, we will be better equipped to judge whether the novels themselves are successful in producing complementing or competing portraits through, or sometimes in spite of, the techniques they have employed.

Reading these novels in light of their relationships with the canonical Gospels is only half of the hermeneutical circle though. Part of the intention of rewrites is to reconfigure the way in which readers view the original sources. When the reading pact, which will be explored below, of these textual relations is fully actualized, readers are propelled to return to the Gospels themselves, usually with an altered perspective and often with new insights or questions.

In order to illustrate how Jesus novels can send readers back to the Gospel sources and stimulate "novel" rereadings of them, the second half of the thesis will offer a different type of case study from the first in which we will focus on one particular event in Jesus' life—the Temptation. After analyzing the portrayals of the Temptation in both a complementing rewrite and a competing one, we will return to the Matthean source to see how the ideas and issues raised in the novels inform an exegesis of Matthew 4:1–11.

One purpose of this work is to serve as an introduction to the important contributions that the study of Jesus novels can make to scholarship. The novels in their own right deserve a place in any discussion of reception history of the Gospels. The first half of this monograph focuses more on this contribution and explores not only the manner in which the canonical Gospels are received and rewritten but also the new Christological portraits

---

3. In fact, one of the novels—Saramago's *Gospel*—has even been dubbed "an example of prototypical rewriting" (Ben-Porat, "Introduction," 5).

that the novels offer to popular culture. Yet critical engagement with the novels can also serve even the more traditional field of biblical studies. By using Mieke Bal's theory of "preposterous" interpretation, which will be explained in the following chapter, we will discover how the novels themselves can have a voice in exegesis of the biblical text and can alert us to "novel" questions to ask and new insights to explore.

Before embarking on our quest, however, we first must begin by addressing some basic questions related to this endeavour, such as what a Jesus novel is and how it interacts with other texts and portraits of Jesus, particularly those found in the canonical Gospels. Therefore, we will begin by offering a prolegomenon to the fictionalization of Jesus before turning to our case studies.

PART I

From Jesus to Jesus Texts

1

Prolegomenon to Fictionalizing Jesus

WHAT ARE JESUS NOVELS?

Jesus Novels As Historical Fiction

WHEN TRYING TO CLASSIFY Jesus novels, we find that the first locus of reference providing some delimitation for their form and content is the larger literary genre to which they primarily, but not exclusively, belong—historical fiction. A simple consideration of this genre's title tells a great deal about the nature of the works contained under its umbrella. The fact that "fiction" rather than "history" is the noun found in the title signals that such narratives are first and foremost fiction.[1] Because a work of fiction is a "literary nonreferential narrative text,"[2] it is by definition not required to be externally referential to the actual world in any prescribed way.[3]

While such creative license might at first lead us to believe that Jesus novels can take on virtually any form and portray Jesus in almost any way imaginable, there are limits, albeit broad ones, to their depictions since Jesus novels are not just fiction but specifically *historical* fiction.

1. Cohn, *Distinction*, 162

2. Ibid., 1. See also Harshaw who defines fiction as "language offering propositions which make no claim for truth values in the real world" (Harshaw, "Fictionality," 229).

3. According to leading theorists, so long as these works are internally consistent, no more need be asked for them to be regarded as "true" or meaningful. For discussions on fiction's distinctive nature in terms of referentiality, see Riffaterre, *Fictional Truth*; Cohn, *Distinction*; or Margolin, "Reference," 517–42.

PART I: From Jesus to Jesus Texts

Fictional Characters in Relation to Real-World Counterparts

The adjectival part of this genre's title restricts the content of the novels found under its wide umbrella and points to historical fiction's tendency to depict historical characters, ones that have "real-world counterparts"[4] whether they be Shakespeare, Genghis Khan, or, in this case, Jesus of Nazareth. These historical imports function in anchoring the novel at one level to the external historical world and to other external texts that describe these persons. Therefore, to qualify as a Jesus novel, the novel's fictional Jesus must be externally referential in some way to its real-world counterpart, Jesus of Nazareth. At the very least, the character of Jesus should share the same name and a similar life story with the one who lived and died in the first-century C.E.[5]

Although such a tethering to the real world might at first appear a simple operation, a number of issues and questions immediately arise. For example, what qualifies as a "similar" life story, and precisely how similar must such a narration be to the more established and "authoritative" versions of Jesus' life? What degree of literary license is permitted in adding or subtracting to this most well known of all life stories, and who or what will arbitrate the limits of this license? Definitive answers to such questions are not easily found even though they are interesting to raise and will be explored as we progress. Suffice it to say that the parameters as to what constitutes "similarity" are highly flexible and diverse depending on the arbitrating categories established at the onset of analysis.

While the *historical* moniker of the genre provides one such arbitrating, albeit broad and subject to varying perspectives, category, it does not

4. Ronen, *Possible Worlds*, 143

5. Zeba Crook, who has also worked on classifying the Jesus novel subgenre, adds that in order for a novel to belong to this category its Jesus must be a main character. Novels, such as Par Lagerkvist's *Barabbas* and Lew Wallace's *Ben Hur*, which are primarily about another character and in which Jesus is a minor or brief character, would not qualify under this definition (Crook, "Fictionalizing Jesus").

While there is an important distinction to be made between a novel, such as Gompertz's *Jewish Brother*, which centers on Jesus and his life, and a novel, such as *Ben Hur*, in which Jesus barely appears, I believe that Crook's definition is too restrictive. It would disqualify, for example, Gerd Theissen's *The Shadow of the Galilean*, in which a Jesus character never even appears although one of the predominant aims of the novel is the construction of a fictional portrait of Jesus and the location of that person within his first-century setting. Perhaps a better qualification in determining what is and what is not a Jesus novel is not the size of the Jesus character's role but the extent to which the novel develops a Christological portrait and the impact that its fictional Jesus, seen or unseen, has on the overall plot and on other characters. While I have chosen in this monograph to limit our case studies only to novels in which Jesus is a main character, I believe that the subgenre of Jesus novels should be extended to such marginal cases.

prevent the metamorphosis of the imported historical elements even though it may limit the extent to which they are changed. Precisely because the novels are historical *fiction*, none of these historical details are ever completely safe from transformation once they have been imported into the novels' fictional worlds. With fictional Jesuses, we see a strange tension between faithful correspondence to their external counterpart and creative freedom to reconfigure that character in a variety of ways.

In addition to its real-world counterpart characters, historical fiction is also known for its creation of imaginary characters. These characters are imaginary extensions of the external historical world, but they have an existence only in the novel's fictional world. There, the real-world counterparts and imaginary characters blend together to create an internally coherent new world.[6]

In Jesus novels, we often see such a mixture taking place. Sometimes new characters are invented to narrate Jesus' life from a different point of view, such as Biff in Moore's *Lamb*, and sometimes they are created to add a new plotline, such as when Jesus falls in love with Avigail in Rice's *Christ the Lord: The Road to Cana*. Whatever their purpose or function, the ability of these imaginary characters to coexist plausibly with real-world counterparts within the new fictional world is a hallmark of historical fiction in general and is seen in Jesus novels as well.[7]

Fictional Worlds in Relation to the Actual World

Besides restraining the extent to which a fictional Jesus can differ from its historical counterpart, historical fiction also restricts the liberty of fiction in its creation of possible worlds. Because Jesus novels are *historical* fiction, they are limited to portraying the actual, physical world of the past—first-century Palestine in the case of Jesus novels. This restriction differentiates them from other fictional novels with Jesus characters, such as J. F. Girzone's *Joshua*, that transport him into the modern world or into any other world for that matter.

Yet like anything imported from the actual world into the fictional world, even the historical setting is not safe from reconfiguration. Jesus novels, such as Vidal's *Live From Golgotha*, sometimes transgress the boundaries of their first-century settings and cross into other arenas of space and time to present multiple historical worlds.[8] As long as the narrative world

6. Harshaw, "Fictionality," 246.

7. Dolezel, "Fictional and Historical Narrative," 257.

8. *Live From Golgotha* is a paradigmatic borderline case in classifying Jesus novels.

that the fictional Jesus inhabits principally resembles the actual first-century one, the work may still be considered a Jesus novel.[9]

Finally, the fact that Jesus novels belong to the genre of historical fiction distinguishes them from Christ-figure novels, such as Graham Greene's *The Power and the Glory* or C. S. Lewis's *The Chronicles of Narnia*. These novels typically are not set in the first-century, nor do they contain a fictional Jesus. Instead, these are better classified as "global allusions" because they appropriate motifs from Jesus' life, such as his martyrdom, that are then refigured in the lives of completely different characters, such as Graham's whiskey priest or Lewis's Aslan.[10]

Jesus Novels As Rewrites

Besides belonging to the genre of historical fiction, Jesus novels also fall under the category of Gospel rewrites.[11] This additional level of external reference, this time to the canonical Gospels specifically rather than to

---

Arguably, it does belong outside the genre of Jesus novels, but its border crossing and portrait of Jesus are so intriguing that it is instructive to include it.

9. Of course, our knowledge of what the first-century world was "actually" like is largely dependent upon ancient texts and artifacts and is itself a textual construction. Thus, the resemblance of these modern Jesus texts to the external ancient world is in large part a question of correspondence to the very Gospel texts that they are rewriting as well as to other ancient texts and artifacts from which historians construct this idea of the "actual" ancient world that shapes our perceptions of what does and what does not constitute a faithful resemblance.

10. Ben-Porat, "Introduction," 4. While in one sense all rewrites, including Jesus novels, are global allusions to their source material, they are more than just allusions by virtue of their intentionality in evoking the original sources and the greater extent to which they import the source material.

11. The idea of Gospel rewrites is similar to the concept of the Rewritten Bible, which was introduced by Geza Vermes to describe post-biblical Jewish literature, such as Josephus's *Jewish Antiquities* or the book of Jubilees (Vermes, *Scripture*, 67–126). Such works retell stories from the Bible in new ways that often include supplementation and interpretation. These fictive supplements to the biblical stories James Kugel calls "narrative expansions." Of them, he says, "A narrative expansion can consist of anything not found in the original biblical story—generally, an additional action performed by one or more of the people in the story or additional words spoken in the course of the events." They can be as small as an inserted new word or as large as entire new episodes (Kugel, *In Potiphar's House*, 6). The difference between Vermes' Rewritten Bible and these Jesus novels, which we are classifying as Gospel rewrites, seems to be one of quantity rather than of quality. They are in essence doing the same type of rewriting, but the novels are lengthier and more sustained in their efforts at rewriting by reproducing multiple episodes from Jesus' life rather than simply one.

ancient Palestine more generally, again limits the extent to which the novel's fictional Jesus can be reinvented.

Rewriting has become a specialty all its own within literary criticism and is popular among those interested in the intertextual nature of texts.[12] In outlining precisely what a rewrite is, Ziva Ben-Porat states that it is "a retelling of a known story in such a way that the resulting text, the rewrite, is simultaneously an original composition and a recognizable rendition, involving a critical rereading of the source."[13]

Rewrites call attention to their intertextual nature by using the original text as the "major building blocks" of their works. Because they build on these earlier works, there is an inherent "reading pact" imbedded within the rewrite, which acts as an interpretative bond between the original and its progeny. When speaking of the "reading pact," we are referring to a set of expectations as to what the text will contain and how it should be read that is activated once the reader becomes aware of the work's particular genre, intended audience, and any other information pertinent to its proper interpretation. This pact denotes a particular way of reading rather than simply pointing out what type of writing a text is.[14] Rewrites depend on the reader's ability to actualize this reading pact encoded within the text's DNA. Once a reader has become aware of the rewrite's connection to the original texts, then those earlier texts can never be discarded as irrelevant because they constantly are being referenced during the reading of the rewrite, and knowledge of them is essential for proper comprehension and interpretation of the rewrite.[15] According to Ben-Porat, "[O]nce a text is perceived as a rewrite it incites the perceiver to read it and process the new information in a particular relation to a declared or assumed source text: mapping from the new text onto the previous one entails the perception of the links as faithful/unfaithful transposition, representations or substitution, and as acceptable/unacceptable omissions, additions and changes."[16] Consequently, the actualization of this reading pact not only affects interpretation of the rewrite but also alters the reader's relationship to and understanding of the original text itself.

In the case of Jesus novels, they are considered *Gospel* rewrites because their "major building blocks" come from the canonical Gospels although

12. Intertextuality, first coined by Julia Kristeva in response to the ideas of Mikhail Bakhtin, refers to the relationships between a text and any other texts that it invokes, whether by implicit allusion or explicit citation (Frow, *Genre*, 48).

13. Ben-Porat, "Saramago's *Gospel* and the poetics of prototypical rewriting," 93.

14. Ibid.

15. Ben-Porat, "Introduction," 5, 6.

16. Ben-Porat, "Saramago's *Gospel*," 94.

additional pieces are also often imported from other texts. These texts may often include the non-canonical gospels, ancient historiographical works, such as those written by Philo or Josephus, and theological treatises.[17] Adele Reinhartz notes in discussing "rewritten Gospels" that in order for a work to qualify as such it must tell a sequential story of Jesus' life based on the Gospel accounts that follow their "overall order and narrative thrust" while still adding supplemental details and presenting the old story in a new and imaginative way.[18] That the Jesus novels are usually rewrites of not just one Gospel but of all four does complicate matters because it means that the reader must constantly be aware of these different texts when analyzing a Gospel rewrite. The four Jesus novels that we will examine as case studies are all clear examples of Gospel rewrites and draw upon material from multiple canonical Gospels.

Readers are first alerted to a novel's status as a Gospel rewrite, and thus to its reading pact that demands engagement with the novel's Gospel sources, by the specific Gospel material appropriated by a novel. There are also other internal cues, such as when a novel refers to itself as a gospel, when a narrator refers to himself or herself as an evangelist, or when the narrator refers to other accounts of Jesus' life, that signal to the reader that the novel is a Gospel rewrite.[19] In addition, paratextual cues, such as titles and information given on dust jackets and introductions, are also helpful in framing the narrative as a Gospel rewrite. For example, the titles *Testament*, *The Gospel according to the Son*, and *The Gospel according to Jesus Christ* all connect the novels with the canonical Gospels and imply that they should be read as other valid versions of Jesus' life.[20]

The varied ways in which each novel engages with the Gospel source material is one of the major areas of interest to this study. Like everything else imported into the fictional world of a Jesus novel, the Gospel material itself is not safe from being transformed. While some rewritings can be mimetic in form and in content, they can also be subversive in their stance

17. Fortney's *The Thomas Jesus* raises an interesting challenge to this rule because its fictional Jesus is more intentionally based on *The Gospel of Thomas'* picture of Jesus rather than on the canonical Gospel Jesus. Yet even this novel is dependent upon the canonical Gospels, particularly for narrative material, which is lacking from the Thomasine sayings gospel, and so also functions as a Gospel rewrite.

18. In her 2009 article, Reinhartz examines the rewriting of the Passion narratives and the characterization of Caiaphas in Sayers' *The Man Born to Be King* and in Asch's *The Nazarene* (Reinhartz, "'Rewritten Gospel,'" 177).

19. Examples of all three of these types of cues can be seen in Saramago's *Gospel*, 192, 200, 204.

20. Ben-Porat, "Saramago's *Gospel*," 94.

toward the Gospels.[21] In fact, subversion or even inversion, particularly of characters' dispositions or roles, are some of the most common practices of rewrites.[22] Such transformations can be achieved not only by calling into question particular events or sayings recorded in the Gospels but also by challenging more essential elements of their narratives, such as their presupposed worldview or their Christological portrayals. The importation of additional characters and events creates further possibilities of subversion by shifting interpersonal dynamics and displaying new facets of the historical characters. How faithful or divergent the rewrite is to its Gospel sources, however, obviously varies with each novel and often from scene to scene within the novel itself.[23] Because the reading pact imbedded within the Jesus novels identifies them as Gospel rewrites, readers are compelled to view these works in light of their relationships with the Gospels and to judge how these novels function as competing or complementing narratives to their sources. This topic is one to which we will return below in section three.

JESUS AND JESUS PORTRAITS

Having established that Jesus novels are primarily works of historical fiction that at least minimally refer to Jesus of Nazareth and to the canonical Gospels, it is important for us to take a step back to examine this person and these sources which the novels rewrite. To do this will involve establishing terminology for the person of Jesus and for his literary portrayals. This endeavor has been aided considerably by Raymond Brown's discussion of different types of Jesus portraits, which he labels the actual Jesus, the historical Jesus, and the Gospel Jesus.[24] A preliminary examination of these "Jesuses" will be helpful since the fictional Jesuses that inhabit these novels correspond to some, if not all, of these portraits.

Actual Jesus

When speaking of the "actual Jesus," Brown refers to the person who lived in Galilee and died in Jerusalem almost two thousand years ago. While many would call this person the historical Jesus, Brown reserves that term for the historiographical portraits that scholars create. He most likely draws this

21. Ben-Porat, "Introduction," 5.
22. Ben-Porat, "Saramago's *Gospel*," 95.
23. Ben-Porat, "Introduction," 6.
24. Brown, *An Introduction to the New Testament*, 105–6.

distinction in order to avoid the confusion between the representation and its referent that often arises with the label "historical Jesus" and with the word "history" in general.[25]

If one were able to create a portrait of the actual Jesus, Brown says that it would portray his life from birth until death. It would include information such as what he looked like, what jokes he laughed at, whether he fell in love, and so on. In short, such a description would include all of the details of interest found in a modern biography. Unfortunately, much of this information has been lost in the recesses of antiquity and is unrecoverable except through imagination. Yet it is precisely "through imagination" where the Jesus novels come in. In their fictional portrayals, the novels answer many of the questions about the actual Jesus that are left unanswered in the Gospel portraits.

Historical Jesus

Moving from the actual person of Jesus to his portrayals, we come to "the historical Jesus." The historical Jesus refers to portraits that are also aimed at recovering and presenting the details of Jesus' actual life. Although the common expectation is that these scholarly reconstructions present Jesus *as he actually was*,[26] their ability to do so is limited by the amount of data

25. Paul Tillich once noted that a great deal of semantic confusion surrounds the term "historical Jesus" because it has been used for both the actual person who lived in first-century Palestine and for the narrative reconstructions of that person based on the results of historical research and written by historians. As Tillich wisely observed, no honest discussion can take place without first distinguishing between these two meanings (Tillich, *Systematic Theology*, 123).

In this monograph, I have chosen to use the term "actual Jesus" when referring to the person who lived in first-century Palestine and "historical Jesus" when referring to the writings of historians about that person. Preserving this distinction is also important for our discussion not only because it helps to avoid confusion but also because it protects us from collapsing the two meanings together and thus falsely assuming that any writing can ever be the same as the people or events about which it speaks. It is a truism that bears repeating—a representation can never be the same as the thing being represented, nor can it be exchanged with its referent (Ankersmit, "Historical Representation," 218; cf. A.C. Danto, *The Transfiguration of the Commonplace*, 120–121).

26. Ranke first popularized the notion that the aim of historiography was to present *history as it actually was* (Ranke, *The Theory and Practice of History*). This conception of not only historiography but also of many of the other "realist" genres is misleading, to say the least (Colie, *The Resources of Kind*, 5; see also Frow, *Genre*, 19). None of their presentations are ever simply and only the subject itself. All inherently involve interpretation in their understanding and reconstructions of actuality. There is no such thing as a genre devoid of subjective perspective and capable of presenting anything merely and only as it actually is or was.

provided by the ancient sources. Also, just as with any Jesus portrait, their depiction is inevitably influenced by the interpretation given to the available source material and by the methodology used in handling it.

When we observe the way in which historical Jesus scholars typically approach the canonical material, we notice that it differs from the method used by other Jesus portrait painters, especially from those who wish to make a harmonized Gospel portrait of Jesus. Whereas harmonizers try to preserve as much canonical material as possible and to unify the evangelists' voices into one seamless narrative, historians usually go behind the Gospels, disassembling their portraits in order to draw out fragments of a historical reality buried beneath the evangelists' theologically redacted layers.[27] Those specializing in this field vary in their opinions on the historicity of the Gospels, with some pronouncing that little of the canonical material can be traced back to Jesus himself and others expressing more confidence in them. As with anything that has been taken apart, the portraits of Jesus reassembled by historical scholars may not be put back together in the same "Gospel" form and typically do not use all of the Gospel pieces, even pieces about whose historicity they are more confident.[28]

Also, the sum of these reassembled historical Jesuses is often more than the individual parts taken from the original sources, and yet the role that interpretation plays in these portraits is not always fully acknowledged.[29] We can see through a quick perusal of the gallery of historical Jesus portraits just how varied their interpretations of what Jesus was *actually* like can be. The works hanging there include portraits as diverse as S. G. F. Brandon's "Jesus the political revolutionary" (1968), Morton Smith's "Jesus the magician" (1978), Géza Vermès' "Jesus the Galilean charismatic" (1981, 1984),

27. In doing this, modern scholars resemble Marcion, who deleted major bits of the Gospels, more than Tatian, who preferred to retain and harmonize all the pieces from the Gospels. Marcion, who accepted only a revised version of Luke's Gospel, rejected the other Gospels as Judaizing Gospels. Hengel compares what Marcion did to modern critics who, in trying to regain the original words of Jesus, strip away whatever they see as redactional layers in order to leave only the actual Jesus sans theological interpretations (Hengel, *Four Gospels*, 32–33).

28. In using a mathematical analogy to explain historical Jesus research, Allison comments, "One can draw any number of curves through a finite set of points to create a thousand different pictures. . . . It is always possible to explain one set of facts with more than one story" (Allison, *Jesus of Nazareth*, 37).

29. Rae criticizes the widespread belief that the actual Jesus can be accessed directly without the "contamination" of interpretation. He censures both those who champion a literal reading of the Bible as a path providing direct access to him and those who believe that the actual Jesus is accessible to any objective observer who uncovers the "neutral" data by stripping back the interpretive layers of the Gospels (Rae, *History and Hermeneutics*, 95).

Bruce Chilton's "Jesus the Galilean rabbi" (1984, 2000), Harvey Falk's "Jesus the Hillelite or proto-Pharisee" or his "Jesus the Essene" (1985), Marcus Borg's "Jesus the spiritual mystic, wisdom teacher, and founder of a revitalization movement" (1987, 1994), or John Dominic Crossan's "Jesus the Galilean Cynic peasant" (1991, 1994).[30] In a separate wing of the gallery, we might peruse the similar "third quest" portraits including such works as E.P. Sanders' "Jesus the eschatological prophet of restoration" (1985, 1993), N.T. Wright's "Jesus the Jewish prophet and forerunner of Christian orthodoxy" (1993, 1996), and Dale C. Allison's "Jesus the millenarian prophet" (1998).

Jesus novelists acquainted with historical Jesus scholarship sometimes intentionally model their fictional creations on different historical Jesuses, and often their approach to the Gospel sources mirrors that of the scholars whose Jesuses they emulate. For instance, with Anne Rice's *Christ the Lord: Out of Egypt*, we see a novel influenced by "third quest" historical Jesus scholarship that expresses more confidence in the historicity of the Gospels and that paints a very Jewish Jesus. In contrast, Steven Fortney's *The Thomas Jesus* provides an example of a fictional Jesus based on the work of the Jesus Seminar that elevates the non-canonical *Gospel of Thomas* as a primary source for uncovering the actual Jesus. By basing their Jesus characters on historical Jesus scholarship, the novelists bolster the historicity of their works and the impression that their fictional Jesuses may represent the actual Jesus.

The Gospel Jesus

The final type of Jesus portrait that Brown discusses is that of the Gospel Jesus. As historical Jesus scholars rightly point out, the Gospel portraits are written from theological perspectives, which make it difficult to discern which parts accurately portray the actual Jesus and which are reflections of the evangelists' faith projected onto that person.

These portraits may seem inadequate and even unhistorical when approached with the assumptions of modern historiography, but that is because they belong to the world of ancient historiography and should be judged according to those standards and not modern ones. Recent genre work on the canonical Gospels has located them within the realm of Greco-Roman

30. Several of these "portrait titles," which are summaries of their works and not official titles, are from Daniel J. Harrington's presidential address to the Catholic Biblical Association cited by Crossan (Crossan, *Historical Jesus*, xxvii–xxviii).

biography or βίος,[31] which David Aune describes as "a specific genre of Greco-Roman historical literature with broad generic features."[32]

Since the chief aim of these ancient biographies was to communicate the essence of a great person and why his or her life was noteworthy rather than to merely detail the facts of that person's life, some events were stressed while others were left unrecorded. Ancient biographies also were not limited to only those events that actually took place, and even fictional elements could be a part of their descriptive portraits. Unlike modern biographies, which require historical veracity, ancient biographies were regarded as truthful representations so long as they were faithful to the person's character by picturing who that person "really" was. Plausibility rather than authenticity was the chief means of distinguishing truth from falsehood in their portrayals.[33]

In many ways, the Gospel portraits are like icons and are even referred to as such in early Byzantine theology.[34] Unlike photographs, which mimetically reproduce their referents with no discrimination to details, icons highlight significant details and suppress those that are less important.[35] They claim to represent what it is most essential about a person and thus are interpretive objects drawing the beholder's gaze to focus on what that person is "really" like. Unlike "realist" genres, iconic imagery draws a distinction between the real and the actual and asserts that reality is more than that which can be empirically observed and reproduced in an imitative fashion.[36] In fact, representing that which is "really real" may require art

31. Burridge, *Four Gospels*, 6–8; Thanks to Justin Smith for his assistance in understanding the issues surrounding genre classification of the Gospels. For further discussions on this matter, see also the following works: Burridge, *What are the Gospels?*; Aune, "Greco-Roman Biography"; Aune, *The New Testament in Its Literary Environment*; Talbert, "Once Again: Gospel Genre," 43; and Talbert, "The Gospel and the Gospels," 33.

32. Aune, *The New Testament in Its Literary Environment*, 29. Richard Bauckham agrees and sees biography as a type of historiography (Richard Bauckham, *Jesus and the Eyewitnesses*, 220, 472–87).

33. Aune, ed. *New Testament*, 64–65.

34. Lepakhin cites Maximus the Confessor from the seventh century as the earliest extant example of someone referring to the Gospels as iconic (Lepakhin, "Text and Icon," 20).

35. Green has a similar discussion comparing images and pictures of God (Green, *Imagining God*, 93–94).

36. Following the ideas of Jüngel (Webster, ed. *Eberhard Jüngel: Theological Essays*, 95–123), Trevor Hart argues for a distinction between actuality and reality rather than an uncritical equation of the two. He says that the future eschatological dimension may very well turn out to be more real than what can be empirically observed in the present (Hart, *Regarding Karl Barth*, 56–57).

that is inherently non-realistic in form, and yet non-realistic should never be equated with completely fictional. Eastern iconic art understands these distinctions and makes a different kind of truth claim than Western "realist" forms of art by asserting that reality can be portrayed, perhaps even better, through non-realistic representations.

When we compare the Gospels to icons, we see that the Gospels also attempt to bring their audiences in contact with different aspects of what the evangelists consider to be the essential features of Jesus' character. Like icons, they train the beholders to see their subject through theological eyes and thus with a clearer gaze on reality.[37] Viewers behold ontological aspects of the real personhood of Jesus through representations that are not entirely actual but are nonetheless real and true, perhaps in even deeper ways.[38]

Also like icons, the Gospels present us with multiple images of Jesus that though different in many aspects are still united on the features that are most representative of Jesus' person. This multiplicity of images helps to prevent viewers from idolatrously equating one image with the person as if it could fully represent or replace that which it signifies. Thus, just as with historical Jesuses, we can speak of many different Gospel Jesuses: the "Matthean Jesus," the "Markan Jesus," the "Lukan Jesus," and the "Johannine Jesus."[39] To these we could add the noncanonical variety, such as the "Thomasine Jesus" or the "Peterine Jesus." When Brown uses the term "Gospel Jesus," he is simply referring to a portrait created by one of the evangelists.

Artists and theologians, however, rarely limit themselves to simply one of the evangelists' portraits when constructing an image of Jesus. In fact, most draw at least a few pieces from each of the four portraits and then reassemble them, often at an unconscious level, to form one new harmonized

37. Paul Tillich likens the Gospels to "expressionist" portraits. He says, "In this approach a painter would try to enter into the deepest levels of the person with whom he deals. And he could do so only by a profound participation in the reality and the meaning of his subject matter. Only then could he paint this person in such a way that his surface traits are neither reproduced as in photography (or naturalistically imitated) nor idealised according to the painter's ideal of beauty but are used to express what the painter has experienced through his participation in the being of his subject. This third way is meant when we use the term 'real picture' with reference to the Gospel records of Jesus as the Christ" (*Systematic Theology*, 133).

38. Likewise, Luke Timothy Johnson has observed that the Jesus whom the Gospels present is real in more senses than can be empirically observed, and therefore, the Gospels are truthful even though the truth that they portray goes beyond actuality (*Real Jesus*, 141–42).

39. Throughout, I will refer to the Gospel authors as "Matthew," "Mark," "Luke," and "John" simply as a shorthand way of referring to the implied authors. This usage does not imply that I am assuming apostolic authorship for these works. The issue of authorship itself is not directly relevant to my work and thus is not addressed.

mosaic of the Gospel Jesus. Of course, each person's harmonized picture of the Gospel Jesus will be different, but so long as the tiles used in constructing that mosaic image are taken from the Gospels and used in a manner complementary to that of the Gospels when repositioned, that image can qualify as a faithful reworking of the Gospel Jesus. When we refer to the idea of the "Gospel Jesus" in this monograph, we are speaking of such a harmonized mosaic, and it is against such a composite portrait that we will compare the fictional Jesuses in each of the novels.

My View of Jesus

In the interest of full disclosure, it is perhaps beneficial to pause and say a word about my own presuppositions regarding the person and portraits of Jesus because my views undoubtedly shape and color much of what follows no matter how much I may strive for objectivity. As a committed member of a Christian faith community, I carry my own set of subjective beliefs that no doubt incline me to have an affinity toward more orthodox views and portraits of Jesus. While I recognize the role of theological interpretation in shaping the canonical Gospels and do not believe that these ancient biographies are simply direct representations of the actual Jesus, I am more likely to join with the proto-orthodox Christian community rather than to contradict it, unless there is compelling evidence to do so, in affirming the Gospel portrayals as faithful and instructive for the Christian faith. Much as Johnson argues, I believe the Jesus encountered in the Gospels to be the "real Jesus" in the sense that his being and person are accurately captured there perhaps precisely because the Gospels do go beyond his earthly actuality and point towards his post-resurrection existence and enthronement.[40] While I agree with historical Jesus scholarship that the theologizing that takes place in the Gospels makes it more difficult to recover the actual Jesus, as a person of faith, I believe that their theologizing is more positive than problematic precisely because it paints a much richer portrait of whom, by faith, I believe Jesus to be.

40. As Johnson argues, the Gospels reveal this real Jesus—the Jesus who was resurrected, who is the Son of God, and who continues to live seated at the right hand of God (Acts 2:34). Their descriptions surpass the boundaries of modern historiographical inquiry and are told from the point of view of resurrection faith. "[T]he *real Jesus* for Christian faith," according to Johnson, "is not simply a figure of the past but very much and above all a figure of the present, a figure, indeed, who defines believers' present by his presence" (Johnson, *Real Jesus*, 141–42).

THE RELATIONSHIP BETWEEN THE GOSPEL JESUS AND FICTIONAL JESUSES, BETWEEN THE GOSPELS AND THE GOSPEL REWRITES

The Fourfold Gospel Boundary

When these novels are examined from a Christian perspective, we find that boundaries are already to some extent established for imaging Jesus. While the plurality of the canonical Gospels may have functioned, at least implicitly, as a stimulus to the production of new Jesus images, this plurality also set limits for the appropriate re-imaging of Jesus. As Richard Burridge explains, "By selecting only four, they [the proto-orthodox Christian community] mapped out the ball park where those who wish to remain in the tradition must play."[41] According to these "rules of play," not all portraits are equally valid, and there are some guidelines by which artists must abide in order for their works to be considered as acceptable orthodox images.

Anyone who has followed the media and witnessed the publicity surrounding the National Geographic's unveiling of the lost *Gospel of Judas* or the Jesus Seminar's inclusion of the *Gospel of Thomas* as the "fifth gospel" offering authentic sayings of the actual Jesus is at least aware that there are more gospels than just the four canonical ones.[42] Indeed, the production of gospels appears to have been a major enterprise during late antiquity.[43] Luke refers to the fact that "many" had written accounts of Jesus' life prior to the writing of his Gospel (1:1). A few of these gospels, although probably not most, may have been roughly contemporary with the canonical Gospels but probably not predecessors of them.[44] So if there were other gospels available, why were only four adopted by the church?[45]

Origen gives an answer to that question when he declares that within the four Gospels the same Lord is being preached (Origen. *Comm. On John,*

---

41. Burridge, *Four Gospels* 177.

42. Funk and Hoover, *Five Gospels.*

43. Aune, ed. *New Testament,* 68. Graham Stanton has counted about thirty Christian writings that designate themselves as "gospels" and were written prior to 600 C.E. (Stanton, *Gospels,* 122).

44. Bauckham, "The Study of Gospel Traditions," 370–71; cf. Stanton, *Jesus and the Gospel,* 88. Crossan is one example of someone who would date some of the non-canonical gospels (e.g., the Gospel of Thomas) or at least some of the earlier sources within those gospels (e.g., the "Cross Gospel" embedded within the Gospel of Peter) prior to the canonical Gospels (Crossan, *Historical Jesus,* 427–29).

45. Stanton says that we have no manuscript evidence that there was ever acceptance of a "fifth" gospel alongside the NT four within mainstream Christianity (Stanton, *Jesus,* 87; cf. Elliott, "Manuscripts, the Codex and the Canon," 87).

5.4 [*ANF* 9:348]). Similarly, Irenaeus writes that it is between the four Gospel pillars that "Christ Jesus is seated" (Against Heresies III.11.8–9 [ANF 1:429]).[46] Since gospels are in essence "Christology in narrative form,"[47] each one, canonical or non-canonical, aims at presenting a Jesus consistent with its author's or community's theological understanding of him. According to the early church's perspective, the "real Jesus" could be found in the four canonical Gospels but not in those other gospels.[48] Therefore, the four Gospels became the canon, the "ruler" against which any other Jesus images should be measured.[49] In order for any of those images to remain within the orthodox camp, their depictions of Jesus needed to fall somewhere between the fourfold boundaries established by the Gospels.

Of course, simply because the Gospels provide a fourfold boundary for orthodox images of Jesus does not mean that they are the only sources from which material can be drawn when constructing a new portrait. As noted above, Jesus novels import material from a variety of places. Many orthodox rewrites freely appropriate material from non-canonical gospels, such as names of unnamed characters in Gospels and additional events. It is not necessarily the sources being used that determine a Jesus novel's relationship to its Gospel sources and the boundaries they have established. Rather, it is the way in which those sources are treated and transformed upon entry into the novel's fictional world that determines whether or not a novel is a faithful rewrite remaining within the fourfold fence.

---

46. Likewise, Burridge suggests, "Somewhere *in between* the four boundaries, running around on the field of play but refusing to be tied down, is the historical Jesus whose character stimulated it all in the first place" (*Four Gospels*, 177).

47. Ibid., 8.

48. Origen comments, "The Church possesses four Gospels, heresy a great many. . . . Many have taken in hand to write, but only four Gospels are recognized" (*Homilies on Luke* 1:5–6). Irenaeus in discussing the canonical Gospels in relation to the non-canonical gospels has this to say: "[T]hese Gospels alone are true and reliable, and admit neither an increase nor diminution of the aforesaid number." He also warns that "all who destroy the form of the Gospel are vain, unlearned, and also audacious; those, [I mean,] who represent the aspects of the Gospel as being either more in number than as aforesaid, or, on the other hand, fewer. The former class [do so], that they may seem to have discovered more than is of the truth; the latter, that they may set the dispensations of God aside" (*Against Heresies* III.11.9 [ANF 1:429]).

49. In a similar manner, Green argues, "God is rendered authoritatively for the Christian imagination in scriptural narrative, [sic] visual images can be judged according to their power to interpret scripture. By this test, even the portrayal of God the Father by Michelangelo has its place in the exegesis of Gen. 1:26–27" (*Imagining God*, 95).

Rewriting the Gospels and Responding to a Gospel Jesus Mosaic

In writing against Valentinian Gnosticism, Irenaeus once described the Gnostic use of Scripture with the analogy of a beautiful jewel-encrusted mosaic of a king. He compared the Gnostics with men who came along and removed the gems from their original positions in that mosaic and rearranged them to form a new picture, one of a dog or a fox, rather than the original image of a king. They then declared their new patterns to be the true ones, and those who had never seen royalty before mistook the picture of an animal for that of a king.[50]

Irenaeus' analogy is also reminiscent of what scholars and artists have done for centuries with the Gospels as they have used them as a mine from which to extract and then reassemble Gospel bits and pieces into new Jesus images. As mentioned earlier, each person begins with some concept of what the Gospel Jesus looks like, and such an idea is usually a mosaic composition drawn from parts of all the Gospels. Then each person responds to that mental image in various ways but typically by becoming either a mosaic mover, one who, like the Gnostics, rearranges the Gospel pieces to form a new pattern, or a gap-filler, one who leaves the Gospel Jesus mosaic in place and works within the spaces between its pieces. This process certainly appears to be at work in Jesus novels as well. Their authors typically function as mosaic movers or gap-fillers depending on the way that they appropriate the Gospels, and their rewrites ultimately relate to these sources in either broadly competing or complementing ways.

Mosaic Movers and Competing Images of Jesus

In glancing back across the centuries at various attempts to rewrite the Gospels, we see that some of the very first "mosaic movers" and "gap-fillers" are the authors of non-canonical gospels. The terms "supplanting" and "supplementing" are often used in speaking of the relationship of these works to the canonical Gospels. For example, in the introduction to Hennecke's *New Testament Apocrypha,* the rationale for considering a work "apocryphal" was not just that it failed to make its way into the canon but also that it either "intended to take the place of the four Gospels of the canon . . . or to stand as enlargement of them side by side with them . . . aimed at supplementing the deficient information which the NT communicates."[51] Similarly,

---

50. Irenaeus, *Adversus haereses* 1.8.1 (ANF 1:326).

51. Schneemelcher, "General Introduction," 28. Likewise, Cullman says, "In the post-apostolic age one of the purposes behind these endeavours was to supplant other Gospels" (*Early Church,* 47).

Bruce Metzger divides the apocryphal gospels into two broad categories: those that intended to supplant and those that intended to supplement the four canonical Gospels.[52] We will address the concept of "supplementing" presently, but for the moment, let us focus on how some modern rewrites may or may not share similar "supplanting" motivations with their ancient predecessors.

Unlike their non-canonical forefathers, many modern rewrites do not necessarily aim to supplant the authority of the canonical Gospels. Like them though, these rewrites often offer images of Jesus that intentionally compete with those of the Gospel Jesus. Because the motivation of modern attempts slightly differs from that of ancient ones, I prefer to use the term "competing" in order to describe not only the intention behind these novels but also the way in which their fictional Jesuses function in relation to the Gospel Jesus once the reading pact between these rewrites and their Gospel sources has been activated.

Like many of their non-canonical predecessors and like many historical Jesus portraits, competing rewrites are not content to leave the structures of the Gospel portraits in place, so they rearrange and remove many of the original pieces and produce an innovative format for their new portraits. Often, these novels intentionally seek to be controversial and provocative when compared to the original Gospel images. Whether one believes that such competing intentions are positive or negative, it can generally be agreed upon that one positive aspect of competing rewrites is that they can be successful as literary works, often unlike their more orthodox cousins, because they are not as constrained by the original pictures but are freed from the Gospel boundaries to be more creative.

While the purposes behind many of the competing rewrites vary, one of them is to challenge the historicity of the canonical Gospels. As Ben-Porat explains, "Rewriters of history assume—and often claim—that their versions are better, more representative of historical truth, than previous attempts to present the same facts."[53] In undermining the historical claims of the Gospels, competing rewrites are sometimes quick to dismiss the miracles that are a part of the Gospel worldview. Instead, they present alternative views of history that eliminate supernatural interventions. For example, Jim Crace's *Quarantine* has Jesus die thirty days into his forty-day fast; Ricci's *Testament* explains how Jesus' reputation as a healer was exaggerated by a rumor mill spinning greater and greater fabrications of the actual events; Lawrence's *The Man Who Died* presents the popular notion that Jesus never

52. Metzger, *Canon*, 166.
53. Ben-Porat, "Introduction," 2.

died but simply regained consciousness in the tomb after passing out on the cross; and Vidal's *Live From Golgotha* promulgates the mistaken identity theory of Judas being crucified in Jesus' place.

At other times, competing novels willingly allow the miraculous into their narrative worlds and challenge the Gospels not on a historical front but on a theological one. For example, many offer extremely low Christological portraits that are not very complementary to the Gospel Jesus. In Mailer's *The Gospel according to the Son*, in Saramago's *The Gospel according to Jesus Christ*, and in Kazantzakis' *The Last Temptation*, Jesus is not simply one who struggles with sin but is sinful himself. Other times, it is Jesus' paternity that is suspect; for example, in Ricci's *Testament* Jesus is the bastard son of Mary and a Roman soldier. Sometimes, it is Jesus' intelligence or his sanity that is in doubt, as in Fortney's *The Thomas Jesus* in which Jesus is just a wee bit crazy or in Crace's *Quarantine* in which he is a naïve and slow-witted simpleton.

As we examine our two case studies of competing rewrites, we will explore some of the methods used in them to undermine either the historicity or the theology of the Gospels, and we shall also examine the competing narratives that they offer. In sum, we will attempt to discern just how complementing or competing their fictional Jesuses are in comparison with the Gospel Jesus.

Gap Fillers and Complementing Images of Jesus

The ancient works that are often deemed "supplementing" have been called so because their aim appears to be not one of replacing the Gospels but of adding to them by inventing extra-canonical episodes for Jesus' life. When scholars who study the non-canonical collection speak of supplementing gospels, they are often referring to the infancy gospels, such as the *Proto-evangelium of James* and the *Infancy Gospel of Thomas*.[54]

As with the term "supplanting," the moniker "supplementing" is not a perfect fit when extending the terminology to include Jesus novels precisely because all Gospel rewrites supplement their sources with imaginative inventions regardless of their stance toward the historicity or theology of those sources. Instead, a better term to distinguish the intent of the more orthodox rewrites is "complementing" because their narratives usually intend to complement the Gospels rather than to compete with them.

Although both competing and complementing rewrites supplement their Gospel sources, the way they go about doing so often differs. Unlike

54. E.g., Cullmann, "Infancy Gospels," 391–92; Cameron, *Christianity*, 90, 98; Evans, "Images of Christ," 60–61.

competing narratives, complementing ones do not set about dismantling the Gospel Jesus mosaic. Because they wish to create orthodox images of Jesus, they strive to stay within the fourfold Gospel boundaries and to work with an intact Gospel Jesus mosaic. Like any mosaic, this one also has many gaps between its pieces, and so orthodox artists usually create within these spaces. There, they add additional jewels that are similar in color, texture, and shape to the original pieces and that hopefully will make the mosaic sparkle a bit brighter and look even fuller.

We can see this gap filling first taking place within some of the non-canonical infancy narratives. Since Matthew and Luke alone of the four canonical Gospels tell anything about Jesus' earlier years, a huge lacuna exists in the Gospel mosaic. To have so much silence surrounding the majority of Jesus' earthly life was not at all agreeable to many of the early Christians.[55] Because it is only natural that whenever "biographical literature shows gaps, legend generally springs up,"[56] it is not surprising that new infancy gospels arose to fill in those gaps. Motivated partly by curiosity about those years,[57] orthodox rewriters, such as the author of the *Protoevangelium of James*, began with the Matthean and Lukan narratives about Jesus' childhood and then filled them in with background stories and further details.[58]

We find an additional motivation for the creation of complementing literature in Tertullian's brief reference to the author of the non-canonical *The Acts of Paul and Thecla*, who decided to fill in the gaps not of Jesus' life but of Paul's. When asked why he composed the work, the writer said that he composed it out of love for the apostle Paul (Tertullian, *De baptismo* 17 [ANF 3:677]).[59]

Much like their non-canonical predecessors, many Jesus novelists appear to be motivated out of a curiosity stimulated by the gaps in Jesus' life and a desire to answer imaginatively the questions left unanswered in the Gospels. Also, as we shall see, particularly in the case of Anne Rice, Jesus novelists often compose out of a devotional desire to draw closer to the one they love by writing about him.

---

55. Cameron, *Christianity*, 98, 113–15.

56. Cullmann, "Infancy Gospels," 364.

57. Metzger, *Canon*, 166–67; cf. Schneemelcher, "General Introduction," 62; Klauck, *Apocryphal Gospels*, 64; Telford, "The New Testament in Fiction," 363. Raymond Brown even argues that this motivation could be at work both in the non-canonical and in the canonical infancy narratives. In both, we may be seeing the work of active Christian imaginations trying to explain Jesus' origination (*The Birth of the Messiah*, 33n21).

58. Schneemelcher, "Gospels," 83–84.

59. I am thankful to Aaron Kuecker for first pointing me to this reference.

Their aim is not to present a different person in the guise of Jesus' name but to re-present the Gospel Jesus to modern audiences through a different medium than the Gospels themselves. Often their hope is that these rewritten versions will reawaken the wonder of Jesus' story that may have been obscured by familiarity with the Gospels or that may have been missed because of the unfamiliar language and style of the first-century writers.[60] Just as words can lose their potency through familiarity, so too the Gospels can be domesticated and the radical challenge of their message dulled. The reinvestment of freshness and vigor to those Gospel stories and the reintroduction of Jesus to a modern audience are partial motivators for some complementing rewrites.[61] We can see such motivation in Rice's preface to the paperback edition of her *Out of Egypt*: "As Christians, I feel most of us in the creative community must seek to be more than scribes . . . I suggest now that we must seize the revolutionary media of our age in the way that those earlier Christians and Catholics seized the printed book. We must truly use the realistic novel, the television drama, and the motion picture to tell the Christian story anew. It is our obligation to tell that story over and over and to use the best means that we have."[62] Retelling Jesus' story with historical realism but using modern language can revive a sense of awe and challenge those whose hearing and eyes have become dull to the Gospels through familiarity.[63]

Finally, a further aim of such complementing projects is an educational one of sending their audiences back to the original Gospels themselves. Dorothy Sayers suggests as much when she says that she hopes that the hearing of her cycle of plays on the life of Jesus would cause Bibles to be dusted off.[64] Likewise, in the preface to his Jesus novel based upon Franco Zeffirelli's film *Jesus of Nazareth*, William Barclay writes that his wish for both the novel and

---

60. Welch, "Foreword," 11, 13. A listener responding to Sayers's play-cycle, *The Man Born to be King*, wrote, "While in language they have been modern, their Gospel has been the eternal Gospel unchanged in substance, though expressed in a manner which would make it more intelligible to the great multitude who never read their New Testament" (14).

61. Sayers certainly lists these as motivations for her play-cycle on the life of Jesus (Sayers, "Introduction," *The Man Born to Be King*, 23).

62. Anne Rice, "Note to the Paperback Edition," *Christ the Lord*, 349–50.

63. Sayers, "Introduction," 23.

64. Welch, "Foreword," 14. Similarly, Barclay argues, "It may well be that there are some who think it is an irreverence to make the life of Jesus into a film, but there are fewer and fewer people who read and more and more who learn by looking at pictures. I therefore regard the writing of this book as an opportunity to be seized" (Barclay, "Introduction," *Jesus of Nazareth*, 7).

the film is that they will inspire their audiences to return to the Gospels and to reread them with a "new intelligence and a new vividness."[65]

In this monograph, we will examine two complementing works that endeavour to work within the Gospel boundaries without rearranging their pieces too much. While analysing this complementary technique of gap filling as seen in these two case studies, we will also attempt to gauge just how complementary their fictional Jesuses are to the Gospel Jesus.

A HERMENEUTICAL CIRCLE:
FROM REWRITING TO REREADING

Up until this point, we have mainly been concerned with how novelists interpret the Gospels and respond to images of the Gospel Jesus in their Gospel rewrites. This topic will continue to be the focus of the first half of this monograph as we explore four different Jesus novels and analyze how each one functions as a complementing or competing rewrite. No less important, however, is the way in which readers respond to these rewrites and how these novels and the reading pacts imbedded within them provoke a rereading of the Gospels themselves. Indeed, this subsequent benefit of stimulating readers to return to the original texts is often pointed out in defense of reading rewrites.[66]

Yet, the Gospels are not merely reread but also reinterpreted, and this reinterpretation takes place in response to the rewrites and often in light of their perspectives.[67] Mieke Bal argues on behalf of this reversal in hermeneutics in which the prior text is interpreted in light of the later one, and she dubs such interpretation "preposterous" because that which came first chronologically (pre-) is now read according to that which was written latterly (post-).[68] Bal defends this inversion of the traditional order of interpretation by suggesting that any exegesis is preposterous by definition because interpreters always return to a text already influenced by their own culture, so inevitably they anachronistically read the original text. Preposterous readings are simply "willful and thoughtful deployment of anachronism in the interpretation of historical artifacts."[69] These readings recognize the effect that intertextuality has on the interpretation of these now rewritten

65. Barclay, "Introduction," 7.
66. E.g., Ben-Porat, "Saramago's *Gospel*," 95.
67. Ben-Porat, "Introduction," 6.
68. Bal, *Caravaggio*, 7.
69. Bal, *Loving Yusuf*, 13.

sources. Beyond simply acknowledging the rewrite's role, preposterous readings welcome its voice into the hermeneutic conversation.[70]

Such a "preposterous" reading of the Gospels will be undertaken in the second half of this monograph. Indeed, we will attempt to complete an entire hermeneutical circle of the reading pact in relation to one particular event in Jesus' life—the Temptation. Beginning with an examination of the Gospel accounts themselves, we then will move on to examine how this episode has been rewritten in two of our Jesus novels, one which complements and one which competes with the Gospel accounts of that story. After comparing these versions with one another, we will return to one of the Gospels (Matthew) and offer a preposterous reading of its Temptation narrative in light of questions and issues raised by the rewrites. It is my intention that the subsequent "novel" exegesis of the Temptation will serve as an apology in itself for the benefit that rewrites can play in NT scholarship and also within the church's understanding of the Gospel Jesus.

---

70. Such preposterous interpretation is not unlike what Kreitzer argues for when he examines the use of the NT in fiction and film in a work appropriately subtitled *On Reversing the Hermeneutical Flow* (Kreitzer, *The New Testament in Fiction and Film*).

PART II

From The New Testament To New Texts

2

Anne Rice's *Out of Egypt* as a Complementing Rewrite

INTRODUCTION

As WE TURN TO examine the Jesus novels themselves, our first case study is Anne Rice's *Christ the Lord: Out of Egypt*, a coming-of-age tale told from the first-person perspective of a seven-year-old Jesus. In the novel, this boy Jesus narrates one year of his life during which he journeys physically from Alexandria to Nazareth while also making an emotional journey to discover both the secret of his birth and what lies ahead in his future.

Out of Egypt is only the first in a series that Rice plans to write about different periods in Jesus' life,[1] but already it has generated a great deal of publicity for Rice and for her overall rewriting endeavour. Remaining on the *New York Times* bestseller list from November 2005 until February 2006, *Out of Egypt* also received accolades from beliefnet.com, which named it the "Best Spiritual Book of the Year" in 2005, and from amazon.com, which listed it among the top ten Christian books of that same year. The nascent Good News Holdings film company even acquired movie rights for the novel,[2] but because of "creative differences," the project was called off.[3] Because of all the publicity and interest surrounding the book, *Out of Egypt*

---

1. *The Road to Cana*, published in 2008, is the second in the series, and the final novel in this trilogy has yet to be finished.

2. Fleming, "Rice Will Trace Faith."

3. Moring, "Egypt Scrapped."

certainly merits attention as an influential example of the contemporary reception and retelling of Jesus' life in popular culture.

More important to the larger agenda of this study is the novel's evident aim to complement the canonical Gospels by filling in their gaps. In using Rice's novel as an example of a complementary rewrite of Jesus' life, we will examine her motivations for attempting such a task, observe some typical complementary techniques used in her novel, and analyze how complementary Rice's Christological portrait turns out to be. Through this case study, we will see how more influences than simply the Gospels themselves affect the final picture of Jesus created in Jesus novels. Finally, we will discuss the problem that can arise with complementary rewrites as they try to be both faithful to their biblical sources and creative in their artwork.

MOTIVATIONS FOR PRODUCING A COMPLEMENTARY REWRITE

A little over a decade ago, Anne Rice, a convinced atheist, the creator of immortal vampires, and the author of soft-core S & M material,[4] hardly seemed a likely candidate for writing novels about Jesus, at least not ones that would complement the Gospels. Yet after finishing her extremely popular *Vampire Chronicles* series, which included well-known works such as *Interview with the Vampire*, *The Vampire Lestat*, and *The Queen of the Damned*, Rice decided to change direction. Thus in 2002, she began her research and writing of a fairly orthodox series about the life of Jesus.

As she explained in the afterword of her book, the event that precipitated such a monumental shift in her literary focus was Rice's 1998 decision to return to her childhood denomination, the Roman Catholic Church. With the passion and thirst of a new convert, she turned all of her attention toward rediscovering this person at the center of her faith. Rice, recalling her zeal for this new endeavour, wrote, "I decided that I would give myself utterly to the task of trying to understand Jesus himself and how Christianity emerged . . . I had to know who Jesus was—that is, if anyone knew, I had to know what that person knew."[5] Soon she began devouring the Bible, researching NT scholarship, and reading primary sources from the first century.

Since Rice was already a gifted novelist, it was not surprising that the fruit of her research and of her newfound faith soon combined to form a

4. Gates, "Gospel according to Anne."

5. Rice, *Out of Egypt*, 309, 313. For the rest of this chapter references to this source will be given in parentheses.

literary portrait of Jesus. Although she knew that such a shift in topic would likely not be popular with her fans, she decided to "do violence" to her career anyway. Abandoning the living dead who had brought her such fame and fortune, Rice vowed to write solely for and about her living Lord. According to Rice, nothing else mattered to her because she had consecrated her work and herself to Christ (309).

Like the author of *The Acts of Paul and Thecla*, Rice was motivated by a love of the person about whom she wrote. She also had a genuine curiosity about Jesus' life that led her not only to investigate but also to imagine what his boyhood was like. Combined with the theological convictions of her Catholic community, these factors led her to try to create an orthodox portrait of Christ, one that would both supplement and complement the canonical infancy material.

Another factor that influenced the bent of Rice's rewrite was an evangelistic desire to share with others this Christ who had influenced her own life. In her interview with *USA Today*, Rice says that through her novel she hopes "to make Jesus real for people who have stopped seeing him as anything other than an icon, and, for non-believers, to bring to life the times that would later spawn a religious revolution."[6] By viewing her novel as a representation of Jesus to believers and as propaganda to non-believers, Rice's aims coincide with those of both the canonical and non-canonical gospel writers.

FICTIONAL GAP FILLING OR MOSAIC MOVING?

Gap-Filling Intentions

In large part because of her faith and her theological stance towards Jesus and the Gospels, Rice became a gap-filler rather than a mosaic mover. Using a harmonized Gospel mosaic as the basis for her rewrite, she filled in its gaps rather than rearranging and remaking the pieces. All of her imaginative additions to that mosaic were purported to be faithful to either the theological contours of the Gospel portraits or to orthodox theology. According to Rice's own admission, she sought to complement the Gospel Jesus rather than to remake him. As she states in her Author's Note, "The challenge was to write about the Jesus of the Gospels, of course! Anybody could write about a liberal Jesus, a married Jesus, a gay Jesus, a Jesus who was a rebel . . . The true challenge was to take the Jesus of the Gospels . . . and try to get inside him and imagine what he felt" (320). That Rice was more interested in

6. Ignelzi, "Rice Takes Leap"; cf. Crosby, "Interview."

creating a fictional Jesus based upon the Gospel Jesus immediately signalled her complementary attitude toward the Gospel portraits.

Of course, such a decision is not a difficult one for someone who believes that the Gospels are accurate depictions of the actual Jesus and of history in general. For Rice, the actual Jesus is not only preserved in the canonical Gospels but also in parts of the non-canonical gospels.[7] Because of these beliefs, Rice makes what some consider a radical decision for the twenty-first century—to treat those texts as accurate depictions of history and to portray them in her novel as such. Unlike mosaic movers, Rice is not the least bit interested in undermining the historicity of the Gospels or in questioning the accuracy of their portraits of Jesus. In fact, her novel aims at defending both the historical and theological truth of their stories. Therefore, in *Out of Egypt,* Rice takes the Gospel stories about angels, foreign magi, and a mad king literally and uses them as the basis for her own story.[8] Upon a mosaic of infancy material drawn from canonical and non-canonical sources, she builds her own reproduction of the first-century world based upon her research of primary and secondary sources.[9] By placing these infancy stories within a historically plausible world created with details, persons, and settings drawn from antiquity, Rice enhances for her readers a sense of the historicity of these events.[10]

7. When questioned about her inclusion of both the *Protoevangelium* and the *Infancy Gospel of Thomas,* Rice says of them, "Ultimately I chose to embrace this material, to enclose it within the canonical framework as best I could. I felt there was a deep truth in it, and I wanted to preserve that truth as it spoke to me" (320). Precisely which type of truth is contained there is not specified. Rice's use of non-canonical material illustrates our earlier point of how the inclusion of such external material itself does determine whether or not a novel remains within the orthodox boundaries.

8. Crosby, "Interview."

9. This is not to say that Rice is not influenced by historical Jesus scholarship. On the contrary, she has read a great deal of such scholarship and says that she has found the work of "Third Quest" authors, such as Sanders, Dunn, and Wright who stress the Israelite context of the actual Jesus, to be extremely helpful in her own quest of constructing a fictional version of Jesus. Indeed, Rice says of Wright that he is the "scholar who has given me perhaps some of my most important insights" (318).

10. For example, Rice supplements the infancy tales with events from Josephus's works. Along their journey back to Nazareth, Jesus' family either witnesses or hears about such historical events as the burning of Herod's palace in Jericho (73; cf. *A.J.* 17.10.6), Judas the Galilean's rebellion (108; cf. *B.J.* 2.4.1; *A.J.* 17.10.5), the subsequent burning of Sepphoris, the enslavement of their people, and the crucifixion of 2,000 men along the road to Jerusalem (121, 207; cf. *B.J.* 2.5.1–2; *A.J.* 17.10.9–10). Perhaps Rice's most successful usage of first-century material can be seen in the novel's settings. She reconstructs ancient Alexandria, Judea, and Galilee with considerable detail describing the landscapes and architecture based on archaeological research that she has studied. For example, after reading about archeological digs in Galilee which uncovered

Yet the mosaic upon which Rice builds is composed not only of bits collected from the canonical and non-canonical Gospels but also of pieces drawn from Catholic teachings and councils about who Jesus is (320). For Rice, there is no conflict between the idea of the actual Jesus, the Gospel Jesus, and her Church's Jesus. For her, they all point to the one real Jesus, whom she calls Christ the Lord.

As Rice writes, she desires for her artwork to be "utterly true to the spirit of Christ as I have received it from multiple sources: the Gospels, my church, my prayers, my meditation."[11] When describing how she went about writing her novel, Rice again makes a similar statement:

> What I did was take the *Jesus of the Gospels*, the Son of God, the Son of the Virgin Mary, and sought to make Him utterly believable, a vital breathing character . . . I had to move in *His world*, and know His world, and that took the immense research . . . I worked within the strictures of *what we have been taught about Christ the Lord*. That's why I used the title.[12]

---

mikvahs and a lack of unclean animal bones, such as those of pigs, in the trash dumps dating to the first half of the first century CE, she decided to make her Nazareth into a predominantly Israelite town (cf. Strange, "First Century Galilee from Archaeology and From the Texts," *Archaeology and the Galilee*, 39–48; Chancey, *The Myth of a Gentile Galilee*; Chancey, *Greco-Roman Culture and the Galilee of Jesus*; Chancey, "How Jewish Was Jesus' Galilee"). She does this by highlighting architectural features such as the mikvah that Jesus' family has at their home for ceremonial washings (141).

A few of Rice's appropriations of historical figures and events, however, are less successful because they involve more use of artistic license than of faithful reproduction. For example, her chronology is quite questionable at points. Her Jesus is seven years old when Herod the Great dies (4 BCE), which would place his birth at around 11 BCE, much earlier than most scholars would date it. Stranger still is the fact that Rice has Jesus not only meet but also befriend an adult Philo during the family's sojourn to Alexandria. Philo is depicted as a wealthy man and a renowned scholar who wishes to take charge of Jesus' education personally (14–15, 17). Rice takes a great deal of artistic license not only with their acquaintance but also in her portrayal of Philo as a fully-grown man and an accomplished scholar. In 4 BCE, Philo would have been about eleven years old if he was born in 15 BCE, as Philo scholars suggest (e.g., Runia, "Philo, Alexandrian and Jew" in *Exegesis and Philosophy: Studies on Philo of Alexandria*, 3).

Another example of Rice's liberty with her sources is in her placement of the tumultuous events following Herod's death, such as the fight between the Jews and the Romans within the temple itself (55–62; cf. Josephus, *A.J.* 17.10.2), at the Passover festival rather than, as Josephus records, at Pentecost.

11. Rice, "A Conversation with Anne Rice." The influence of her Roman Catholicism comes out most strongly in her portrait of Mary as a perpetual virgin (51). When Jesus asks why Joseph does not sleep with Mary, his uncle tells him, "He never touches her because he does believe [in Mary's purity and in Jesus' conception by the Holy Spirit]. Don't you see? How could he touch her after such a thing?" (47).

12. Rice, "A Conversation with Anne Rice"; emphasis added.

Christ the Lord is indeed an appropriate title for this series because Rice begins with a high Christological portrait composed of a mixture of her Catholic theology and a harmonized portrait of the Gospel Jesus with a few bits from non-canonical gospels thrown into the mix. With this mosaic in place, she then goes on to fill in the gaps and to construct a more detailed narrative about a seven-year-old Christ.

Preserving the Gospel Mosaic Structure

When we survey the novel's structure, we again see how Rice functions as a gap-filler by leaving in place a harmonized version of Gospel events and then filling in the spaces between them with new stories.

The novel's main action and its enactment of biblical material both begin with Joseph's decision to take the family back to Israel after receiving news in a dream about Herod's death (18; cf. Matt 2:19–20). Both also end with another event from the infancy narratives—Jesus' visit to the temple and his three days spent there (282–97; cf. Luke 2:42–52). Interspersed between these two appropriated biblical events are allusions to earlier stories within the Matthean and Lukan infancy narratives. Instead of providing an unoriginal and thus dull re-enactment of the sequential order of these earlier events, Rice chooses to weave descriptions of them naturally into conversations throughout the novel's discourse.

Thus, we are told about John the Baptist's birth (84, 87; cf. Luke 1:5–25); the Annunciation (33, 46, 292–93; cf. Luke 1:26–38); Mary's visit to Elizabeth (84; cf. Luke 1:39–45); Mary's virginal status (e.g., 19, 46, 50–51, 286; cf. Matt 1:18, 25; Luke 1:34–37), which in accordance with Catholic tradition is retained perpetually (47); Joseph's two other angelic visitations during which he was instructed to take Mary as his wife (293; cf. Matt 1:19) and to later flee to Egypt (294–95; cf. Matt 2:13); the census that necessitated their journey to Bethlehem (294; cf. Luke 2:1–3); Jesus' birth in Bethlehem where he was wrapped in swaddling clothes and placed in a manger (259; cf. Matt 1:24–25; Luke 2:6–7); the shepherd's visitation (20, 260–261, 294; cf. Luke 2:8–20); the magi's visitation (20, 238, 260, 263, 294; cf. Matt 2:1–12); and the holy family's eventual flight to Egypt (294–95; cf. Matt 2:13–14). Principal among these imported pieces are the multiple references to the slaughter of the innocents (e.g., 12, 31; cf. Matt 2:16–18) including its eventual recounting by a priest (286–87) and then by Mary (295). Since repetition alerts us to narratival importance, the frequent reprisal of the slaughter of the innocents event speaks to its centrality in Rice's novel.

Rice carefully transports each of these biblical events into her novel. Unlike their use by mosaic movers, these pieces arrive in *Out of Egypt's* narrative world virtually undisturbed. When pieced together by the reader at the story level, they follow a harmonized chronological order of the Matthean and Lukan infancy narratives even though not all of the events are enacted in the novel and some of the pieces are recounted at different points during the novel's discourse.

Although Rice tries to remain true to the biblical narratives and claims to take as little artistic license as possible, it should be noted that she does make a few interesting changes to the imported Gospel material.[13] For example, she places Jesus' visit to the temple in his eighth rather than in his twelfth year, as Luke records. She also has the character Mary Cleopas die during Jesus' childhood even though the Gospel of John has Mary Cleopas alive at Jesus' crucifixion (John 19:25). Aside from these revisions, her work remains close to the canonical Gospels and provides a faithful harmonization principally of the Matthean and Lukan infancy narratives.

GOSPEL FORESHADOWINGS

In line with many complementing novels that focus on Jesus' hidden years, *Out of Egypt* retells Gospel events that concur with its own narrative time span and also references those that occur prior to it. In addition, the novel foreshadows events and characters that appear in the story line of the Gospels after the period of Jesus' life that *Out of Egypt* rewrites. When these foreshadowings are consistent with those later events, they serve as another clue alerting us to the complementing character of the novel. In *Out of Egypt,* we see this technique of faithful foreshadowing of the Gospels throughout the novel. For example, accusations and insinuations that will later be hurled at the Gospel Jesus are prefigured in words thrown at Rice's fictional boy Jesus. Just as Gospel characters will later accuse Jesus of working miracles by the power of Satan (e.g., Matt 9:34; 12:24), so now in the novel Eleazar's father accuses Jesus of being demon-possessed after witnessing Jesus' ability to kill and then raise his son (8). Likewise, the future insinuation in the Nazareth synagogue about Jesus' questionable paternity (Mark 6:3) is anticipated during Jesus' first Sabbath visit to that synagogue (161) and again when he

---

13. In regard to artistic license, Rice says, "When it comes to this book, artistic license does not really exist . . . Of course I created fictional scene and dialogue. But it is all within an immense and solid frame. This was a huge challenge. I had to move in His world, and know His world, and that took the immense research. But license? I took as little as possible" (Rice, "A Conversation with Anne Rice").

returns there to study with the Rabbis (173–80).[14] Like the Gospels and unlike competing accounts, however, *Out of Egypt* vigorously affirms that Jesus is begotten of God (296; cf. Matt 1:20; Luke 1:33–34; John 1:14, 18; 3:16, 18), a point so important and central to the narrative that the novel ends with Jesus saying, "Father, I am your child" (301).[15]

Other examples of foreshadowing occur when later Gospel characters come on the scene at an earlier stage in this novel. One instance of this is the introduction of the future high priest Caiaphas as the young man Joseph Caiaphas, who coincidentally is a distant relative of Jesus' family. The family camps outside his resplendent home in Bethany when they arrive for the Passover. Foreshadowing his future position, Old Sarah remarks, "Perhaps Joseph Caiaphas may be High Priest someday?" (253).

Sometimes foreshadowings are statements or occurrences that precipitate later Gospel events. In *Out of Egypt*, Jesus is disheartened to discover when he visits the temple that it is not a peaceful place of prayer but a noisy marketplace (270). During that same visit, a blind Rabbi reminds Jesus that, according to Zechariah, one day the traders will no longer be in the house of the Lord (279). Both of these statements anticipate the Gospel Jesus' future cleansing of the temple when he casts out the merchants who are making his Father's house into a den of robbers rather than a place of prayer (Matt 21:10–17).

Not surprisingly, one event that is almost always foreshadowed in complementing novels is Jesus' future death. From the descriptions of those crucified at Sepphoris (133, 143) to the willingness of Jesus' male relatives to die for their family, the multiple references to crucifixion in *Out of Egypt* invoke for the reader familiar with the Gospels a foreboding of Jesus' ultimate earthly fate. Jesus' own realization that everyone *is born to die* and the italicization of these words at the end of the novel also point forwards and speak to the importance of his future death (300).

Most significant and interesting of the various ways in which *Out of Egypt* foreshadows the Gospels are the multiple miracles that the boy Jesus performs. Similar to the *Infancy Gospel of Thomas* and to Greco-Roman childhood biographies, Rice prefigures Jesus' future greatness during his boyhood specifically by having this child prodigy work miracles. For example, Rice's fictional Jesus demonstrates his powers when he mends his own cuts and bruises (16), cures his uncle Cleopas from an illness (98), and

14. Although many view Mark 6:3 as a slanderous remark regarding Jesus' conception, others, James Dunn for one, contend that the basis for this inference is not very strong (Dunn, *Jesus Remembered*, 346–47).

15. We will see with our two competing examples, *Testament* and *Gospel*, that rewriting Jesus' paternity and attributing it to a human father are often done in revisionist works.

restores sight to a blind man (279–80). All of these miracles prefigure the Gospels' portrayal of Jesus as a great healer. In addition to performing healing miracles, Rice's Jesus makes the rain stop (170–171) and creates snow (239)—two miracles that anticipate the Gospel Jesus' power over nature, which is later displayed in miracles such as the calming of the sea (Matt 8:23–27), the miraculous catch of fish (Luke 5:1–11), and the multiplication of the loaves and fishes (Matt 14:13–21).

In order to prefigure the Gospel Jesus' power over death, Rice draws upon a tale from *The Infancy Gospel of Thomas*. She begins the novel with a rewriting of the Thomasine scene in which Jesus curses the bully Eleazar, who falls down dead (3; *Inf. Gos. Thom.* 4–5 A and B; cf. *Pseudo Matthew* 29), and continues to follow that infancy gospel by recounting the subsequent raising of the child from the dead (6; *Inf. Gos. Thom.* 8 A; cf. *Pseudo Matthew* 29). Another Thomasine miracle appropriated by Rice is used to prefigure the Gospel Jesus' transformative powers, which are seen, for example, when he changes water to wine (John 2:1–11). In this miracle, the boy Jesus transforms clay sparrows into real birds (5; *Inf. Gos. Thom.* 2(A) 3(B); cf. *Pseudo Matthew* 27).[16]

Throughout the novel, Rice makes a concerted effort to prefigure the adult Jesus' mighty deeds during his childhood. In fact, the only type of miracle that Rice fails to foreshadow is that of demon exorcism. The repetition and variety of ways in which the boy's miracles foreshadow those of the Gospel Jesus alert us to the importance that Rice places on his miraculous abilities, a discussion to which we will return later.

OT TYPOLOGICAL PORTRAYALS
OF CHARACTERS AND EVENTS

Another technique sometimes used by complementing novels and reminiscent of the Gospels themselves is the typological portrayal of characters. According to this practice, NT figures are related to OT characters or events. The NT stories then are interpreted in light of their OT predecessors, which in turn are recast as foreshadowing these later NT characters and events.[17]

16. Rice not only includes apocryphal material from the *Infancy Gospel of Thomas* but also from the *Protoevangelium of James*. The events drawn from this other non-canonical infancy gospel include Mary's selection as one of the virgins to sew the temple veil (174, 223), Salome's attendance as a midwife at the birth of Jesus (259–60), the explanation of Zechariah's death as at the hands of Herod's officers (88), and the escape of John and Elizabeth into the mountains (88; *Prot. Jas.* 23:1–3).

17. Stegner, *Narrative Theology*, 4, 5. According to Michael Fishbane, typology "sees in persons, events, or places, the prototype, pattern, or figure of historical persons,

Sometimes these typological comparisons are simple and explicit such as when Elizabeth places herself in the roles of Sarah and of Hannah (84). Sometimes, the typology is more sophisticated, such as the framing of the novel within a journey motif that has the holy family reliving the exodus experience of Israel as they come *Out of Egypt* and into the Promised Land. Rice makes this typological comparison even more apparent by having the family travel to Jerusalem in order to celebrate the Passover immediately after their own exodus from Egypt.

Just in case the events themselves were not enough to alert the reader to the typology at play, Rice has the character Cleopas, Jesus' uncle,[18] explain the meaning of their journey:

> Because in each of us, you must realize, is the full story of who we are. We were in Egypt, as were our people long ago, and as they did, we came home. We saw battle in the Temple, as our people did under Babylon, but the Temple is now restored. We suffered on our journey here, as our people suffered in the wilderness and under the scourge of the enemies, but we came home (234).

After Cleophas interprets the meaning of their travels, understanding dawns on Mary and Joseph. Joseph responds, "Yes. . . . Now it does seem that way. It was our journey through the wilderness" (234).

If all of these clues were still insufficient, the passage that Rice chooses as the novel's epigraph makes her typological framing of the novel abundantly clear. The words that begin Psalm 114—"When Israel went out of Egypt, the house of Jacob from a people of strange language; Judah was his sanctuary, and Israel his dominion"—present the entire narrative as a typological reenactment of Israel's journey.

With both these subtle hints and overt explanations regarding the meaning of the holy family's sojourn, we see Rice's astute perception of the theological import of that event. She clearly recognizes the OT typology already in place in the Matthean infancy narrative and uses it in her own narrative. Like the Matthean Jesus, Rice's Jesus symbolically relives his nation's history so that Israel's Messiah assumes Israel's earlier experiences (311). That Rice makes this point effectively through her narrative is one of the stronger aspects of her novel and also demonstrates how she complements the Gospels.

---

events or places that follow it in time" (*Biblical Interpretation and Ancient Israel*, 350).

18. According to Hegesippus, a second century bishop of Jerusalem, a Cleopas/Clopas was the brother of Joseph, not Mary as Rice has it in her novel, and thus was an uncle of Jesus. He was also said to be the father of Simon, who followed his cousin James as the leader of the Jerusalem church (Eusebius, *Hist. Eccl.* 3.11; 4.22.4).

That Rice fails to draw any distinction for her readers between what happens to the actual Jesus in history and how he is typologically portrayed in her own infancy narrative may demonstrate her affinity to the Gospels, but it also displays her divergence from modern scholarship. While many scholars recognize the holy family's Egyptian sojourn as a typological reproduction of the OT Exodus motif that is important to Matthew's theological portrait of Jesus, they would disagree with Rice's portrayal of it as an actual historical event.[19] Even though Rice has read enough biblical criticism to be aware of this distinction, in her novel she portrays the entire episode as a God-ordained event that has to take place in actual space and time. Only if Jesus relives Israel's history in his own actual history can he then become the ultimate representative for Israel.

Her insistence on the historicity of these events as seen in the literal portrayal of them within her fictional world perhaps exceeds the intentions of the author of Matthew and the expectations of that Gospel's original audience. If ancient authors and audiences understood that ancient biographies could contain some inventions so long as they were plausible and faithfully portrayed the person's character,[20] then Rice's preoccupation with defending the historicity of these events is perhaps unnecessary. Of course, we can never know for certain the precise intentions of ancient authors—or modern authors, for that matter—but the likelihood that their historical concerns differed greatly from the more modern ones displayed by Rice is a point well worth considering when assessing just how complementary *Out of Egypt* is to the Gospels.

COMPLEMENTING OR COMPETING NARRATIVE WORLDS AND WORLDVIEWS?

Also complementary to the Gospels are the narrative world and the theological worldview displayed in *Out of Egypt*. The same moral polarities as those seen in the Gospels exist in the novel: God is good and the source from which all goodness flows; Satan is the prince of chaos and also Jesus' antagonist (196).

As we have already noted, the narrative world of *Out of Egypt* also complements that of the Gospels, for in both worlds miraculous events occur and supernatural beings appear. No demythologizing of Jesus' miracles or of angelic visitations is necessary.

19. E.g., Brown, *Birth of the Messiah*, 225–29.
20. Burridge, *What are the Gospels?* 247; Aune, *New Testament*, 64–65.

Perhaps most complementary to the Gospels though is the religious nature of the world in which Rice's Jesus lives, moves, and has his being. In both the Gospels and in the novel, the Jesus characters are soaked in an Israelite context.[21] For example, Rice's Jesus is part of an observant family that repeats the Shema every morning (114); observes the Sabbath (17, 158); studies the Torah, the Prophets, and the Writings (19, 153); participates in ritual cleansings in mikvahs (267) and in traditional purification rites at the temple (200); goes on pilgrimages to Jerusalem three times a year (298); and always keeps the Passover (281). Members of Jesus' family repeatedly quote the psalms in their conversations and continually retell biblical stories of Israelite heroes, which shape the identity of the children in Jesus' family whose own narratives, as we have seen, are interwoven with those from Israel's past. One example of this takes place when the family arrives at the Jordan. The children are thrilled to see the famous river that is a part of many of the stories they know so well. Joseph stops to tell them about Elisha and the leper who washed in the river, and the children excitedly run in and bathe in that same river (94–97). Because the children, including Jesus, are nurtured in this type of context, they naturally learn to interpret events and to find meaning in their lives through their Scriptures and their Israelite traditions.

COMPLEMENTING OR COMPETING CHRISTOLOGICAL PORTRAIT?

As we have seen, Rice's construction of Jesus is based upon not only the infancy Gospels, both canonical and non-canonical, but also upon the teachings of the Catholic Church. According to her Author's Note, one of her goals is to create a Christ child who would be both God and man and thus faithful to the Council of Chalcedon's declaration (320).

Even though such an explicit Christological definition of Jesus' person cannot be found in the Gospels themselves, Rice, along with many theologians, would argue that the theological portraits in the Gospels are part of the basis from which this "fully human/fully divine" doctrine is derived. For example, some suggest that Jesus' powers in the Gospels to work miracles and his ability to know the thoughts of others or information that is typically not accessible to humans point towards divine qualities such as omnipotence and omniscience. If such is the case, then the "fully divine" statement of the Chalcedonian Council is simply a more overt description of Jesus' personhood as it is displayed in the Gospels. If then this more explicitly

21. Here, we also see the influence of "third quest" scholarship on Rice and the Israelite context of her Jesus.

articulated Chalcedonian Christology can be viewed as complementary to the Gospels and if *Out of Egypt* is successful in faithfully portraying such a Christology, then we again would have reason for regarding the novel as complementary to the Gospels even though its portrayal and development of Jesus' personhood certainly go beyond what is overtly stated in the Gospels themselves.

Fully Divine

In order to be faithful to her Church's theology, which in turn she would argue is faithful to the Gospels, Rice endeavors to depict a Jesus who is fully divine. Of course, portraying a fully divine seven-year-old boy who is also fully human and a believable character is quite a challenge. In fact, trying to portray the infinite through finite means is always problematic and is an issue for all artists and theologians, not just for Rice. Somewhat ironically, Rice hopes to solve this dilemma not by portraying the presence of Jesus' divinity but its absence. In her Author's Note, she claims to adopt a kenotic Christology, which is based upon an interpretation of Phil 2:7, according to which Jesus "empties" himself of his divine qualities (320). Unfortunately, Rice is inconsistent in her Christological portrait and, as we shall see, ultimately unsuccessful in creating a fully divine Christ child.

An Omniscient Seven-Year-Old?

In *Out of Egypt*, the *kenosis* of Jesus' divinity extends only to his omniscience, or as Rice calls it, "his Divine awareness" (320), and of this quality, Jesus is emptied only some of the time. At other times, this boy Jesus fully experiences his omniscient powers. One such experience Rice's Jesus describes in the following way: "And there came in a flash to me a feeling of understanding everything, *everything*! It was gone as soon as it had come" (215; cf., 98, 99, 196). All of the knowledge of the universe floods his mind but then recedes like a wave. Indeed, Rice portrays his omniscience much like a car that is having trouble cranking. Sometimes the engine growls loudly, but at other times, it remains strangely silent.

In the novel, Cleopas comments that members of Jesus' own family do not know what to do with the divine child (47) who will one day give them all the answers (215). It is clear that Rice struggles with what to do with him and his divine knowledge as well. Rather than displaying a form of *kenosis*, Rice instead offers us an embodiment of *krypsis*, a Christology in which Christ's divine omniscience is hidden, but not entirely. She gives us a Christ who is divine in fits and starts—now he is omniscient; now he is not. His knowledge has been poured out, but now it comes rushing back to him. The result is confusing and unsuccessful as an example of both kenotic Christology and omniscience.

Rice's attempt to portray both omniscience and *kenosis* points to the fundamental problem of trying to do both since the very definition of *kenosis* negates any tangible portrayal of omniscience. If Rice were to depict a Christ child fully "emptied" of his divine attributes, then we would not see any signs of omniscience. Yet if we could not see any evidence of omniscience, then how could we know that she intends to portray his character as divine? It is a paradoxical problem of portrayal and one that Rice is not alone in struggling to solve.

While Paul in his letter to the Philippians may appear to be more certain about such divine emptying, the evangelists themselves seem more confused over the issue of omniscience and *kenosis*, that is, if these were even issues about which they were aware. In the Gospels, we see a similar tension to that found in *Out of Egypt* in that Jesus seems to have extraordinary knowledge at some points but not always. For example, the Gospel Jesus can predict signs of the coming end of the age but still declare that even he does not know when these events will take place (cf. Mark 13). There also seems to be tension between the Gospels themselves regarding the amount of awareness Jesus has about his own identity. In the Synoptics, there appears to be more of a process of discovery in which Jesus grows in wisdom (cf. Luke 2:52) and even in self-awareness whereas in John, Jesus seems to know all about his own identity, his relationship with his Father God, and his destiny. In fact, most of Jesus' teachings in John center on these topics. If the Gospel writers themselves had difficulty in deciding whether and how to portray an omniscient Jesus, then perhaps we should not expect Rice to have such a complicated issue solved and depicted perfectly either.

An Omnipotent Seven-Year-Old?

While the omniscient part of his divinity supposedly has been poured out, at least partially, Jesus retains another part of his divine nature—his omnipotence, which is displayed through his miracles. As Mary explains to Jesus:

> "You are the son of the Lord God!" she said. "That's why you can kill and bring back to life, that's why you can heal a blind man as Joseph saw you do, that's why you can pray for snow and there will be snow, that's why you can dispute with your uncle

Cleopas when he forgets you're a boy, that's why you make sparrows from clay and bring them to life" (296).

Because Rice sees Jesus' miraculous powers as tied to his divine nature,
she reasons that Jesus would have displayed special powers as a child. Precisely why, since Rice endeavors to portray *kenosis*, an emptying of these divine powers does not take place along with his divine knowledge is unclear.

In deciding to depict Jesus as possessing miraculous powers at a young
age, Rice follows the lead of the non-canonical infancy gospels and, as we
have seen, draws some of her boy wonder's deeds from them. Her decision
to begin the novel with the Thomasine tale of Jesus' slaying of the bully Eleazar and the subsequent raising of that child from the dead not only sets the
tone of the novel but also tells the reader a great deal about the Christological presentation to come. Throughout the novel, we see a picture of a little
boy full of miraculous powers that he does not quite know how to control.

Unlike the *Infancy Gospel of Thomas, Out of Egypt* cannot be accused
of the same type of docetic portrayal of Jesus "as a god walking around in a
little boy's body, performing one miracle after another."[22] Yet Rice's picture
of the boy's omnipotence is neither without its own problems nor perhaps
without its own form of doceticism.

The belief seen in *Out of Egypt* that Jesus' mighty deeds are expressions
of his divinity is what D. S. Cairns calls the traditionalist view of miracles.
The assumption behind this view is that only a divine being could have performed such powerful acts.[23] Cairn contends that this position is in fact
incongruous with the presentation of miracles in the Synoptic Gospels. For
one, it negates the role of human faith reiterated as an essential component
for many of these works. For another, in ascribing these miracles to Jesus'
divinity rather than to his perfect humanity, this position negates the transference of those powers from Jesus to his disciples described in the Gospels
and thus calls into question the validity of stories found throughout the NT
of decidedly non-divine followers of Jesus performing miracles. Cairn and
many other scholars argue that miracles are not an outflowing of Jesus' omnipotence but are the result of the indwelling of God's Spirit within Jesus.[24]
According to this view, Jesus in his full humanity prefigures his disciple's

22. Talbert, "Once Again," 354. In her note to the paperback edition, Rice addresses
the concerns expressed by some of her readers about the inclusion of the apocryphal
infancy gospels, which some view as possible Gnostic material. She responds that she
made a conscious effort to remove any docetic elements from the early legendary material and that her purpose was to present a truly human and orthodox child Jesus (Rice,
"Note to the Paperback Edition," 347–48).

23. Cairns, *Faith*, 25.

24. E.g., ibid., 29–30; Baillie, *God*.

later abilities to perform mighty deeds through the Spirit. An equation of the miraculous with Jesus' divinity comes at the cost of his full humanity and could be even be construed as a form of doceticism.

Also problematic with Rice's portrayal of Jesus' divinity is the presence of divine power without any divine awareness. This combination produces not only a very confused little boy but also one who is capable of performing immoral deeds, such as the Thomasine slaying of Eleazar. It is no wonder then that the neighbors in both Rice's tale and in the Thomasine gospel all fear Jesus. Who would not be afraid with such a dangerous mixture of omnipotence sans omniscience? Thankfully, as the novel progresses, Jesus learns to pray to his Father and to ask his will before performing miracles, such as the healing of Cleopas (98) and that of the blind man (280), but sometimes miracles still seem to spring unbidden, such as when the rain ceases (170–71) or when the snow begins (231).

Complementing Ancient Biographies and the Non-Canonical Infancy Gospels

Instead of successfully embodying a kenotic Christology that Rice and others would claim as a faithful representation of the Gospel portrayals and of Catholic theology, Rice's Jesus more successfully embodies the assumptions of ancient biographies in general and of the non-canonical infancy gospels in particular that personhood is fixed and consistent over one's lifetime. Because later in life Jesus demonstrates omniscient characteristics, the novel depicts similar traits in Jesus as a boy by portraying him as a highly intelligent pupil whose wisdom far exceeds his years.[25] Likewise, since the adult Jesus will later show omnipotence through the miracles he performs, Rice has the boy Jesus perform similar mighty works. Rather than portraying the absence of Jesus' divinity as suggested in the Author's Note, *Out of Egypt* consistently tries to depict the presence of that divine nature by displaying the characteristics of omniscience and omnipotence through acts that foreshadow those of the adult Gospel Jesus.

This portrait of a miracle-working, all-knowing seven-year-old Jesus is not in keeping with the Gospels, which delay portraying Jesus with such abilities until after his baptism. It is, however, more in line with the non-canonical infancy gospels.

---

25. Jesus is a star pupil (10, 13–15) who garners the attention of no less than Philo himself, one of the greatest Israelite scholars.

Fully Human

When we turn to Rice's portrayal of Jesus' humanity, we see that Jesus is pretty much the perfect child. He is obedient to his parents, helpful at home, and diligent in his study of the Scriptures. He also has a fairly normal childhood within a supportive and loving extended family. He spends his mornings in synagogue school with the rabbis and his afternoons working with his father and uncles doing carpentry. Aside from living in the tumultuous times following Herod the Great's death, Jesus has a fairly uneventful and idyllic life in pastoral Nazareth.

Apart from the unintentional doceticism that results from the attachment of his miracle working to his divinity, nothing else threatens the picture of Jesus as a fully human child. Like other children, he is not exempt from normal childhood illnesses. Also like them, he is capable of feeling fear, a point that Rice overemphasizes.

While such a portrayal is safe from competing either with the Gospels or with Rice's Catholic theology, it does little to provide the reader with an engaging tale or with a character with whom readers can connect. Of course, the characters with whom readers can most empathize are those who are inherently flawed, and such a portrayal of Jesus is ruled out from the start by any author who wishes to remain within orthodox circles and so must portray a sinless character.

One area of Jesus' humanity, however, remains available for authors to exploit in order to engender an empathetic connection between their readers and their Jesus characters. That aspect is the inevitable loneliness and isolation that such a fully human and thus sinless person would have felt from the rest of humanity.[26] It is surprising that Rice does not explore this theme more given that it is a major one in many of her vampire novels. A few times, she does allude to the isolation that Jesus feels from those around him (290, 299), but it is not until her second book in the series, *The Road to Cana*, that she really makes use of this topic. There, she imagines what it would have been like for Jesus to be in love with a young woman named Avigail and yet to know that he can never have her. This Jesus, who not only struggles with the absence of romantic love but also with the growing isolation from his family, becomes a more believable character and undergoes one truly human experience with which readers can empathize—loneliness.

26. This line is in fact taken in Moore's *Lamb*. While readers can more readily identify with Biff, who struggles with problems like controlling (or not) his sexual urges and always being the sidekick overshadowed by Jesus' presence, the one characteristic of Jesus with which they can relate is Jesus' incredible loneliness. This motif running throughout the novel is epitomized in the scene with the Abominable Snowman with whom Jesus feels an ultimate kinship because both of them are unique creatures that are utterly alone.

CONCLUSION: THE PROBLEM OF COMPLEMENTING NOVELS AND THE PRODUCTION OF ART

Rice's relatively benign portrayal of Jesus raises the question as to how a Jesus novel can successfully remain true to its source material while also producing an original and engaging work of art. This dilemma is further complicated by Rice's attempt to produce a theologically orthodox image of Jesus—a figure who is one of the best known in history and about whom people are very protective and sensitive.

As Rice recognizes, it is easier to write about a married Jesus, a gay Jesus, or, as would have seemed more probable for her, a vampire Jesus. In the case of revisionist accounts, the author is not necessarily constrained by the canonical portrayal, by the historical context, or by Christological creeds and can reinvent Jesus in almost any way imaginable. Because of the larger scope of artistic license provided to them, these revisionist attempts have a better chance of producing creative literature.

Like most novels, competing rewrites "embody art and (relative) lack of piety,"[27] but complementing rewrites are often more like devotional writing in that they embody genuine piety but often lack art. According to her Author's Note, Rice is primarily concerned with producing a work of devotion rather than with producing a successful work of fiction. While *Out of Egypt* may be successful in creating devotion in readers and has been called by one reviewer a work of "restrained piety and devotion,"[28] such fidelity to the original source material may come at the cost of creating a compelling work of art. The reviewer of Rice's novel for *Time* magazine focuses on this duality of purpose and the difficulty of meeting both goals when he writes:

> *Christ the Lord* is, as any retelling of Jesus' life must be, cleft: it's both a work of devotion and a work of fiction, and one reads it with a divided mind. The religious reader wants it to hew closely to the known facts and spirit of Jesus' life, to show respect and be plausible. The novel reader wants drama and action. Seven-year-old Jesus is largely the good little kid you would expect, and he makes the novel reader in you a teeny bit impatient. When Jesus bumps into Satan in a fever dream, Satan says to him, mockingly, "I'm watching you, angel child! I'm waiting to see what you mean to do." It's hard not to have a little sympathy for the devil.[29]

27. Anderson, *Eros Sophistes*, 63.

28. Hughes, "Review of *Christ the Lord*," 833.

29. Grossman, "Junior Jesus."

As an artistic piece of literature, *Out of Egypt* is not as successful as some of Rice's earlier works. Her characters are flat and undergo little development through the novel. Jesus is somewhat an exception to this rule, but his growth has more to do with the normal development that occurs in childhood rather than with character development. Perhaps this is in part because of the assumption seen in the apocryphal infancy gospels and in Rice's novel that Jesus' person must have been in many ways fixed. In keeping with Luke 2:52, Rice pictures him growing in knowledge and in maturity but in little else.

Another adverse factor in her characterization is the paucity of emotions that her characters undergo. For some reason, their emotional responses appear limited to fear and laughter, and these two emotions are so overused that a blogger once reviewing the book quipped that if one more character laughed or cried in the book then she was going to cry too. This lack of emotional range is perhaps due to Rice's decision to narrate the story from the point of view of a seven-year-old. Breaking perspective at one point, Jesus remarks, "But as I am trying to tell you this story from the point of view of the child that I was, I will leave it at that" (41). Because of this breach, the reader knows that the novel is being narrated by an older Jesus (how much older is not stated), and so Rice's choice to try and limit the narration to the vocabulary and observational skills of a seven-year-old seems strange. It is unclear why she does not follow autobiographical novels, such as *Jane Eyre* or *David Copperfield*, whose namesakes narrate their own childhoods in first person but from their later adult perspectives that enable greater insights and better descriptions of events. Also, even though Rice's Jesus claims to be narrating the story from his childhood perspective, there are still many terms used and explanations given in the narration that would be beyond the verbal and mental capabilities of a seven-year-old child. Thus, the severe limitation of emotional descriptions seems out of place and certainly weakens the narrative. It also aids in inhibiting an empathetic attachment between readers and characters that Rice so easily enables in some of her earlier novels.

Regarding plot construction, Rice fails to create tension or an impetus to follow Jesus' search for the truth about his birth perhaps because many readers are already familiar with the "mystery" surrounding Bethlehem. Readers are not carried along in Jesus' quest as they were, for example, when her vampires Lestate or Louis delved into their own mysterious origins.

Artistically, *Out of Egypt* fails to live up to the standards of Rice's earlier works. As a Gospel rewrite and as a devotional work, however, it is more successful. The novel certainly exhibits the intention to provide a storyline and a portrait of the boy Jesus that are complementary to the Gospels. For the most part, individual Gospel stories and the overall narrative world are preserved in their transference from the original sources to this rewrite. The fictional portrait of Jesus as a seven-year-old boy, however, is arguably less complementary to the adult Gospel version. In the end, Rice provides her readers with a fairly complementary rewrite of the Gospels but at a literary cost.

3

Neil Boyd's *The Hidden Years* as a Complementing Rewrite

INTRODUCTION

NEIL BOYD IS THE pseudonym of Peter De Rosa, a former Catholic priest from Ireland. He is best known for the 1970s *Bless Me, Father* series that was later turned into a popular British television show.[1] Presented as the fictional autobiographical adventures of Father Neil Boyd, a novice priest serving in a small parish outside London, these works were loosely based on De Rosa's own early experiences in ministry. In 1984, De Rosa published one further novel under his *nom de plume*, but this time his subject was the life of Jesus himself rather than the humorous escapades of one modern-day disciple.

As one might surmise from the title, *The Hidden Years*,[2] like *Out of Egypt*, focuses on Jesus' earlier "hidden years," that large, looming gap in the Gospel narratives. Rather than beginning with Jesus' childhood, as *Out of Egypt* and other "hidden years" novels do, Boyd's narrative commences with a Jesus fully grown and depicts the final four years of his life prior to the start of his ministry.

---

1. These works include *Bless Me, Father*; *Bless Me Again, Father*; *Father before Christmas*; *Father in a Fix*; and *Father under Fire*. The first of these works inspired the television series, which ran for three seasons.

2. Page number references to this novel will be provided throughout the chapter in parentheses.

When the novel's storyline reaches the period of Jesus' public life, it follows the structure of a typical Gospel harmonization blending early events from John's Gospel with those of the Synoptics: John the Baptist appears and baptizes Jesus (179–82; 200–202; cf. Mark 1:2–11; John 1:29–34); John and Andrew find Jesus and visit where he is staying (140; cf. John 1:35–39); Jesus is impelled by the Spirit into the desert where the sequence of his tests follows the Matthean order (205–40; cf. Matt 4:1–11); and finally, Jesus returns to Nazareth to preach in his own synagogue, where he is rejected by his neighbors (245–51; Luke 4:16–30).

Because the novel's timeline overlaps very little with those of the Gospels, its designation as a complementing narrative cannot be based solely on how it handles imported Gospel pieces. With that said, whenever *The Hidden Years* does rewrite Gospel scenes it remains close to the biblical presentations. Such faithfulness to the original sources is a telling bit of evidence in ascertaining this rewrite's relationship to the Gospels.

Instead of focusing solely on how the novel handles Gospel material, we will attempt to understand how *The Hidden Years* acts as a complementing narrative by examining several common techniques found in the novel that are often used in more orthodox Jesus novels. These hallmarks of complementing narratives include fictional gap filling, Gospel foreshadowings, backgrounds for later teaching material, OT typological portrayals of characters and events, and a fairly orthodox Christological portrait.

FICTIONAL GAP FILLING OR MOSAIC MOVING?

One of the essential literary techniques used in all Jesus novels is that of filling in the narrative gaps of the Gospels with imaginative extrapolations. Even though all fictionalizers fill gaps, their methodologies differ and are often influenced by their theological outlooks. Many pious Christians are motivated out of love and curiosity to explore imaginatively and to experience vicariously more of the life of their Lord. These rewriters typically believe that the Gospels offer faithful portrayals of Jesus, so their aim is not to disassemble those portraits but simply to add to them. The plots of these complementing novels often are based on traditional Gospel harmonizations that attempt to respect, as much as possible, the chronology and theological formation of those events in their original Gospel settings.

To use the mosaic analogy once again, complementing novels use a harmonized Gospel Jesus and try to leave that picture intact. They prefer to add additional jewels in the spaces between the original mosaic pieces in the hope of making the portrait of the king become even more lively and beautiful. *The Hidden Years* is one such gap-filling novel. Like many other orthodox novels, this one appears to have been written with pious intentions spurred on by curiosity about the life of Jesus. From its pages emanates a great deal of love for Jesus and respect for the evangelists' portrayals of him. As we have already noted, when the novel's timeline intersects with that of the Gospels, it leaves the Gospel pieces in place and does little to reformat them. The novel faithfully complements the testimonies of the evangelists while also filling out their reports with further details, dialogue, character analysis, and, of course, a very large section about Jesus' earlier years. Because of these features, *The Hidden Years* qualifies as a gap-filling novel rather than a mosaic-moving one. As we shall see more clearly in a moment, Boyd's life of Jesus presents a portrait in miniature of a much larger mosaic whose structure the novel has been careful to maintain.

GOSPEL FORESHADOWINGS

Even more important than offering a complementary plotline is the fact that complementing novels do not go against the theological contours of the Gospel portraits. Regardless of the stage of life portrayed in these novels, the fictional Jesus' character remains consistent with that of the mature Jesus painted in the Gospels. In fact, much of what the Gospel Jesus will later do and say is foreshadowed in these fictional versions of his earlier life.

The second hallmark of complementing novels that we observe in Boyd's novel is this foreshadowing of Jesus' later life as it is portrayed in the Gospels. These foreshadowings anticipate anything from events to teachings to future characters. For example, in *The Hidden Years*, major Gospel characters, such as the disciples, Jesus' mother Mary, and Mary Magdalene, are introduced during Jesus' hidden years. Minor characters, such as the women who will later travel with Jesus (139; cf. Luke 8:3) and the siblings Mary, Martha, and Lazarus (169–70; cf. Luke 10:38–42; John 11:1), are mentioned as well. We also see that Jesus' later Gospel teachings are consistent with his "earlier" opinions expressed during these years. For example, the Gospel Jesus' later response to the question about the greatest commandment (Matt 22:34–40) is anticipated by this fictional Jesus' statement about true religion being loving God and doing his will (123) and in his "big idea" that we are to "love everyone as we love ourselves" (138). Many of the Gospel Jesus' parables are also prefigured in events that take place during the novel; one such instance is the incident in the temple with the proud Pharisee praying loudly and comparing himself to Levi, the tax collector, who humbly sits at the back and refuses to even lift his head towards heaven (172–73; cf. Luke 18:9–14).

We can see additional examples of the foreshadowing of future Gospel events in *The Hidden Years*. When Boyd's Jesus visits the Court of the Gentiles and says that it looks more like a market than a place of prayer (163), this incident anticipates the Gospel Jesus' future cleansing of the temple (cf. Matt 21.12–13; John 2:14–22). Likewise, Simon Peter's later walking on water in the Gospels is foreshadowed throughout the novel with the running joke between Simon and Jesus that one day Jesus will teach him to walk on water (129, 140, 152, 203–4; cf. Matt 14:28–33). Other examples of Gospel foreshadowings are the allusions to the Gospel Jesus' future ministries and conflicts seen through various relationships and interactions that Boyd's Jesus has. In the novel, Jesus' relationships with Mary Magdalene, the prostitute (108–11), and Levi, the tax collector (148), cause people to spread rumors and question his integrity as others will later do during the Gospel Jesus' ministry (148; cf. Matt 9:11–13; 11:18–19). Also similar to the original versions, this Jesus conflicts with San-hedrin officials (62–65) and with Pharisees (152–53), whom he considers hypocrites (cf. Matt 23:1–36). Like the Gospel Jesus, Boyd's Jesus also cares for the poor, the gentle, and the lowly (125, 224; e.g., Matt 11:5); loves children (46, 58, 76; e.g., Matt 9:13–14); and pays more respect to females than is typi-cal in his society (73; e.g., Luke 10:38–40; John 4:42).

Even Jesus' own suffering and its atoning quality are alluded to in Boyd's novel. When Jesus carries a tree downhill after felling it, he appears to be carrying a cross. Jesus comments, "[I]t felt like the weight of the world," and someone observing him says, "You'd think he was on his way to crucifixion" (31). Later, Jesus will tell Asuph, the foreign camel driver, that he will give his own life for him (73), and during his baptism, Jesus looks like "a lamb about to be slaughtered" (201).

Essential to the complementing classification is not only the existence of these foreshadowings but also the manner in which the Gospel material is anticipated. These proleptic descriptions must be consistent in character and in trajectory with the later Gospel material, and, as the above examples show, the Gospel foreshadowings in *The Hidden Years* are.

BACKGROUNDS FOR TEACHING MATERIAL

The Hidden Years, like many complementing novels focusing on Jesus' ear-lier years, explains who influenced Jesus and from where he learned much of what he would later teach. Not surprisingly, Boyd's Jesus learns a great deal from his mother Mary who focuses on the present day and refuses to worry about tomorrow.[3] One of Mary's other core beliefs is that the poor

---

3. Mary would often say, "Tomorrow's bread has no taste for me. . . . Today's is sweet

are particularly important to God. Always willing to share whatever she has with anyone in need, she teaches Jesus to do the same (e.g., 14–15; cf. Matt 5:3; 19:21; Luke 4:18; 14:12–24).[4]

Besides his mother, Jesus is most influenced by the village Rabbi Ezra, a fictional but historically plausible character rather than a Gospel import. Ezra is a beautiful example of a leader who ministers to his congregation in many ways—by taking their sorrows upon himself (38), by carrying the people on his back (239; cf. Matt 11:28–30), and by offering his own body up for them (51; Luke 22:19–20). Through observing their relationship, the reader sees how Jesus learns to love his people by watching Ezra's example. In addition to these two characters, Jesus is influenced by the Rabbi Hillel's version of the golden rule (18; cf. Matt 7:12). He also admires Rabbi Samuel, who uses simple parables to show the people the unimportance of outward expressions of piety like wearing amulets (165–66; cf. Matt 6:1–4).

Explaining Jesus' sources for much of his teaching is a prime example of fictional gap filling in Jesus novels. That their teachings match those of the later Gospel Jesus is a particular hallmark of complementing narratives.

OT TYPOLOGICAL PORTRAYALS OF CHARACTERS AND EVENTS

Another way in which *The Hidden Years* complements the Gospels is by its stylistic imitation, particularly of Matthew's Gospel, of using OT typology when describing characters and events. For example, the Rabbi Ezra is frequently portrayed as one of the OT prophets, speaking to God for his people (37–38; 50–54).[5] The Nazarenes are pictured as the Israelites wandering in the desert, grumbling against God because of their lack of food, and wanting to return to Egypt (37, 52). The drought in Nazareth is compared to Jeremiah's prophesies of Judah's suffering (62–63), and the locust invasion is

---

enough." Reflecting on his mother, Jesus thought, "Tomorrow was as distant for her as a hundred years hence. If you look to the future, try to live in it, you only cheat yourself of the present" (13; cf. Matt 6:25–34).

4. Also like most complementing novels and contrary to competing ones, Jesus and Mary have a very loving and uncomplicated relationship. Wangerin's *Jesus*, however, would be an exception to this rule of thumb because in this novel we see a very complex and often acrimonious relationship between the two.

5. In the synagogue, he was known to address the assembly "as if he were Elijah mocking the false prophets of Baal" (53) or to speak to God in their hearing as Abraham and Moses used to do (51). Like the prophets, he would physically enact his messages by doing crazy stunts like placing an iron chain over his shoulders while quoting Amos (51) or pouring out a bag of dead locusts and telling God that this is their congregation's offering to God (38).

likened to the plagues of Egypt (32). Jesus himself typifies the Song of Solomon by becoming the lover and viewing the people as the bride to whom he is pledged to marry (30), and in the temptation scene, he is connected with both Moses and Israel (211, 212). These typological descriptions of events and people bring this new rewrite even closer in line with its biblical progenitors.

COMPLEMENTING OR COMPETING CHRISTOLOGICAL PORTRAIT?

One final characteristic of complementing novels that appears in *The Hidden Years* is a complementary Christological portrait. The character and opinions of Boyd's Jesus are consistent with those of the Gospel Jesus. He loves his people and wants to show them God's love and care (80). He believes that all men need saving (161; cf. John 3:17) and prefers to suffer himself rather than see anyone else suffer (116). He frequently talks about God's kingdom (e.g., 138), and as Simon observes, it appears that Jesus believes there can be "a family, a kingdom of nothing but right and goodness" (117; cf. Matt 12:49–50).

Also through his actions, this fictional Jesus often resembles the Gospel Jesus by embodying in word and deed his counterpart's teachings. He loves enemies (72, 113–14, 142, 161) so much so that he has no enemies (130) and prays for those who persecute him, such as the Sanhedrin official (65), his unjust employer (54–55), and Herod Antipas (116; cf. Matt 5:43–48). In fact, this Jesus sets no limits on forgiveness (140; cf. Matt 18:21–22). His prayers are simple and direct rather than babbling and long-winded like those of the Rabbi in Capernaum (144; cf. Matt 6:5–8). He is first to serve and last to receive (140) and never minds taking the lowest place (169; cf. Matt 19.30; 20:16).

In *The Hidden Years*, Jesus is pictured as "a true son of Israel" who spends hours learning Hebrew and pouring over the Scriptures (23). He is referred to as Israel's Savior (209) and as the one who will fulfill his people's destiny (176). He displays a special relationship with God, whom he addresses as Abba (11). Although he is called the Son of Man (210), his identity as the Son of God is only hinted at and not explicitly stated. Even so, many recognize that God's Spirit is upon him. For example, Simon insightfully realizes that "God's word has become flesh, so to speak, in this carpenter from Nazareth" (131; cf. John 1:1, 14) and that in Jesus "God came to the Lake of Galilee" (144).

Finally, the Christology of *The Hidden Years* challenges docetism, the idea that Jesus was a divine being who only appeared to be human. Boyd's Jesus is in solidarity with the rest of humanity so much so that for the first chapter and at a few other critical moments (e.g., 208) he is only identified as "the Man." This "Man" displays many typical human qualities that would preclude any docetic understanding: he hungers during the drought (12), has a pimply face as a teenager (22), snores during a boring sermon (120), laughs at the pompousness of others (23), has a sense of humor,[6] and weeps when he holds a dying child (58–59). Boyd's Jesus is portrayed as a real human in every way, one who joins the suffering of all humanity and who undergoes real temptation (cf. Heb 2:17–19).

COMPLEMENTING OR COMPETING NARRATIVE WORLDS AND WORLDVIEWS?

One final feature of complementing narratives displayed in *The Hidden Years* is that of a narrative world and a theological worldview consistent with those of the NT Gospels. In Boyd's novel, God is still the good Creator, and Satan remains the evil tempter. Good is equated with doing God's will, and evil is anything that is contrary to it. The Israelites continue to have a special relationship with God, and the religious calendar of Sabbaths and festivals organize the days and weeks of the characters, who are all soaked in the Torah and the traditions of their forefathers.

There is one aspect of *The Hidden Year's* narrative world that is at odds with that of the Gospels and that betrays a modern worldview. The novel is more ambiguous than the Gospels themselves as to the occurrence of supernatural events. Such events are never explicitly denied, but they do appear to be demythologized and alternative natural explanations are given for their supernaturally explained Gospel parallels. For example, at Jesus' baptism, there is no description of the heavens opening and a dove alighting on Jesus, but there is a depiction of Jesus himself appearing to John *as a dove* when he approaches the river in his white Sabbath robe with his arms outstretched (200). Likewise, when the "angels," which are described in Matt 4:11 (cf. Mark 1:13), arrive to minister to Jesus after his wilderness sojourn ends, they turn out to be Jesus' own disciples and not supernatural beings (236–37).

---

6. When Jesus breaks the Sabbath to find food for the starving child, he sends a message back to Jerusalem with the investigator, "Tell Caiaphas that Jesus of Nazareth is leaving his ass behind to keep the Sabbath in his stead" (65).

Still, *The Hidden Years* does hint at the possibility of miracles in other passages, such as in the Sea of Galilee scene when a dramatic storm on the lake mysteriously parallels Jesus' own emotions. It begins when he expresses anger at Herod Antipas, who is on the lake and subsides when Jesus begins to worry that Antipas and his crew will perish in the storm and utters the words "Peace. Peace" (112–16). The novel leaves open the possibility of the miraculous but does not vigorously affirm its existence as do the Gospels.

CONCLUSION

The Hidden Years is an exemplary model of a complementing narrative in that it successfully balances faithfulness to its Gospel sources with an original and artistically successful narrative. It takes the Gospel portraits as its basis and translates Jesus into the modern genre of a novel by fleshing out his character with more details—psychological, social, situational, and relational. The pious Christian reader can immediately feel comfortable with this fictional Jesus who is like the Gospel Jesus in essential matters. Unlike competing narratives, *The Hidden Years* refrains from challenging any orthodox Christological categories or characteristics.

Boyd manages to provide a rewrite that avoids disassembling and challenging the Gospel Jesus mosaic while still providing a fictional Jesus that is extremely engaging and compelling. Boyd's Jesus is at once both loving and easily loveable, both human and humane. He is "an individual rich in humanity, without malice or sin, endowed with a heart capable of deep, faithful, gentle affection."[7] Like the Lukan version of Jesus, this one too grows in wisdom (cf. Luke 2:52) about himself, his mission, and the world as he humbly learns not only from his heavenly Father but also from those around him. Because he is not presented as a divine being hovering slightly above the earth but as one who identifies with humanity, readers are enabled to identify with and to approach him. Yet this novel does not allow the Christian reader to simply sit back and enjoy a nice, pretty picture of gentle Jesus, meek and mild. Just like a good sermon, *The Hidden Years* makes Jesus come alive, penetrates to the heart of his message, and uses his example to challenge its audience.

Boyd's Christological portrayal also complements the Christology of at least the Synoptic Gospels better than most other orthodox novels, including Rice's *Out of Egypt*, precisely because it hints at Jesus' divinity rather than shouting about it. Simon can say that listening to Jesus was "like listening to a voice out of the burning bush," but he does not say that he is

7. Gomez, "Review of *The Hidden Years*."

listening to God himself (138). Other complementing novels, such as those written by Holmes, the Thoenes, and even Rice, display a more fully developed Christology than the Gospels themselves. As we have seen through Rice's example, however, such portrayals also tend to run into problems trying to represent these more developed Christological notions, such as omniscience and *kenosis*. In some of the complementing novels, there is never a question about Jesus' divine identity because often characters know from a very early stage that Jesus is God incarnate. *The Hidden Years*, like the Gospels themselves, is more circumspect and has its characters gradually come to understand who Jesus is.

What makes this novel so powerful and more successful than many other complementing narratives is that, unlike them, it presents a Jesus who questions and struggles with serious theological dilemmas, a trait that is often only seen in competing novels. Many works of popular Christian piety feature a Jesus who is completely confident in his identity and certain of his mission. While these works are pious and complementing, they are also bland and lifeless. They mundanely retell the Gospel stories and fill in a few gaps here and there, but typically, they offer little critical reflection and appear almost afraid to do so.

The Hidden Years, however, does not hesitate to ask the hard questions and to point out problematic areas in Christianity by having its Jesus expose similar issues in Israel's religion. During the novel's temptation scene, Satan accurately summarizes the character of Boyd's Jesus and also hits on the reason why many complementing novels prefer a Jesus who has all the answers rather than one with multiple questions. He says, "You are a man who insists on asking, Why, Why, Why? And whoever asks why, him religion destroys . . . *Any* attack on religion, however heinous religion is, is judged by religious people to be blasphemy; and blasphemy is an 'insult to God'" (227).

Boyd through his Jesus character can playfully satirize the pompousness and insipid nature of much of his own tradition through scenes like the Capernaum synagogue, the temple official's visit to Nazareth, and the rich Pharisees' prayers in the temple. His criticism, however, is constructive because it aims to correct aberrations rather than to condemn either Christianity or the Gospels' portrayal of Jesus, two motivations that are common among competing narratives. The Johannine Jesus' image of pruning a vine to bear more fruit (John 15:1–5) springs to mind as an accurate description of what Boyd attempts to do with his Jesus character and his implicit (and sometimes explicit, as in his temptation scene) castigations of Christianity.

In literary terms, the novel is a success because it does not simply parrot the Gospel Jesus' words or replay the same scenes. Boyd takes Jesus' words and repackages them in a format more accessible to modern readers, and he places his Jesus character in new situations where his actions display a likeness to those of the Gospel Jesus. Boyd successfully transforms the Gospel Jesus into a fictional one and gives him new stories to tell and new adventures to experience. With *The Hidden Years*, a reader can enjoy a novel that is literarily unique while also remaining within the Gospel boundaries with its fictional Jesus. As a paradigmatic example of complementing narratives functioning according to their intentions, this novel makes the fictional Jesus and his world come alive and can easily provoke its readers to return to the Gospels with a fresh zeal for understanding their world and their portrayals of Jesus.

4

Nino Ricci's *Testament* as a Competing Rewrite

INTRODUCTION

In 2002, Canadian author Nino Ricci published a new version of Jesus' story in the novel *Testament*. The child of Italian immigrants, Ricci was raised in the Roman Catholic Church and dabbled in evangelicalism before finally leaving Christianity all together. Ricci says that while by his early adulthood he could no longer call himself a Christian he was still never able to forget about Jesus. *Testament* is the product of his wrestling with this larger-than-life figure, with the complexities he sees within the Gospels, and with the problems he has with the Christian religion. For his efforts with the novel, Ricci has garnered many critical accolades, such as the Trillium Award, the U.S. Booklist Choice for Top 10 Historical Novels of the Year, and U.K. Times Literary Supplement Book of the Year.

With this novel, we arrive at our first case study of "mosaic moving" seen in this overt attempt to challenge the Gospel portrayals of Jesus and to encourage doubt regarding the credibility of their testimonies. In the first part of this chapter, we will focus on the ways in which the novel attempts to undermine and call into question the Gospel forms in which the pieces were originally placed. We will do this by first exploring how Ricci sets the stage for a comparison between *Testament* and the Gospels with the form in which he casts the novel. Then, we will look at the direct and indirect use of Gospel material in *Testament* and summarize the various ways in which the novel supports, subverts, or rejects outright the testimony of the evangelists. Next, we will consider how *Testament* questions not only the evangelists' testimony but also its own witnesses by framing them as unreliable narrators. Through this analysis, it will be shown that the novel attempts to subvert the Gospel testimonies both on a mirco level, by challenging presentations and interpretations of specific events given by the evangelists, and on a macro level, by calling into question the reliability of the Gospel narratives themselves. Finally, we will examine the portrait Ricci constructs in place of the Gospel Jesus and compare these portraits with one another before offering a response to Ricci's attempt at competing with and subverting the Gospels. By using Ricci's *Testament* as a case study for competing novels, we shall be better able to recognize competing techniques used in other Jesus novels and also become familiar with an important example of Jesus imagery in modern literature.

FICTIONAL GAP FILLING OR MOSAIC MOVING?

As noted in the prolegomenon, images often conflict with one another, and sometimes one even succeeds in supplanting another. Often this occurs unintentionally, but in the case of removing the gems belonging to one mosaic and repositioning them into a starkly different pattern, it is hard to imagine that such action has been taken without at least some intention to challenge the original form. When artists remove pieces from their original positions in the Gospels and replace them in new works that offer competing Christologies, their actions suggest that these "mosaic movers" have some sort of problem with the original portraits.

Mosaic Moving Intentions

The problem, of course, varies depending on who is looking at the Gospel images and on what they hope to find in them. In Ricci's case, as well as that of many historical Jesus questers, the problem appears to be that while he wants to find the actual Jesus in the Gospels the evangelists were more interested in painting portraits that captured who they believed Jesus really was and not solely how he appeared in actuality. In one interview, Ricci states, "My idea in *Testament* was to try to look at the figure of Jesus in purely human, and hence non-Christian, terms. In other words, if we supposed that some *actual historical figure* lay behind *the myth of Jesus* as it was handed down, what might he have been like, stripped of the interpolations and inventions of Christian tradition?"[1] In this search to find the actual Jesus behind what he believes to be layers of myth hiding Jesus in the Gospels, the influence of modern historical criticism on Ricci is evident.

Challenging the Original Form and Supplanting the Testimony of the Gospels With a New Testament

Instead of deriving his portrait from the final form of the Gospels or from any Gospel Jesus mosaic, Ricci has more confidence in the historical Jesuses constructed by various Jesus Seminar participants. As Ricci himself states in his Author's Note, his own narrative portrait of Jesus is influenced more by their work than by the original Gospel pictures themselves (457).[2] In fact, with *Testament,* Robert Funk, the founder of the Jesus Seminar, has finally gotten his wish for a fictional narrative that places Jesus within a different narrative context. Even better than having only one new "gospel" as Funk desired, Ricci provides him with four![3] The parodied gospel form used by Ricci is intentionally subversive.

Also, because the novel is presented as a recognizably fictitious narrative of Jesus' life, Ricci is apparently making a statement on what he and others, such as Funk, perceive to be the fictitious nature of the canonical Gospels. If this is his aim, then Ricci is not the first to attempt such a maneuver. Celsus, one of the earliest critics of Christianity, once created a fictional dialogue between a Jewish Christian and other Jews in which he couched his own criticisms of Christianity. One of the more covert intentions behind Celsus' decision to use a fictional genre for his attacks was that its use would be likely to expose what he deemed to be the "fictitious" nature of the canonical Gospels. The aim of such writing was that after reading the work the audience would agree with the implicit suggestion embedded in the fictitious form—that the Gospel stories are just as fictional as the fictions Celsus created.[4]

Ricci challenges the claim that the Gospels are reliable testimonies of Jesus' life and mounts his assault against the evangelists' portraits by using both dismantling and constructing techniques. As in Irenaeus's analogy, he first pulls the image of the Gospel Jesus "all to pieces" and then reshapes and rearranges these pieces while adding new ones as well so that they fit

1. Ricci, "An Interview with Nino Ricci"; emphasis added.

2 All page references to Ricci, *Testament,* will be given in parentheses throughout this chapter.

3. Funk, "Jesus," 12.

4. Bowersock, *Fiction,* 3–4.

together in a new narrative structure that offers a competing fictional portrait of Jesus. In a word, *Testament's* ultimate aim is to supplant the testimony of the Gospels by undermining their original form and replacing the
evangelists' testimonies with new recognizably fictitious parodies of them.

TAKING THE GOSPELS "ALL TO PIECES": COMPETING TECHNIQUES

Setting the Stage for a Comparison Between Testament and the Gospels

*Parodying the Structure of the Four Gospels and Providing Four
New "Evangelists"*

The reader first learns that she is meant to compare the testimonies of *Testament* with those of the Gospels through Ricci's structural parody of the
four-fold Gospel. His narrative provides alternative testimonies to those of
Matthew, Mark, Luke, and John given instead by Yihuda of Qiryat (Judas
Iscariot), Miryam of Migdal (Mary Magdalene), Miryam (Jesus' mother
Mary), and Simon of Gergesa. The first three of these four "gospels" are
written by "evangelists" whose characters are based on historical persons
described in the Gospels and which have been imported into *Testament's*
fictional realm. There, they are recreated and transformed by Ricci's narrative to fit their new surroundings, but at the same time, they also retain
many of their historical features. Since their historical counterparts are all
first-century Israelites and therefore would have spoken Aramaic, the characters in the novel are also identified by the Aramaic form of their names,
and throughout their narratives, they use the Aramaic forms for people and
place names.[5] In doing this, Ricci attempts to surpass the Gospel narra-
tions by making *Testament* more historically accurate to the language that
Jesus, his disciples, and these witnesses would have used rather than using
the Greek form used by the evangelists.

   Unlike the first three narrators, Simon, the fourth narrator, has no historical counterpart, although he is a historically plausible character, an imaginary

---

5. Using the more foreign, at least to the modern reader, Aramaic form of names
not only increases the novel's historical accuracy by tying its narrative world to the
external, historical world, but it also serves to defamiliarize a very familiar story and to
accentuate the feeling of distance between the modern reader and the story's ancient
setting (Crook, "Fictionalizing Jesus," 39). For simplification purposes, I have chosen
to use the more familiar Greek or Latin version of the names throughout this chapter
rather than follow Ricci's use of the Aramaic names.

extension of the first-century Palestinian world and of the Gentiles to whom Jesus reportedly ministered. Because his character is a Greek-speaking farmer from Gergesa on the Gentile side of the Sea of Galilee, in his narration all of the Aramaic names and places used in the first three testimonies shift to the more familiar Greek forms. For example, Yihuda of Qiryat becomes Judas Iscariot, Notzerah is Nazareth, and Yeshua is Jesus.

The externally referential characters (i.e., Judas, Mary Magdalene, and Mary) with other imaginary extensions, such as Simon, blend together in this new fictional world modeled after the historical one. That both historical and fictional characters can plausibly coexist within the new fictional world is a feature of historical fiction that Ricci uses to great effect. That Ricci has chosen Gospel characters for three of his four witnesses further increases the comparison between *Testament* and the Gospels. Their "Gospel" status gives weight to their testimonies and to their ability to challenge the testimonies of those Gospels.

Using the Form of First-Person Testimony

In his discussion on the reliability of testimony, Richard Bauckham describes two ways in which a testimony can be called into question: first, when it is not internally consistent or coherent and second, when it conflicts with external evidence.[6] Certainly, one of the major sources of external evidence that elicits doubt about a testimony is that of conflicting testimonies, and this second route is the one that Ricci has chosen in his competitive endeavor.

Testament is able to challenge the Gospels by beating them at their own game, so to speak. Like the works of the four evangelists, *Testament*'s four alternate testimonies are presented as having been written within living memory of the events themselves. The novel's "gospels" one-up the canonical Gospels, however, because they are not only based on eyewitness testimony but are the testimonies of *the* eyewitnesses themselves, told in first person and with their own voices.

As is typical in the genre of historical fiction, Ricci uses the technique of narrating the past via first-person memoir and thus provides readers with an intimate view of the events and characters involved in them.[7] One of

6. Bauckham, *Eyewitnesses*, 506.

7. Leo Tolstoy believed that this type of narration was important because, according to him, even fictional versions when told from the perspective of characters involved in those events could bring readers closer to the truth than historical narratives (Cohn, *Distinction*, 151–52).

the purposes of framing *Testament* through these first-person memoirs is to establish a perspective that purports to show *what really happened* before rumors and myth-making covered up the truth, and only eyewitnesses are able to do this. That the testimonies in the novel differ significantly from those of the evangelists is an intentional device meant to undermine the Gospels as reliable testimony.

Importing External Historical Referents Into a Fictional World

Finally, Ricci imports not only historically referential characters but also draws upon external historical sources when constructing *Testament's* fictional world. In addition to the historical Jesus portraits created by members of the Jesus Seminar that Ricci imports (457),[8] he also brings in ancient historical sources like the noncanonical gospels,[9] Josephus,[10] Philo,[11] Tacitus,[12] and either Celsus or the Talmud.[13]

The majority of imported material in *Testament*, as in any Jesus novel, however, comes from the canonical Gospels. Ricci mixes these bits with those from his other sources, stirs them together, and forms his own new fictional Jesus and fictional world. This appropriation of pieces from the Gospel Jesus mosaic draws the reader's attention to those original images and prompts a comparison between Ricci's fictional Jesus and the Gospel Jesus.[14]

---

8. According to the website of the publisher Houghton Mifflin Harcourt, Crossan's *Historical Jesus* is one of Ricci's main sources for material.

9. For example, Ricci appears to draw from the following sayings in the *Gospel of Thomas* (137, cf. *Gos. Thom.* 3, 78; 179, cf. *Gos. Thom.* 53; 137, cf. *Gos. Thom.* 113a, 113b) and from these chapters in the *Infancy Gospel of Thomas* (239, cf. *Inf. Gos Thom.* 6–8; 241–43, cf. *Inf. Gos Thom.* 14, 15).

10. *A.J.* 17.10.9; 18.3.1; 18.5.2; *B.J.* 2.5.1; 2.9.2; 2.9.2–3

11. Pilate and the standards incident (61–62, cf. *Legatio ad Gaium* 38).

12. Pompey's entering into the Holy of Holies and discovering that it is empty (259, cf. *Historiae* 5.11–12).

13. Jesus' conception as a result of Mary sleeping with a Roman soldier (227, cf. Origen, *Cels.* 1.69 [*ANF* 4:428]; *b Sanh 67a*, 104b); the accusation of Jesus being a frivolous disciple (243, cf. *b Sot 47a*; 107b); the accusation of Jesus using magic that he learned while in Egypt (51, 146, cf. *b Sanh 43a*, 104b, 107b; *b Sot 47a*).

14. While I agree with Crook that speaking of Ricci's Jesus "is almost as complex as distilling a single portrait of Jesus from the four canonical gospels" (Crook, "Fictionalizing Jesus," 50), I do think that it can be done. When we look at the discourse level of the novel, there are four varied portraits of Jesus, and they certainly do offer different interpretations. When we look at the story level of the novel, however, there is a fairly coherent portrait of Jesus that emerges after comparing the different testimonies. On this level, we can speak of Ricci's fictional Jesus.

The Use and Analysis of Gospel Material in Testament

Direct and Indirect References to Gospel Material Within Testament

Now that we have seen some of the ways in which the novel is intentionally structured to create a comparison between it and the Gospels, we can turn to an analysis of the ways in which Gospel material is reused and presented in *Testament*.

Most Jesus novels are not simple harmonizations that import direct quotations from the Gospels and rearrange that material into a new order.[15] They are literary works in their own right (some more so than others) that create their new Jesus characters and do not always use a great deal of biblical material. When they do use Gospel stories, they often transform them to such an extent that they are not easily recognizable. *Testament* is one such novel that is sparse on biblical allusions. Often Ricci succeeds in making imported Gospel material almost unrecognizable. Indeed, he goes a step further than most Jesus novelists and almost never has his Jesus character utter a direct quotation from the Gospels. For example, in the first of the novel's four testimonies, Judas directly quotes Ricci's Jesus approximately sixty-five times.[16] Only six of those can be characterized as possible allusions to sayings uttered by the Gospel Jesus, and most of these are placed in completely different contexts and often are altered to carry variant connotations from their biblical counterparts.[17]

15. It is true that some of the older, more conservative novels do little more than have their Jesus characters parrot the red-letter lines of the Gospels, but more recent, and certainly more successful, novels avoid such verbatim quotation.

16. Certainly part of the reason for the paucity of biblical allusions in the direct quotations of Ricci's Jesus within Judas's testimony is that most of his lines (approximately half) take place within new dialogues between him and Judas created for the novel. Still the lack of biblical sayings for Ricci's Jesus and the way in which the few that are used have been transformed and transferred to other contexts are suggestive of the author's attitude towards the canonical Gospels.

17. Here are the six statements that appear to be allusions to Gospel material:
- When followers asked why he continues to be kind to Rakiil, a tax collector who persists in cheating them despite their graciousness to him, Jesus replies, "How honest would my kindness to him be if it were only a means of seeking more favourable treatment from him?" (53; cf. Matt 5.43–47; Luke 6.27–35; and possibly Luke 14:12–14). The Jesus seminar ranked the idea of "loving your enemies" as the third highest among the statements that were likely to have come from the historical Jesus (Funk and Hoover, *Five Gospels*, 147).
- "Why are you coming with weapons against me?" (55; cf. Matt 26:60; Mark 14:48; and Luke 52). Jesus asks this question not of soldiers coming to arrest him in Gethsemane but of a crowd at Korazin that barred his entrance in to the town because of his work with lepers.

When we broaden the search beyond just the direct quotations of Ricci's Jesus, we find that the number of possible allusions to Gospel material increases. I have found almost two hundred such allusions, although there are probably more. Not surprisingly, the testimonies of Judas and Mary Magdalene contain the most allusions (sixty-two and fifty-seven respectively) since their narratives cover a greater amount of Jesus' public ministry. Simon of Gergesa's narrative, which has the next highest amount (thirty-nine), focuses on the end of Jesus' ministry and his life. His tale begins when Jesus branches out to the Decapolis area, continues with his pilgrimage to and last week in Jerusalem for the Passover, and concludes with his death. Mary's testimony has the fewest (twenty-nine), and this too is understandable because her narrative, unlike the others, focuses predominantly on Jesus' life prior to his ministry.

Analysis of Which Witnesses Tend to Be the Most Faithful to the Gospels (Color Coding)

In order to better discern Ricci's techniques and intentions, after compiling a list of these allusions, I decided that it would be helpful to analyze them in relation to how closely they matched their Gospel antecedents. By doing this, I was able to offer a general summary of each witness's stance towards the Gospels by looking at how often each one supported, transformed, subverted, or rejected outright the Gospel versions. I also was able to categorize some of the main techniques used to challenge the evangelists' testimonies while still using Gospel material or at least referencing it. I then color-coded the allusions red, pink, grey, or black according to

- "It's what's inside you that pollutes you, not what's outside" (55; cf. Matt 15:17–20; Mark 7:18–23). This statement is also made in the controversy over his ministry to the lepers and not in relation to food laws, although in both situations, the issues raised concern OT purity laws.
- "What kind of a doctor ignores the sick?" (56; cf. Matt 9:12; Mark 2:17; Luke 5:31). Jesus says this when his followers beg him to refrain from visiting the lepers because he is losing the crowds for their sake and not, as in the Synoptics, in the context of being criticized by the Pharisees for eating with tax collectors and sinners.
- "'If someone comes with only the truth, it's not enough for them,' he said, growing bitter. 'They have to have wonders'" (91; cf. John 4:48).
- When Judas tells Jesus who will accompany him when he goes off alone, Jesus responds, "So you see how the last are first" (96; cf. Matt 19:30; 20:16; Mark 10:31; Luke 13:30). This quotation takes place in the context of Jesus choosing Judas as one of the three who will accompany him on a journey instead of choosing the usual suspects (Peter, James, or John) whereas in the Synoptics the statement takes place in the context of eschatological judgment.

how closely they resembled their biblical referents, red being the closest and black being the most unlike them. Because Ricci seemed most interested in recovering the actual Jesus through these fictional testimonies, I paid particular attention to the level of historicity that *Testament* gave to these biblical allusions through the way in which they were portrayed or presented in the narrative. The following is an explanation of the criteria used and also a summary of some of the main ways in which the Gospel material was handled in the novel.

RED:

Red was ascribed to those allusions that were very consistent with a least one Gospel version and seemed to support the historicity of the material referenced.[18]

- Often these were simply statements of historical details—Jesus once went to Tyre to preach (25, 154, cf. Matt 15.21; Mark 7.24); Simon was nicknamed "the Rock" (26, 128, cf. Matt 16.18); Judas carried the common purse (John 13.29); etc.

- A passage was colored red when it agreed with and provided a generalization of something that the Gospel Jesus often taught. For example, Simon of Gergesa says that Jesus used to teach that there was no "point of worrying whether you had enough money or if your barns were full enough" (331; cf. Matt 6.25–34; Luke 12.16–32).

- Finally, red was given to a part that detailed a typical perception of the Gospel Jesus by other characters noted in the canonical versions. That Judas and Mary Magdalene both relate that Jesus was accused of healing through sorcery by the strength of the devil is an example of these type of red passages (51, 144–46; cf. Matt 12.24; Mark 3.22; Luke 11.15).

PINK:

Pink was used for passages that were fairly clear Gospel allusions that had been transformed or twisted in Ricci's text so that they were in some way inconsistent with the Gospel versions. In a pink passage, Ricci's witnesses

18. I am not interested in determining with which Gospel they were most consistent but only with confirming whether or not they were consistent with some version of the story found in at least one of the canonical Gospels. Analyzing them according to Markan, Matthean, Lukan, or Johannine consistency would have complicated the study too much.

suggested that there was at least a historical basis for these events or sayings even if later accounts (that is, the Gospels) distorted them.

- Different methods were used to achieve this transformation such as placing a biblical event within a different narrative context or keeping the context the same but changing the action or dialogue within it.

  - An example of the first type is when Ricci's Jesus says, "It's what's inside you that pollutes you, not what's outside" (55, cf. Matt 15.11; Mark 7.15). Instead of making this statement in the context of questioning ritual purity on the basis of food, as the Gospel Jesus does, Ricci's Jesus makes this statement in regard to leprosy and in answer to those who seek to bar him from entering their town because they believe he has been polluted through his ministry with lepers. The situations are similar in that they both have to do with the issue of ritual purity, but the historical contexts for the statements are different. Here, we see how Ricci puts into narrative form what so many biblical scholars have come to believe: that many of Jesus' sayings may have had their genesis in settings other than those in which the evangelists placed them in their Gospels.

  - An example of the second type would be Jesus' trial before Pilate (430–434, cf. Matt 27.11–14; Mark 15.2–5; Luke 23.2–5; John 18.28–38). While the context is that of a trial before Pilate in the praetorium, the dialogue varies.

- Also, a biblical event could be interpreted in a significantly different way in Ricci's version from those of the evangelists. Typical of passages that I designated pink was the demythologizing of the miracles in the Gospels. An example of this is the healing, not exorcism, of the Phoenician woman's daughter. In Ricci's version, the girl suffers from the trauma of a rape and an unwanted pregnancy and not from a demon as the mother suspects and as the Gospel versions state (27–30; cf. Matt 15.21–28; Mark 7.24–30). Ricci's Jesus "heals" the girl by gently wiping her face, which calms her down, by giving her some food, and by providing her mother with some herbs from which to make a brew if she ever suffers from another attack.

GREY:

- Passages were grey for different reasons. First, they received a grey mark if they appeared similar enough to something in the Gospels to suggest that from the basis of a very small historical kernel a larger, mythical Gospel story could later grow, but at the same time, they were presented in such a disguised manner that it was difficult to connect them with the Gospel versions at all. For example, all of *Testament's* witnesses refer in various ways to the fact that after John's arrest, some of John's acolytes, of whom Jesus was one, went into the wilderness to hide (21, 126, 286, and 367–68). Judas notes that when he meets Jesus after he has come out of the wilderness that it was not quite two months (thus close to forty days) since John the Baptist had been arrested (21). While there is no temptation by Satan during this time, Ricci appears to be alluding to the wilderness episode narrated in all three Synoptics (Matt 4.1–11; Mark 1.12–13; and Luke 4.1–13). The implication is that over time, the simple fact of Jesus retreating to the wilderness, which *Testament* records accurately, could morph into a cosmic battle between the Son of God and Satan.

- Second, I categorized something as grey whenever a completely new event or saying resembling something that the Gospel Jesus would have done was narrated. These parts fit a pattern of the Gospel Jesus but were not drawn from the Gospels themselves. One such example was when Judas tells of Ricci's Jesus healing a boy with a broken shinbone (35). While not found in the Gospels, this story is similar to the many healings the Gospel Jesus performed and implies that on the basis of such "historical" events, which may have been lost or left unrecorded, Jesus' reputation as a healer or a teacher could have developed.

BLACK:

Finally, passages were given a black coding when they referred to a story in the Gospels but contradicted it by describing almost the exact opposite of what the Gospels claimed.

- This subversion could happen by presenting a different, but still historically plausible, account of events. Perhaps the best example of this type of passage is Simon of Gergesa's suggestion of the "non-Resurrection." Under the cover of darkness after the crucifixion, Simon watches as the family of one of the other crucified criminals bribes the tomb guards to remove a relative's body. Later when Simon hears the rumor that Jesus resurrected, he wonders whether that family mistakenly took Jesus' body and whether that is why the women who came the next morning could not find his body (450–451).

- This also could be done by presenting a Gospel saying or event in Ricci's narrative as a complete fabrication not based on an actual historical event. For example, Simon narrates the Markan story of Jesus healing the blind man at Bethsaida with spit and the laying on of his hands (Mark 8.22–26), but in the novel, this miracle has no basis in reality but is merely an invention by the prankster Jerubal (340–341).

The Witness Who Is Typically Most Faithful to the Gospel Versions

Biblical Allusions in Mary Magdalene's Testimony (57)

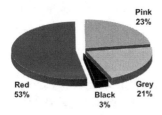

Pink 23%

Red 53%

Grey 21%

Black 3%

Next, I used the number of red, pink, grey, and black passages found in each of the testimonies of the four witnesses to determine which witnesses were more likely to confirm the perspectives of the evangelists and which were more likely to supplant them. Mary Magdalene was the witness whose testimony most often resembled that of the Gospels with more red passages than any of the other witnesses (thirty in total). Within her own testimony, there were more red allusions than any other color, but her testimony, like the others, had a high percentage of pink and grey passages with only a few black interspersed.

Judas had the next highest number of red passages, which was surprising to find given the skeptical tone throughout his narrative. More in keeping with that tone, however, was the fact that his allusions were more likely *not* to be red. This indicates that Judas typically took a doubtful stance towards the historicity of the material reported in the Gospels or at least towards the interpretation given to that material. A theme

Biblical Allusions in Judas' Testimony (62)

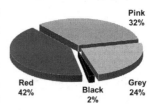

Pink 32%

Red 42%

Black 2%

Grey 24%

especially prevalent in his narrative was how the supernatural events in the Gospels were in reality only natural occurrences in reality.

Mary, Jesus' mother, had the smallest number of red allusions (only nine) of any of the witnesses, but she had an almost identical percentage of them within her own narrative, as did Simon. Only about a third of their versions of biblical events tended to agree with those of their Gospel

Biblical Allusions in Mary's Testimony (30)

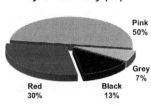

Pink 50%

Grey 7%

Red 30%

Black 13%

counterparts, but Mary and Simon differed as to the ways in which they tended to transform or undermine the Gospel testimonies. Mary was more likely to twist the Gospel material than to contradict it outright. Most notable of her contradictions is her version of Jesus' conception. Her story confirms the rumor reported by Celsus[19] and related in the Talmud[20] that Jesus is the bastard son of Mary and a Roman soldier, which goes against the Synoptic claim that he is the Son of God born of the virgin Mary (cf. Matt 1:18–25; Luke 1:31–38).

Simon of Gergesa's testimony was the most complex in relation to the Gospel material. He had the highest percentage of both grey and black allusions of any of the witnesses. Several of his black passages, such as Jerubal's invention of Jesus healing the blind man (340–41), implied that the biblical versions were complete fictions founded on either invented stories or misunderstandings.

Biblical Allusions in Simon's Testimony (41)

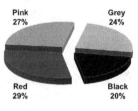

Pink 27%

Grey 24%

Red 29%

Black 20%

Thus, all of the witnesses aided to some extent, but at different levels, in subverting aspects of the Gospels by transforming or contradicting their material and by engendering doubt about the testimonies of the evangelists. The findings were intriguing not only because of the above ways in which Ricci's narrators challenged the Gospels by changing their material but also because of the following implicit ways in which *Testament* suggested that the Gospel testimonies should be doubted.

Complementing Or Competing Narrative Worlds and Worldviews?

Contradictory Narratives and Unreliable Narrators

The collection of Gospel material used within *Testament* allowed for a comparison of the witnesses' testimonies whenever they narrated two versions of the same biblical event. While the four testimonies did not overlap very much, there were a few occasions when they used the same Gospel story.

In general, when two narrators used the same material, their accounts agreed with one another either in support of the biblical versions or against

19. Origen, *Cels.* 1.69 (*ANF* 4:428).

20. *b Sanh 67a, 104b.*

them. There were, however, a few interesting examples of different versions of the same event, or at least varied interpretations of the event's meaning. These contradictory narratives, which are those "in which more than one 'incompatible and irreconcilable' version of the story appears,"[21] not only cast *Testament*'s narrators as unreliable but also served to instill doubt regarding the biblical event to which they alluded.[22]

The unreliability of its narrators is perhaps the most apparent way in which *Testament*'s narrative world differed from those of the Gospels. In the Gospels, the evangelists present themselves as trustworthy, as those who through careful investigation and on the basis of eyewitness accounts are capable of delivering faithful and true narratives of Jesus' life (cf. Luke 1:1–4; John 21:24). Even when no overt claims are made by the evangelists (i.e., Mark and Matthew) regarding the trustworthiness of their accounts, there is never any suggestion that they are to be doubted. The same cannot be said in *Testament*'s narrative world where uncertainty is engendered regarding its own narrators and extended to question the reliability of testimony in general.

To understand how this facet of *Testament*'s narrative world develops, we will focus on the character of Mary Magdalene. While all of *Testament*'s narrators could be classified as "unreliable," Mary Magdalene is the one whose testimony is presented as the most unreliable.

Guilt by Association: How the Other Witnesses Characterize Mary Magdalene As an Unreliable Narrator

In Ricci's novel, the unreliable nature of the witnesses becomes apparent not solely through the existence of different portrayals of the same event. More subtly, the integrity of the narrators is questioned by their co-narrators, and even by themselves sometimes, as they establish motivations for why their testimonies should be doubted. This is certainly true in the case of Mary Magdalene.

---

21. Keen, *Narrative Form*, 96.

22. To say that a narrator is unreliable suggests that the author "deliberately exploits readers' awareness that the version of the story retailed [sic] by the narrator should be treated with skepticism." As narrators become more overt and personified, as they do in first-person memoirs, the chances for unreliability increase (ibid., 42). Such is certainly the case in *Testament*.

Keen's definition of the unreliable narrator is slightly different from the one first suggested by Wayne Booth. Booth simply defines the unreliable narrator as one whose views or presentation is discordant with that of the implied author (Booth, *The Rhetoric of Fiction*, 158–59).

All three of the other witnesses are united in the opinion that Mary Magdalene has strong feelings about Jesus. Judas talks about the way that all the women hover like Greek furies around Jesus and how Mary Magdalene in particular competes with Judas for Jesus' time, never wanting to leave him alone (44). Simon of Gergesa comments on the way that she "wanted to possess the man" and how she barely let him out of her sight (365). Mary, Jesus' mother, makes the most telling observation when she says, "I saw how besotted she was with him and how she worshipped him, so that she could not see him clearly" (314). She also says that she can tell Mary Magdalene wishes she were Jesus' wife (291). Even Mary Magdalene herself betrays signs of a romantic interest in Jesus, at least at first. Her first impression of Jesus when her father brings him to their home is that he is a potential suitor (126). When he leaves their house the first time, she acts like a girl in love, crying when he goes and wanting to take the mat he had slept on for her own (127–28). Later on, she portrays herself as having moved past being interested in things like marriage (196) and seems to love Jesus more as a worshipper and disciple rather than as a lover.

Another charge against Mary Magdalene is that of a lack of intelligence or at least of discernment capabilities. When Judas meets Jesus' followers, he comments that there was not one among them who was an educated person (41). Mary accuses Mary Magdalene of being "a simple girl of Galilee, with the credulity of Galileans" (314). As we shall see in a moment, Mary Magdalene is presented as credulous through her acceptance of the testimony of another character. Even by her own testimony, she presents herself as one who is superstitious enough to believe in pagan magic (170).

According to one literary theorist, plausible clues for determining that a narrator is unreliable include such things as a heightened psychological state, a low IQ, and extreme youth.[23] The co-narrators establish each of these as reasons for Mary Magdalene's unreliability as they portray her psychological state as that of a woman in love obsessed by the object of her worship and question her intelligence. She is also presented as a young girl, little more than a child (291) but one of a marriageable age (126).

The Example of the Transfiguration Accounts

Let us take a moment to examine how the gullibility of Mary Magdalene, and therefore her unreliability as a narrator, is contrasted with the calm and reasonable testimony of Judas on the issue of the transfiguration. According to Judas' version, which I designate as a pink passage, Jesus journeys to

23. Keen, *Narrative*, 42–43.

Mount Hermon with Simon the Canaanite, Judas, and John as companions rather than with Simon Peter, James, and John, as the Synoptics say (cf. Matt 17.1–9; Mark 9.2–10; Luke 9.28–36). They camp at the base of the mountain in the middle of a fog, and Jesus wanders off in the night. When Jesus' companions discover he is missing, Simon frantically runs after him leaving the others behind. Because it is dark and the fog is too thick to find either of them, Judas and John have to wait for morning to search.

Soon after setting out, they find Simon in an agitated state coming down the mountain. He shouts that he has found Jesus and that he is up on the mountaintop with "the others." Judas notes that Simon was babbling and that they could not calm him down.

As they climb the mountain together and pierce through the fog, they find Jesus at the top by himself. Simon swears that earlier there had been angels with Jesus, but Jesus himself assures them that he had always been there entirely alone, noting, "If there had been angels, I would have been the first to see them" (102). Still, Simon cannot be dissuaded, and Judas tells the reader that when they return to Galilee, "it was Simon's version of things, being the most fantastical, that seemed at once to gain currency" (103). Even before they reach Galilee though, Judas says, "I was surprised to discover that tales of the miracles he had wrought on Mount Hermon were already circulating, along with Simon's story of the angels; it was amazing to me, this hunger people had for wonders, and the speed with which they published them" (110).

Judas' narration of the events comes across as objective and measured. In addition, according to his testimony, even Jesus himself denies the appearance of any supernatural beings. In contrast, Simon has already been described by Judas as being in a state of fear and panic induced by his belief that his former gods are coming back as demons to torment him for his desertion of them to follow Jesus. Judas characterizes Simon as "growing more and more crazed" and as suffering from a "kind of madness" (100) so that the reader is leery to believe the tale told by one whose mental capacities are impaired.

Before reaching Mary Magdalene's narrative, which is strategically placed in the novel after Judas', the reader knows not to trust the crazy Canaanite's version of the transfiguration. Unfortunately, Mary Magdalene does not know better, and it is Simon's version that she records. Her acceptance of his story does nothing to bolster faith in her judgment capabilities.[24]

---

24. She briefly writes, "Simon the Canaanite told how he had seen huge ghosts in Yeshua's company on Mount Hermon, and how Yeshua himself had stood transfigured and white as if the very light of the Lord had glowed inside him" (216).

The reader now has two conflicting interpretations of the same event, and here we see a typical ploy in historical fiction of narrating the event and then showing how that event is told quite differently by participants in it.[25] This strategy leads to discrediting eyewitness testimony. By first having Judas narrate the event and provide a calm, reasonable, and natural explanation and then contrasting it with Simon's incredible supernatural explanation, which is retold again in Mary Magdalene's narrative, *Testament* teaches the reader to become more cautious in crediting the testimony given by Mary Magdalene.

The Effect of Linking Mary Magdalene's Testimony with the Gospel Accounts

When explaining how to determine whether or not a narrator is unreliable, Keen says that it often comes down to the question of motivation: "What effect would the author produce by rendering the narrator unreliable?[26] Therefore, we must ask, what would be the effect of establishing Mary Magdalene as the most unreliable of the four narrators?

As noted earlier, Mary Magdalene's testimony is more closely aligned with the Gospel accounts than any of the other testimonies. Hers is the one with the highest number of red allusions. In addition, Mary Magdalene is presented in the novel as the only one of the four witnesses who could be classified as a true disciple.[27] In all four of the testimonies, each of the narrators connects Jesus with the Johannine image of a gate or doorway (10:9), but Mary Magdalene is the only one who passes through it to travel with Jesus.[28] She is the one who is able to believe in and to love Jesus in a way that the others, though they regard him highly, cannot. They can never shake

25. In *Testament*, however, the events themselves are always told within a testimony by a first-person narrator and never by an objective, unseen third-person narrator. The third-person point of view gives readers the impression that they are reading the events exactly as they happened whereas a first-person narration draws attention to the subjective viewpoint from which the events are being retold.

26. Keen, *Narrative*, 42–43.

27. Jesus specifically says that Judas was the one they could not win over (217). One of the discussion questions provided on the website of publisher *Houghton Mifflin Harcourt* picks up on the contrast between her and the other three: "Of the four narrators, Miryam of Migdal is the one who could most closely be described as a true follower of Yeshua."

28. Compare the following quotations to understand the different positions each of the witnesses has in relation to faith in Jesus (all italics are added):

Judas: "And even now, *though I had left him*, I often saw him beckoning me as towards a *doorway* he would have had me pass through, from *darkness to light*" (122).

their doubts enough to follow him as she does. Yet, it is precisely that love and that belief that work against her reliability as a narrator.

Mary Magdalene also appears to be the only one of the four who remains as a follower after Jesus' death when the group returns to Capernaum and tries to keep Jesus' teaching and ministry going.[29] It makes sense that her version of the events would most "affect" the proto-Christian community and so most resemble what that community's descendants will one day write in the Gospels.

Linking the most unreliable narrator, the witness who is presented as the most gullible, whose judgment is impaired by love, with the Gospels has the effect of undermining their credibility. *Testament* delivers one further blow by having even the most credulous witness, the one whose narrative is most likely to coincide with those of the evangelists, often question their versions of events with her own narrative. As the chart above shows, only a little over half of her allusions remain like their Gospel counterparts without some sort of transformation or denial of their accuracy.

A Competing Worldview?

If even the testimony of Mary Magdalene, the one disciple-narrator, conflicts with many of the reports given in the Gospels, then it is not surprising that the other testimonies more blatantly question the Gospels' historicity.

Mary Magdalene: "Rather it was as if a *door* had suddenly opened, or a passage been granted to a country you'd hoped might exist but had never quite dared to imagine. I could smell the air of this other place on him, feel the wind of it, see its different sunrise, and felt inside me the sudden sure thought that *I must travel there with him*" (128).

Mary: "Indeed it seemed that since Yeshua had gone from me I had put from my mind all thoughts except those of the marriage of my daughters and sons, and that the *doorway* he had opened for me *had been closed*" (285). Mary also compares her faith with that of Mary Magdalene's: "Yet it was true that when she spoke of my son the wonder I heard in her voice was not so different from what I myself had felt, that sense of a *doorway* Yeshua stood before, to some new understanding. Except that *she had passed through it*, and saw things in a different *light*" (314).

Simon: "And for a moment it was as if some curtain had been pushed aside in my head and *I had a glimpse* of something I understood but couldn't have put into words, like some beautiful thing, so beautiful it took your breath away, that you saw for an instant through a *gateway or door, then was gone*" (455).

29. Judas leaves the group at Jericho on the journey down to Jerusalem for Passover (383). We are never told what happens to Mary, but out of Jesus' family only her son Jacob (James) is mentioned as returning with the group to Capernaum and taking over for Jesus (452). Simon goes back to his home in Gergesa and never has much to do with the group again (452).

One of the main aspects of the worldview found in the Gospels that comes under fire in the novel is that of miracles. Unlike the Gospels, *Testament* operates under a modern materialistic worldview that leaves little room for anything miraculous.

Part of Ricci's anti-religious agenda appears to be a narrative demonstration of the process of oral transmission that form critics suggest led to these supernatural tales found in the NT. Right before our eyes, we see the transformation from historical fact to Gospel fiction occurring as stories are passed along and embellished. By describing this process, the novel demythologizes many of the miracles recounted in the Gospels. Through their four reminiscences, Ricci's witnesses tell how the simple reality of Jesus, the man, came to be transformed through rumors started by both his enemies and his followers and finally enshrouded in myths and legends that turn out to be strikingly similar to the stories in the canonical Gospels.

Crook in his work on the novel has noted that the power of rumor is a constant motif running throughout the narrative.[30] As Jesus' mother relates, frequently "tales of him were spread around, and grew more fantastical with each retelling" (296).[31] Nothing Jesus does seems to quell their growth. Judas describes how at one point Jesus grew so frustrated with the crowds' desire for wonders that he withdraws from them. His retreat from the public instead of calming the rumors only serves to enhance them. He says, "As what had once been freely offered became more inaccessible and rare, so did the stories grow of the wonders that Yeshua [Jesus] was capable of and of the miracle cures he had brought about" (91). He even has to make his own disciples promise not to spread rumors after he "heals" Lazarus, but it is no use (403). The rumors continue to grow.

Simon of Gergesa, speaking like a faithful disciple of Strauss,[32] offers the key quote that seems to sum up *Testament's* perspective regarding the creation of myths that begin to cover up the actual Jesus:

> It was probably the shock of Jesus' death that started twisting them, and that they had to strain to make sense of the thing, and that in time, with someone like Jesus, things got distorted. Now for every little thing he did when he was alive some story gets put in its place, and if he'd lanced somebody's boil it turned out he'd saved a whole town, and if there were fifty in a place who'd followed him, now it was five hundred . . . But however things

30. Crook, "Fictionalizing Jesus," 52; cf. 27–28.

31. "Fantastical" and its derivative "fanatic" seem to be favorite words of Ricci's because they are used repeatedly to describe the stories told about Jesus and those who follow him (e.g., 33, 82, 103, and 296).

32. Strauss, *The Life of Jesus Critically Examined.*

get remembered, you can be certain it won't be how they actually were, since one man will change a bit of this to suit his fancy, and one a bit of that, and another will spice it to make a better story of it. And by and by the truth of the thing will get clouded, and he'll be simply a yarn you tell to your children. And something will be lost then because he was a man of wisdom (453, 454).

The reader picks up on the implied point that as in this novel where the truth of events becomes more "fictional" as they are passed on from one person to another, especially when passed on by superstitious and credulous individuals, perhaps too the miraculous deeds described in the Gospels are only fictional constructions built up over time from the basis of very natural events to ever increasing "fantastical" heights. As Simon suggests, when there is a considerable gap between the events and their narration, the possibility of the perception of the events being altered by time and memory increases.[33] Stories about these events blossom and grow even further out of control after Jesus' death, and the resulting myths are what become entombed in the Gospels.

Another one of Ricci's implied points appears to be that such a morphing was possible only because the Gospels were written not by eyewitnesses, unlike the testimonies offered in Ricci's novel, but by later Christians who were removed from the events and who, like Mary Magdalene, were infatuated with the idea of Jesus. According to ancient historiographers, the best history is that which is written by insiders because they are most likely to get at the truth of the events. Eyewitness testimonies rather than stories transferred and transformed over a long process of oral transmission are more likely to be trustworthy, and it is eyewitness testimony that *Testament*, supposedly in contrast to the Gospels, provides.

With the transfiguration story, however, Ricci subverts even this assumption and also ironically one of the main themes of the novel—that the rumor mill is responsible for the creation of many of the myths surrounding Jesus. This incredible, supernatural account of the transfiguration flows not from rumors that gather speed and form over time but springs directly from Simon the Canaanite, the eyewitness himself![34]

As Crook has noted, Ricci's explanation for the development of these miracle stories is a complex one. In *Testament*, there is often some sort of historical basis for the later myths.[35] Jesus is a gifted healer, but over time

33. Such a narration is known in literary criticism as a dissonant narration (Keen, *Narrative*, 36).

34. Thanks to Kathleen Burt for first suggesting this idea to me.

35. Crook, "Fictionalizing Jesus," 47–48.

and through rumors spread by both followers and enemies, the natural medical assistance that he gives transforms into supernatural healings and exorcisms. These myths, however, can also spring directly from the "witnesses" themselves who, like Simon the Canaanite, are superstitious and misinterpret events or, like Jerubal, are jokesters and enjoy seeing just how big of a tale people will believe.[36]

COMPETING OR COMPLEMENTING CHRISTOLOGICAL PORTRAIT?

At the end of her testimony, Mary Magdalene makes the following comment: "Thus it was that everyone who heard him or laid eyes on him formed an image of him, and believed him a holy man or a madman, a heretic or a sage, with deepest certainty" (223). Certainly if there is any Jesus novel that captures the issue of diversity in Christological interpretation especially in Jesus portraits, that novel is *Testament*.

In turning to examine the image of Jesus painted in *Testament*, we will be able to see just how possible it is to produce a different image while using the same gems extracted from a kingly mosaic. We will then be in a place to critique the final portrait that Ricci has produced by using and reshaping Gospel pieces within a new narrative setting.

The Christology of the Gospels Taken to Pieces

As we demonstrated earlier in this chapter, the novel's four narrators hold differing opinions of Jesus and often conflict in their testimonies. Even so, there is much that they agree on, and consistent themes regarding Jesus' identity run throughout their narratives. Before we attempt to overview Ricci's fictional Jesus constructed from the four witnesses' testimonies, it behooves us to examine which aspects of the Gospel Jesus or of traditional orthodox Christology are "taken to pieces" in the novel. When we do so, we find that the three main Christological titles or roles challenged in the novel are those of Messiah, Savior, and Son of God.

Much like the historical Jesus of William Wrede and others,[37] Ricci's fictional Jesus leads a very un-messianic life. He never makes any claims to be the Messiah although some of his disciples secretly hope that he may be

---

36. As Jerubal says, "[T]he bigger the lie, the more people fell for it in the end" (359).

37. Wrede, *Messianic Secret*.

(421–22). Similar to the way in which Ricci demythologizes the miraculous, he also paints a convincing picture of how the Messiah legend could grow up around a very un-messianic Jesus.

First, fodder for this belief may have come from some of Ricci's Jesus' own careless comments. Judas records one such statement that Jesus makes in reply to detractors who chastise him for allowing his followers to break the Sabbath by walking long distances to pray with him. He answers them saying, "How can you fault them for coming to pray with their teacher?" (81). When his challengers respond saying that there are teachers in their own towns with whom his disciples could pray, Jesus replies: "'And if the Messiah came . . . would you tell them to keep to their towns rather than worship him?'" When Judas reflects on Jesus' statement, he concludes, "This kind of provocation struck me as foolhardy, particularly as there was no shortage of fanatics attached to him now who might be inclined to take such statements literally" (82).

Second, the Messiah legend arises from some of Jesus' followers whom Simon of Gergesa describes as having hopes that were too high. In hearing Peter's messianic dreams regarding Jesus, Simon of Gergesa calls him childish and says that he was too taken with Jesus (421–22). Ricci offers a combination of ill-chosen words on Jesus' own part and the wishful and foolish beliefs of his credulous followers to explain how the Messiah legend developed around the actual, un-Messianic man.

Likewise, Ricci presents Jesus not as a Savior by whose death the world is ransomed. Yet, even so, there is still a salvific element to his death in *Testament* and to that of Jerubal's, who dies with Jesus. Because these men are sentenced to death, the others who have been captured with Jesus are set free by Pilate, who seems to have had enough of condemning men and feels that he has made a sufficient example with the crucifixions of Jesus, Jerubal, and a few other criminals (435–36). Once again, we see Ricci offering a small kernel of historicity (a sacrificial death that saves a few) around which a legendary husk can develop (a salvific death for the world).

Finally, Ricci offers theories as to how the traditional belief in Jesus as the Son of God, an erroneous identity according to *Testament*'s witnesses, could spring to life. One suggestion as to how he transitioned from a human man to a divine god is based on the almost supernatural knowledge that Jesus seems to possess about certain people, such as the information he knows about Ribqah's dad (135). Another foundation upon which Jesus' followers build is his amazing healing abilities. Both Mary and Simon of Gergesa comment on how Jesus' followers blow out of proportion these events and Jesus' own person (314, 402). There is also the suggestion that Jesus' divinity may have developed from comments taken out of context, such as Lazarus' statement after Jesus heals him. After Lazarus opens his eyes, Jesus asks whether he knows who Jesus is. To this question Lazarus replies, "You must be the son of god himself, if you brought me back from the dead" (402). While everyone present at the event, including Jesus, knows that the response is a joke, one can imagine how the statement's context-less and consistent repetition could develop into a quite different understanding of the person of Jesus.

Overview of Ricci's Fictional Jesus

While denying Jesus' divinity, *Testament* goes to great lengths to emphasize his humanity. In the novel, he is described as "fallible, mortal, and unsure" (110). Simon of Gergesa's testimony particularly focuses on his humanity as he describes sleeping next to Jesus, who had "a body like the rest of us. He had a smell to him just like anyone" (413). Simon also relates how at the crucifixion Jesus dies just like anyone else. According to him, "Jesus wasn't any different than the rest, crying out with the pain—he was made of flesh like them, which was what such treatment reduced you to, just skin and blood and bone and the ache of them. It was strange to see him that way, as if all of his notions, all of his sayings and his stories, counted for nothing now, and it was only his animal nature that mattered" (446–47).

In imitation of the nineteenth century liberal quests and of modern quests that have followed in their stead, *Testament* emphasizes that Jesus was a mere man, and his primary role in the novel is that of an ethical teacher (cf. 91–93, 330, 454). While his charisma draws people to him, he never wants the responsibility or the power that others try to hand over to him. Instead, he wants them to think for themselves (261), and as a good teacher, he seeks to show them how. Judas describes how Jesus taught like one of the Greek philosophers who turn questions back to their questioners so that they can find their own answers (48). In fact, Judas' portrait of Jesus most resembles that of Crossan's Cynic peasant. On multiple occasions, he refers to Jesus' teaching style as akin to that of the Greeks, the Cynic philosophers in particular (cf. 11, 26, 47, 48, and 51).

Placing Gospel Pieces Into a New Narrative Structure

Like many scholars and artists before him, Ricci recognizes that the Gospels are not constructed according to chronology or causality. Also like them, he turns this recognition into a license to wrench the Gospel mosaic pieces from their narrative structures and to rearrange them according to whatever new grid he chooses. Not surprisingly, when such pieces are placed into a new narrative context, they often take on very different meanings.

We have already seen when discussing the "pink" passages that this technique is typical in Ricci's narrative. Let us now examine one very important tile found in the Gospels that Ricci appropriates and uses as a bedrock piece for his new fictional Jesus and discuss how its new narrative context affects the Christological portrait in *Testament*.

The integral piece that Ricci lifts from the Gospels and places within a completely different context is that of Jesus' unorthodox conception. Both of the canonical infancy narratives relate how Jesus' mother Mary became pregnant out of wedlock and not by her future husband Joseph (Matt 1:18–25; Luke 1:26–38). The Gospel context in which this information is placed is that of a larger narrative that paints Jesus as the Son of God. In that story, Mary's unorthodox pregnancy is used as a piece of evidence to further prove Jesus' identity as the Son of God, the Messiah. This same information when used in *Testament*, however, instead of pointing towards Jesus' divine sonship serves to confirm his identity as a bastard. While Mary becomes pregnant out of wedlock in Ricci's narrative just as she does in the Gospel versions, the paternity of her child in *Testament* is far from divine. There, Jesus is the bastard son of a Roman soldier and as such is forever barred from the Israelite assembly.

In the novel, Jesus' bastardry haunts him for his entire life and becomes the psychological key to explaining Jesus' person and ministry. Jesus' inclusive ministry that extends the kingdom of God to outsiders, such as pagans, lepers, and women, is tied to his own exclusion from Israel. Each of the four witnesses notices the way in which Jesus identifies with the socially marginalized although only two of them know the truth—that Jesus more than identifies with them but is actually one of them.[38] Ricci does an excellent job offering human explanations for Jesus' character formation, and his bastardry is by far the most essential key to unlocking his complicated psyche and to explaining his ministry.

---

38. Here are a couple of examples of how Jesus' own exclusion connected him with the marginalized:

> Judas: "I thought I understood something in him then, though I could not quite have expressed it, that indeed he was like the lepers in some way, or even Rakiil, all those who were marked, though he had a prince's bearing and the looks of one" (60).

> Mary: "So I heard how he accepted pagans among his followers, and rejected circumcision and the law, yet still proclaimed the one God. All this, I thought, must come from the knowledge of his own bastardy and his exclusion from God's assembly, such that he sought all means to make a place for the outcast and thus justify himself" (296).

In the end, however, Ricci's Jesus ironically turns out to look very much like the Gospel Jesus because of his concern for including outcasts and for expanding the kingdom of God. Yet the character motivation for doing so is precisely opposite what we see in the Gospels. There, Jesus' central identity as the Son of God motivates him to draw all people into his Father's kingdom. In the novel, Jesus' central identity as a bastard and thus an outcast from Israel's kingdom motivates him to be more compassionate and to include others into "his god's special kingdom" (330). By placing just one key piece from the Gospel mosaic—Jesus' unorthodox conception—into a new narrative context, Ricci both transforms the person of Jesus but at the same time ironically produces one who, like his Gospel counterpart, makes a part of his central message the inclusion of outsiders into the kingdom of God.

CONCLUSION

Postmodern works often not only question traditional historical assumptions but also the notion of any absolute historical truth. They are able to cast doubt on the authority of traditional authoritative texts by emphazing the role of interpretation and narrative within them. Texts that claim any absolute truth are looked upon with suspicion and are often thought to be the products of the powerful elite used to justify their positions by creating a particular version of history.

Ricci and his novel are products of both postmodernity and modernity. From the former, Ricci draws a skepticism of authoritative texts and of historical truth, both of which the Gospels claim to be. From the latter, he has developed an assumption as to what in reality can and cannot exist, and thus, according to such a modern view, the miraculous simply is not possible and must be explained in some other manner.

By starting from this position, Ricci sets out to challenge the accuracy of the Gospels' testimonies, particularly regarding their interpretations and claims regarding history. The means by which he subverts their testimonies are threefold. On one level, he calls into question the Gospel narratives by providing counter-narratives that contort or explicitly contradict the evangelists' testimonies regarding specific events and sayings.

On the second level, he ties the least reliable narrator's testimony with those of the "later" evangelists. Since Mary Magdalene was the only one of the four witnesses who by the end of the novel is said to still be a part of the early Christian community, it can be assumed that her unreliable, credulous, and emotional views are the ones that have the greatest effect upon the evangelists' writings. This implicit link does little to bolster faith in the

Gospels when the reader, following the cues of the novel and actualizing the reading pact, makes the connection between them and Magdalene's rewrite.

On a third level, Ricci undermines the very notion of testimony by framing all of his own witnesses, Mary Magdalene in particular, as unreliable narrators. By discrediting its own witnesses, *Testament* successfully undermines faith in testimony in general and in the Gospels in particular. It does so, however, at the cost of reflexively undermining its own narrative since the reader is left questioning whether these testimonies offer the truth and whether there is ever any real truth to be found or only interpretation. In this manner, *Testament* could be a poster novel for postmodernity. Ricci likely sees the undermining of his own witnesses as worthwhile so that his readers may make the comparison between his witnesses and the Gospel evangelists and accept the point that just as Ricci's witnesses were wont at times to invent so too were the evangelists. If testimony in general should be doubted, then why should anyone trust the Gospels in particular?

Yet the doubt that Ricci attempts to create is not the same as disproof, and in order for skepticism to be true to its aims, it must turn back and question even itself and the doubt that it has engendered. Ordinarily throughout the novel, the idea of critiquing the novel's own skeptical position does not occur. There is one occasion, however, when one of Ricci's narrators does just this. Right after discounting the resurrection myth circulating about Jesus, Simon of Gergesa becomes skeptical about his own skepticism and says, "For all I know, it might have happened that way—wasn't I there myself when Jesus brought Elazar [Lazarus] back, who'd been dead as a stone" (453). Such an admission of the uncertainty of his own doubt is an admirable, if infrequent, one on Ricci's part.

By dismantling the credibility of the Gospels and by foregrounding the role that interpretation obviously plays in any telling of history, Ricci presents himself as a heroic liberator whose keen objective and unbiased skills of deduction have aided in freeing Jesus' life from superstition and theological bias. While Ricci presents his aim as solely that of uncovering a "factual" account of the simple man from Nazareth, his motives are far less neutral and are influenced by an undeclared anti-religious agenda. Far from being free of the distorting suppositions of religious belief that he attacks, Ricci's account is influenced by his own views on the nature of reality and what is possible, which are as contestable as the views he seeks to call into question.

Ricci also fails to recognize that an admission of the likely inclusion of imaginative or interpretative elements within the Gospels does not automatically discredit their ability to function as reliable testimonies. A proper understanding of the Gospels within their literary genre of ancient biographies explains how inventive interpretation can coincide with reliable testimony: the aim of these biographies is to testify to the person and character of Jesus by providing a portrait that is a faithful representation of the person's character not by providing a video recording or a literal transcript of each event. Thus, even fiction is a possible medium to be used when painting a truthful portrait of Jesus so long as its colors remain faithful to his character and person. Ricci acknowledges no distinction between actuality and reality and makes an uncritical equation of the two that prevents his understanding of the Gospels as iconic representations of the real Jesus.

When seen from an alternative perspective, many of the critiques that Ricci makes of the Gospels appear as strengths. For example, the characteristics used to cast Mary Magdalene as an unreliable narrator and which are implicitly applied to the evangelists as well may be viewed from another angle as validations of her testimony. Is not love a way of knowing that allows the lover to understand the beloved in a manner not possible for those outside the relationship? Some things have to be experienced firsthand in order for them to be understood.[39] While Mary Magdalene is derogatively characterized as credulous, perhaps it is simply that she possesses faith, and is faith not another way of knowing that is possible only as one takes that Kierkegaardean leap and enters into belief? Finally, although Mary Magdalene may be young, was it not Jesus himself who said that we each must become children in order to enter the kingdom of God?

Even *Testament* leaves open the possibility of an affirmative answer to these questions. Immediately after discrediting Mary Magdalene because of her worship of Jesus and her credulous nature, Jesus' mother momentarily suspends her skepticism and remarks:

> Yet it was true that when she spoke of my son the wonder I heard in her voice was not so different from what I myself had felt, that sense of a doorway Yeshua stood before, to some new understanding. Except that she had passed through it, and saw things in a different light, and who was I to say that the miracle she had witnessed had not occurred, for those who had eyes to see it (314).[40]

39. Even Judas discusses the necessity of experiential knowing for truly understanding Jesus' teachings: "But many of Yeshua's notions, I came to learn, were not the sort that could be reduced to simple principles; rather they had to be felt, as it were, and lived out, so that it was only the experience of them that could bring you to understanding" (46).

40. Judas says something similar when he reflects on Simon's faith, love, and understanding of Jesus: "So the others could not accept me, because I reduced to merely a man the great notion that Yeshua was to them, the notion of their own betterment and redemption. I had understood this in an instant when Kephas had come and made his greetings, and I'd seen how he ached with emotion at Yeshua's return and with the things he wished to say to him but held himself back on my account. And though I had

5

José Saramago's *The Gospel According to Jesus Christ* as a Competing Rewrite

INTRODUCTION

José Saramago, who recently passed away in 2010, was born in poverty in 1922, published his first novel at the age of twenty-five in 1947, and became the first Portuguese-language writer to receive the Nobel Prize for Literature in 1998. Extremely prolific, Saramago dabbled in almost every literary genre, including poetry, essay, drama, short story, and, of course, novel.[1]

An atheist and a life-long Communist party member[2] whom some critics refer to as a "political moralist,"[3] Saramago frequently displays these ideologies in his writings. Nowhere is this seen more clearly than in his 1991 critically acclaimed but highly controversial version of Jesus' life *O Evangelho Segundo Jesus Cristo* (translated in 1994 by Giovanni Pontierro as *The Gospel according to Jesus Christ*, hereafter referred to as *Gospel*).

---

never held Kephas to be a man of great intelligence, I wondered now if he did not see Yeshua more clearly than I did, because he understood him with his heart, while I had always striven to find the argument that would defeat him" (111–12).

1. For a bibliography of Saramago's works, see Klobucka, "Bibliography of José Saramago." For a bibliography of secondary literature (most of which is in Portuguese) and short critical reviews in English on each of Saramago's works, see Tesser, "A Tribute to Jose Saramago."

2. Cousland, "José Saramago's *Kakaggelion*, 56n55.

3. Klobucka, "Interview."

Saramago's revision of Jesus' life has generated a wide range of responses, from being considered blasphemous by some and to being hailed as sublime by others. In 1992, the Portuguese government blocked the novel's nomination for a European literary prize because it was deemed offensive to the country's Catholic religion. Saramago, in protest over the offense, left his homeland and moved to Lanzarote.[4] In contrast to the government's reaction, critics like Harold Bloom praise the novel calling it "imaginatively superior to any other life of Jesus, including the four canonical Gospels."[5]

Alternatively loved or hated, praised and censured, the novel has certainly elicited numerous responses, but the one point that all readers could probably agree upon is that it intentionally tries to compete with the gospel story. Critics have labeled it a "subversive rewriting of the Gospels,"[6] the *kakaggelion* or "badspel" according to Jesus Christ, and an "extended and bitter satire on the Bible, the Gospel genre, and the message contained in the Gospels."[7] In his 1998 Nobel Prize speech, Saramago himself called it a "heretical Gospel."[8]

If reader response and authorial intention were all that were needed to categorize *Gospel* as a competing novel, then we would have already made our case. In order to analyze better *Gospel*'s stance towards the Gospels, however, we must examine not only the opinions of others but also the novel itself, particularly how it appropriates and transforms its biblical source material. Therefore, we shall examine this "heretical" rewriting by paying attention to how it subverts the Gospels' characters and their worldview in order to produce this *kakaggelion*.

FICTIONAL GAP FILLING OR MOSAIC MOVING?

Overview of Gospel's Stance Towards the Gospels

Like *Testament*, *Gospel* spans the actual Jesus' entire life, beginning with his conception and ending with his crucifixion. Thus, there is a great deal of potential for the use of Gospel material within this Jesus novel.

Although the way in which a Jesus novel moves and manipulates the biblical source material is usually very telling regarding its stance towards the original Gospel portraits, in the case of *Gospel*, its use of the biblical

4. Ibid.
5. Bloom, "The One with the Beard Is God."
6. Ben-Porat, "Saramago's *Gospel*," 97.
7. Cousland, "*Kakaggelion*," 55, 60.
8. Saramago, "The 1998 Nobel Lecture."

material is not as overtly subversive as that of other competing narratives, such as *Testament*. While offering a competing message to those of the evangelists, *Gospel* neither moves nor reshapes the Gospel mosaic pieces quite as much we would expect in a subversive rewrite. Most of the individual bits and pieces imported arrive in Saramago's new narrative surprisingly intact. By assessing the novel's handling of its source material according to the same color-coding scheme that was used with Ricci's novel, we find, perhaps surprisingly, that a large proportion of the Gospel material remains red with a few splatterings of pink and a handful of obvious black redactions.[9] As the following summary of *Gospel*'s use of source material in its plot construction will demonstrate, the novel retains a harmonized plot structure essentially faithful to that of the Gospels while at the same time shifting the sequence of some events.

Plot Summary of Gospel Material Used in Gospel

In *Gospel*'s opening chapter, we meet Joseph and Mary, a young married couple living in Nazareth.[10] After having intercourse one morning (13; cf. Matt 1:18; Luke 1:34–37), they conceive their firstborn son. Four weeks after, not prior to, Jesus' conception, an angel disguised as a beggar visits their home and *announces* Mary's pregnancy (16–17; cf. Luke 1:26–38). Months later, the couple is forced because of a Roman census to travel to Bethlehem (28; cf. Luke 2:1–5). There in a cave, Mary gives birth to Jesus with the help of a midwife named Salome, and soon shepherds bearing gifts visit the young family (56; cf. Luke 2:6–20).[11]

9. The events that are most obviously shaded black in the novel are the sexual histories of Joseph and Mary and of Jesus and Mary Magdalene. When we first meet the holy couple, they are already married and on that very morning are busy consummating their marriage with an act that will produce Jesus nine months later. While we later learn that God mixed his own seed with that of Joseph's on that fateful morning (according to the novel's perspective, perhaps "fatal" would be the better adjective), this revelation does nothing to redeem Mary's virginal reputation.

Likewise, Jesus himself is no celibate but becomes involved with the prostitute Mary Magdalene with whom he continues to live until his death. Although we are never told in the Gospels anything about Jesus' sexual or marital status, Christian tradition has almost uniformly depicted Jesus as an unmarried virgin, and certainly nothing in the canonical Gospels themselves would contradict this tradition. Some suggest, however, that from some of the non-canonical Gospels, a romantic relationship between Mary Magdalene and Jesus could be construed (e.g., *Gnostic Gospel of Philip* 28, 48; *Gospel of Thomas* 21). Perhaps Saramago bases his portrayal of the couple on these gospels.

10. All page references to *Gospel* will be given in parentheses throughout this chapter.

11. Here we see the influence of the *Protoevangelium of James* with the inclusion of a cave for the birthplace and a midwife named Salome (*Prot. Jas.* 18–19).

Next comes Herod's slaughter of the innocents, which Jesus manages to avoid not because of an angelic messenger's warning but because of some loose-lipped soldiers whom Joseph overhears discussing their orders (80–85; cf. Matt 2:13–18). After hiding in their cave to avoid the slaughter, the not-so-holy family returns to Nazareth rather than fleeing to Egypt (94; cf. Matt 2:14), where Jesus leads an uneventful childhood helping in Joseph's carpenter shop while attending the synagogue school and studying the Torah. At this point, the source material runs out, and *Gospel*, like other Jesus novels, fills in Jesus' hidden years with new material.

After turning thirteen, Jesus' life changes forever when Roman soldiers mistakenly crucify his father Joseph in Sepphoris after they squelch Judas the Galilean's uprising and burn the town to the ground.[12] Jesus then literally and figuratively steps into his father's shoes, inheriting not only his sandals but also his nightmares about the slaughter of the innocents in Bethlehem and the guilt that Joseph felt over his complicity in that event. This revelation compels Jesus to visit the temple (169–74; cf. Luke 2:41–52) to ask the elders if a son can inherit his father's guilt.[13]

During his hidden years, Saramago's Jesus has other adventures, such as working as a shepherd for four years with the mysterious Pastor, meeting God for the first time in the wilderness and making a covenant with him there, traveling to the Sea of Galilee where he meets some of his disciples and where the first miraculous catch of fish occurs (228; cf. Luke 5:1–11), falling in love with Mary Magdalene, and finally being rejected by his family when he claims that God has a special mission for his life. After this rejection, Jesus returns to the lake with Mary Magdalene at his side, and the novel resumes following its biblical source material.

During this period, miracles, like those described in the Gospels, begin to occur wherever Jesus goes—storms are calmed (282, 296; cf. Matt 8:23–27); water turns to wine (290; cf. John 2:1–11); the fever of Simon's mother-in-law vanishes (295; cf. Matt 8:14–15); demons are exorcised from a Gadarene lunatic (296–300; cf. Mark 5:1–20); a fig tree is cursed and

12. Saramago's depiction of this incident actually mixes two different uprisings in Galilee. The first took place among the many other outbreaks of violence immediately following Herod the Great's death. It was during this first uprising that Sepphoris was burned (cf. Josephus, *A.J.* 17.10.09; *B.J.* 2.05.01). Two thousand Israelites who had besieged Jerusalem were also crucified at that time (cf. *A.J.* 17.10.10; *B.J.* 2.05.02). The second rebellion led by Judas the Galilean broke out almost ten years later after Archaeleus was deposed, and it took place in response to Quirinius calling for a census and a new tax (*A.J.* 18.01.01; *B.J.* 2.08.01).

13. In *Out of Egypt*, the boy Jesus also has an emotional breakdown when he learns about the slaughter of the innocents, and he too suffers on behalf of the murdered children (Rice, *Out of Egypt*, 286–91).

dies (302–3; cf. Matt 21:18–22); and five thousand are fed (303; cf. Matt 14:13–21). Here, we see how Saramago, like most Jesus novelists, harmonizes events from all four Gospels.

After the climactic testing scene on the lake during which Jesus discovers his true identity as God's Son and what that identity entails (cf. Matt 4:1–11), which we shall discuss at length below in chapter 6, Jesus continues performing biblical miracles, such as the healings of a leper (338; cf. Matt 8:1–4), a paralytic (339; cf. Matt 9:1–8), and a mute man (351; cf. Matt 15:29–31). This time though, he not only heals but also preaches. Surprisingly, his main message—that people must repent of their sins and prepare for God's new era (304)—is very similar to that of the Gospel Jesus (cf. Matt 4:17). Also like his Gospel counterpart, Saramago's Jesus instructs the twelve disciples and sends them out to spread his message (342, cf. Matt 10:1–42). While the disciples are gone, he and Mary Magdalene travel to Bethany where they stay with Mary's siblings Martha and Lazarus (342ff.; cf. Luke 10:38–43; John 11:1). Although Jesus is able to heal Lazarus of one illness (348), he does not raise him from the dead when he later dies (361–62; cf. John 11:1–44). When the disciples return, they inform Jesus about a prophet called John who is baptizing and preaching by the Jordan (353–54; cf. Matt 3:1–12). Now at the end of his ministry rather than at the beginning (cf. Matt 3:13–17), Jesus goes to be baptized by John (355). Also contrary to the Gospel versions, it is Jesus who seeks out John in order to discover if Jesus is the Messiah who is to come (354, 356; cf. Matt 11:2–6).

Next, Jesus leads an attack on the moneychangers at the temple (359; cf. Matt 21:10–17), but it is not this event that leads to his arrest (contra the Synoptics). Instead, John the Baptist's arrest and beheading (355–56; cf. Matt 14:1–12) prompt Jesus to tell his disciples everything about God's plans for global domination and their own martyrdoms. Jesus, wanting to make sure that none of these predictions come to pass, tries to thwart God's will by quickly arranging to die as the "King of the Jews," a political pretender to the crown, rather than as the Son of God before God can realize what Jesus has done. Judas offers to help by betraying Jesus to the officials and arranging for Jesus' arrest (370; cf. Matt 26:14–16). After undergoing two trials, one with the Israelite religious leaders (372–73) and one with Pilate (373–75), that are similar and yet different from those detailed in the Gospels (cf. Matt 26:57–75; 27:11–14), Jesus is crucified between two criminals under an inscription proclaiming him "Jesus of Nazareth, king of the Jews" (375–76). Unfortunately, God knew all along what Jesus was doing and shows up in person at the crucifixion. Thwarting Jesus' intention and using Jesus' death for his own purposes, God declares, "This is My beloved son, in whom I am well pleased" (376; cf. Matt 3:17; 17:5) so that everyone will know Jesus' true identity and so that the religion of Christianity will be founded on the Son of God's martyrdom.

A New Type of Mosaic Moving

As we can see from the description of source material used in *Gospel*, even though some details are changed and others are left out, Saramago, for the most part, retains the basic integral structure of a harmonization of the Gospel narratives. At the same time, he revises that structure at various points and adds to it with details and incidents from apocryphal gospels and other ancient sources.[14]

Saramago's wider and more consistent use of the Gospel material alerts us to the fact that he is a different type of mosaic mover than Ricci. In *Testament*, there is a subtle suggestion through its reshaping and rearrangement that the original mosaic pieces themselves had been painted over and placed incorrectly in the canonical pictures. Ricci presents his aim as simply one of restoring the original, undistorted picture of the actual Jesus rather than the covered-up version of the Gospel Jesus by moving the pieces back to their original shapes and positions.

Saramago makes no such pretense of uncovering the actual Jesus. In describing his own rewriting efforts, Saramago says that his *Gospel* "was not a matter of looking behind the pages of the New Testament searching for antitheses, but of illuminating their surfaces, like that of a painting, with a low light to heighten their relief, the traces of crossings, the shadows of depressions."[15] While Saramago's principal interests are not historical as Ricci's are, they are certainly not as benign as simply "heightening" the relief and shadows of the original Gospels. Also, although he does indeed retain and use the "surfaces" of the NT Gospels for his own story, Saramago is not terribly forthcoming about the alternative ideologies he inserts to undergird and ultimately to transform even those surfaces.

Gospel turns out to be a theological remaking of the Gospels and of the characters that inhabit their worlds. In the novel, Saramago reformats Jesus according to his own philosophy and then uses Jesus to promote his own gospel of humanitarian compassion. As Cousland has astutely noted,

---

14. The inclusion of material from apocryphal sources is often a clue in categorizing the novel because it is more common among competing narratives. As we have seen with Rice's use of the apocryphal infancy narratives, however, such imports are not conclusive evidence for calling a novel a subversive rewrite of the Gospels.

15. Saramago, "1998 Nobel Lecture."

Saramago uses the Gospel events and settings only "to provide a convincing costume for the very different figure that lies beneath them."[16]

In *Gospel*, Saramago presents us with a new type of mosaic moving that may be an even more devious way of subverting the Gospels than Ricci's because the Jesus character in *Gospel's* new mosaic still resembles its original self in some essential ways. We are lulled into uncritical acceptance by the similarity in features between the original and the remake as we are lured into the narrative. Then we are shocked awake when we realize that by changing the whole of the Scriptural worldview in *Gospel*, Saramago also has changed the Jesus who inhabits that world. In order to see how Saramago performs this transformation, we must now turn to the narrative world and the characters that exist there.

COMPLEMENTING OR COMPETING NARRATIVE WORLDS AND WORLDVIEWS?

If we were to base our opinion of *Gospel's* relationship with its biblical source material solely on the initial impression given by the novel's outward adherence to the plot imported from the Gospels, we might be misled to conclude that the novel is only slightly subversive in its stance towards the Gospels. Also misleading is the fact that *Gospel* allows miraculous events and divine characters to intrude into its world. On this score, Saramago's novel appears on the surface to be more in line with the Gospels' worldview than even Boyd's novel was.

The presence of supernatural features in *Gospel*, however, does not necessarily imply that the novel has adopted the Gospel's worldview. In fact, Ben-Porat attributes the appearance of miracles to Saramago's adoption of the Latin American style of magical realism rather than to any faithful adherence to the Gospels' theological perspective on supernatural and miraculous incursions into the natural world.[17] While Saramago certainly adopts the magical realism mode in some of his other novels, such as *The Stone Raft* (1986) or *Blindness* (1995), it is less certain that magical realism is really what lies at the heart of the miraculous and magical events in *Gospel*.

16. Cousland, "Kakaggelion," 69.

17. Ben-Porat, "Saramago's *Gospel*," 96; cf. Duarte, "What Is It That Saramago Is Doing?"

Saramago's Use of Magical Or Magic Realism?

Magical realism is a term used by literary theorists "to refer to all narrative fiction that includes magical happenings in a realist matter-of-fact narrative, whereby, 'the supernatural is not a simple or obvious matter, but it *is* an ordinary matter, and everyday occurrence—admitted, accepted, and integrated into the rationality and materiality of literary realism."[18] Magical realist texts are known for being subversive because they break down the barriers between what is assumed to be real and that which is not by placing both magical and realist elements side by side without any hieracrchy of order or authorial instruction as to their legitimacy. Because this mode questions the notion of absolute truth in relation to reality, it is also inherently suited to questioning and breaking other boundaries, such as those that are political, geographical, or, in Saramago's case, ontological.[19] It is often used in postcolonial literature as a way to subvert the dominant historical narrative of colonialism, but in Saramago's novel, we see that his target is the subversion of the traditional narrative of Christianity. Just as magical realist texts are often used by those on the margins of society, those speaking from the position of the "other," to critique the powerful elite, dictators, or other dominant forces of society, so too we see Saramago using his novel to cast God in the dictatorial role and humans in the marginalized, oppressed peasant role. The view of the "other" espoused by Saramago is that of the atheist, a minority in a Christian-dominated culture.

While it is true that *Gospel* carries many characteristics of magical realism, such as excess, fantastical elements, a sense of mystery, metafiction, intertextuality, parody, and certainly a type of political critique, the novel perhaps is not best categorized as a work of magical realism. Certainly Saramago does not deny the reality of the miraculous or the magical, and he does not try to explain these events away as a more modernist author, such as Ricci, would by giving plausible scientific explanations for them. He willingly admits such intrusions into his narrative world, but the difference in *Gospel* is that such events are intrusions into the narrative world and are not presented as a natural, ordinary part of it. When magic or the miraculous happens, such as the appearance of the shining dust after the annunciation, Jesus's inheritance of Joseph's dreams, or the traditional miracles of Jesus' ministry, characters are always surprised. They question the existence of miracles and sometimes seek natural explanations or accept them as divine

---

18. Bowers, *Magic(al) Realism*, 2.

19. Zamora and Faris, "Introduction," 5; Bowers, *Magic(al) Realism*, 4.

invasions into their world rather than understanding them as part of the natural order.

Perhaps here we see Saramago using even the miraculous elements of the narrative to promote his humanist agenda because in the final analysis these magical happenings are viewed as unwelcome and unneeded. The miraculous in Saramago's world, unlike the miraculous in the worlds of most magical realist novels, is not the vehicle of deliverance or subversion for the oppressed but the means of oppression by the deity. It is intrinsically tied to the Christian church and its God and as such needs to be rejected just as Jesus tries to reject the magical powers bestowed on him by his Father.

Instead of looking for divine and miraculous deliverance from their problems, humanity is encouraged by Saramago to be their own solution and to celebrate the beauty of the natural order. In this way, *Gospel* resembles more the magic realism of Europe than the magical realism of Latin America since in the European variety the ordinary is given a mysteriousness and a marvelous quality whereas in Latin America the genre focuses more on blending the real and the magical together in such a way that both are common and ordinary in the narrative world. We can see an example of this difference in the birth narrative of *Gospel* in which Saramago celebrates the marvelous ordinariness of the sexual encounter between Mary and Joseph and its ability to bring new life into the world. Yet he also mixes magic into that act with the appearance of the beggar and his magic dust and the claim that God mixes his seed with that of Joseph's. Unlike Latin American magical realism, the intrusion of these extraordinary characters and of this event is not presented as commonplace but as extraordinary and as a matter of much concern and discussion among the peasant villagers in Nazareth. Also as we see later in the novel, God's miraculous interference with this natural act is seen as unwelcome and as the beginning of disastrous consequences for humanity.

In sum, it appears that Ben-Porat is perhaps mistaken in attributing Saramago's inclusion of miraculous elements to magical realism rather than to an adherence to the Gospels. Instead we find that Saramago includes such events precisely because they are a part of the traditional Christian narrative, but he adopts them in order to subvert them once they are imported into his narrative world. There they are rejected as impositions of the divine dictator. Saramago, in resemblance to the magic realism of Europe, prefers to champion the marvelousness of the ordinary and the majesty of the natural order.

The "Universal" of Saramago's World: Compassionate Humanism

By digging a bit deeper into the narrative world of *Gospel*, we find that in other ways the novel is not as complementary to the Gospels as an initial glance at its imported structure and affirmation of the miraculous might suggest. In fact, *Gospel* turns out to be the most subversive of the Gospel rewrites that we have examined because it intentionally inverts the metaphysical framework and the moral polarities of the Gospels.[20] As Ben-Porat and other critics have already noted, "The most irreconcilable element with faithful representation is, of course, the seemingly complete reversal of roles between God and Satan."[21] Yet even though *Gospel* reverses the moral characters of God and Satan, it does not invert the nature of good and evil themselves. In the novel, we see that realism rather than nominalism rules its world since on the surface there clearly are universals, qualities such as "goodness" and "beauty," that have real ontological value and that exist apart from the entities that possess those qualities. These universals do not have an existence simply because God wills them to be as they are or because they are an outflow of God's own nature. In fact, the reader cannot rely on the fact that God himself possesses "goodness," "beauty," or any other positive quality traditionally ascribed to God. Judgment on what is good and evil in *Gospel*'s world is not dependent upon God's verdict, and even God himself can be critiqued according to these standards that exist above and apart from God.

In *Gospel*'s world, the defining criterion for calling any of the characters "good" is whether or not they show humane compassion for others, which on a macro level manifests itself in the elimination of unjust and oppressive structures afflicting humanity and on a micro level occurs with the performance of even the smallest acts that alleviate the suffering of others. Here, we see Saramago's own beliefs seeping into *Gospel*'s worldview and begin to understand why critics refer to him as a "political moralist."

Once, when asked to summarize precisely what his moral philosophy entails, Saramago did so with a short quote from Karl Marx and Friedrich Engels: "If the human being is shaped by his circumstances, then it is necessary to shape those circumstances humanely."[22] One critic has observed that "the novel serves as an evangel for the humanistic communism Saramago espouses."[23] Throughout *Gospel*, structures, such as Christianity, and characters, such as God, that Saramago portrays as inhumane are critiqued. The real

---

20. Cousland, "Kakaggelion," 55, 60.
21. Ben-Porat, "Saramago's *Gospel*," 98.
22. Klobucka, "Interview."
23. Cousland, "Kakaggelion," 67.

heroes of the novel, who also happen to be faithful disciples of Saramago's humane philosophy, emerge as those who oppose these inhumane structures and strive to show compassion to their fellow creatures. These disciples do all they can to proclaim Saramago's gospel by announcing that God's inhumanity to man is the true tragedy that needs to be met with some "good news."

COMPLEMENTING OR COMPETING CHARACTERS?

Portrait of Satan

The first disciple of Saramago's new gospel is his Satan character, and nowhere is Satan's humanitarian compassion better portrayed than in the wilderness episode. In a parody of epic proportions, Satan poses as a shepherd called Pastor. While in biblical literature God is often referred to as the shepherd of God's people (e.g., Gen 48:15; Ps 23:1; 80:1; Isa 40:11) and Jesus is called the good shepherd (John 10:11, 14), in Saramago's *Gospel*, it is Satan who plays the role of the good shepherd, tenderly guarding sheep that are not even his own. Implicit in the name is the suggestion that this "Pastor" is better able to shepherd and care for humans than God. The new "gospel" that Pastor preaches is "precisely about shaping humane circumstances for humans and their fellow creatures"[24] and is strikingly like Saramago's own philosophy.

Pastor not only preaches but also enacts his humanitarian gospel particularly through his care for the sheep. For example, he shears them only to keep them from suffering under the weight of the wool in the summer, will not use their wool for profit, and refuses to sell the lambs for sacrificial purposes. A practitioner of euthanasia, Pastor kills sheep only when they are too old or sick to keep up with the rest of the flock (190). These mercy killings are just one side of Pastor's humanitarian philosophy that promotes a "natural" order for life—death for the aged is acceptable but for the young and innocent is wrong and unnatural. In accordance with his philosophy, Pastor can condemn the sacrifice of lambs in the temple while committing the slaughter of the aged in his own flocks. Pastor's compassion, however, extends beyond sheep to humans. For example, he abhors the slaughter of the innocents in Bethlehem and has "compassion" on Jesus when he hears God's plan for Jesus' martyrdom (312).

In *Gospel*, it is not Satan who is responsible for the structures that cause humanity so much suffering and fear. He tells Jesus, "I don't recall having invented sin and punishment or the terror they inspire" (325–26). No, in this narrative world, it is God who bears that responsibility, and "[n]o

24. Ibid., 63.

one in his right mind can possibly suggest that the devil was, is, or ever will be responsible for so much bloodshed and death" as God is (328). As the reader learns in the traveler's tale, in the devil's alternative universe Satan would deny humans nothing so that there would be no problem of sin (195). Satan desires for humans to be happy and to enjoy their lives. In fact, the only person to whom the devil ever denies anything is himself (263).

Perhaps the most prominent symbol of Satan's compassion and his particular care for the life of Jesus is the bowl that appears at key scenes throughout the novel.[25] In the "annunciation" scene, it functions first as an extension of Mary's compassion as she gives food to Satan who is disguised as a beggar.[26] He returns it to her with compassionate words about the condition of humans, who are only "[e]arth to earth, ashes to ashes, dust to dust" (16–17), words embodied by the luminous earth left in the bowl. Jesus' own growing existence parallels this strange earth, and, like it too, Jesus is also held in a fragile chalice, his mother Mary's womb.[27] In this scene, it is Satan, not God, who commemorates Jesus' entry into the world as a frail creature, and it is Satan, not God, who pities the destiny awaiting Jesus and all humanity.

The bowl appears throughout the novel always connected with either Jesus or Satan and usually related in some way to the frailty of humanity and used as a symbol of compassion for their plight. It last materializes at the foot of the cross where it collects Jesus' blood as it drips down (377). Aside from the Eucharistic symbolism, the bowl acts as Satan's final gesture

25. Compassion for the frailty of humanity is symbolized by two other bowls in the novel as well. First, after learning that his neighbor is dead, Joseph stays in Sepphoris to tend a stranger instead of returning safely home. He holds a bowl to the boy's lips sharing life-giving water with him. The bowl embodies the compassion that Joseph has finally learned to give, and the scene functions as a reversal of the slaughter of innocents when Joseph put his own family's well being ahead of the lives of the Bethlehem families (277).

Second, when Jesus runs away to Jerusalem where he finds himself alone and without any food, a Pharisee has compassion on him and buys him a bowl of food. In that scene, the narrator explicitly links the earthenware bowl with fragility and the precarious nature of humans, who, like the bowl, are so easily broken (168).

26. Bloom mistakenly thinks that the beggar who appears to Mary and the shepherd at Jesus' birth are both appearances of God rather than of Satan (Bloom, "One with the Beard," 163–64).

27. Cousland has also noticed the intended comparison between the two chalices and says that the bowl "serves as an effective image for the annunciation—a divine child sired in the earth of Mary's jar-like womb." Coulsand sees in the motif a Gnostic influence in that the "image of glowing earth in the bowl furnishes an instance of the divine light imprisoned in the medium of earth—human clay" (Cousland, "Kakaggelion," 58).

of compassion.[28] As it was at the beginning of Jesus' life, so it is at the end. Satan, not God, marks Jesus' passing and values his life as symbolized by the blood he collects in the earthenware bowl.

Clearly Saramago's Satan has little in common with the Satan of the Gospels but much in common with Saramago's humanist philosophy. Even within this dramatic character revision, Saramago's Satan does retain one classical satanic feature—that of functioning as God's antagonist. Although in outward appearance God and Satan could be twins except for the beard that God has (310, 314), they are neither identical in character nor in purpose. Saramago's Satan still tries to oppose God's will and also tempts Jesus to do the same. The only difference is that in this nightmarish inversion of reality Satan is justified in his opposition. Instead of tempting Jesus to evil, Satan tempts him to have compassion on humanity, something that is apparently not part of his Father's plan.

Portrait of God

In many ways, the God of *Gospel*'s world is Satan's antithesis. He is a deity who "chooses to suppress compassion" (321)[29] and for whom humans, including Jesus, are simply tools to be used and exploited for his purposes.[30] Saramago's God sacrifices both sheep and humans on the altar of his consumptive desires and feels no remorse for what happens to them (329).[31] As Satan tells us, God does not sleep and so is able to "avoid the nightmares of remorse" (193). In short, Saramago's God is the polar opposite of a compassionate humanitarian and of his Gospel counterpart.

It is precisely on humanist grounds that Saramago not only creates but also critiques God's character. For Saramago, the atheist, God is merely a human invention[32] and therefore can be reinvented by Saramago as he sees fit. Because Saramago looks at the actual world and sees atrocities committed in the name of God, he creates a God in his alternate universe reflective of those actions. He makes a God who is capable of countenancing all the blood

28. I am grateful to Allison Connett and Whitney Drury, who participated in a seminar discussion that first sparked the idea of a connection between Satan's compassion and the bowl at the cross.

29 As Bloom rightly observes, Saramago's God "manifests neither love nor compassion for Jesus or for any other human being" (Bloom, "One with the Beard," 155).

30. Cousland, "Kakaggelion," 65.

31. Here, I refer to God's global domination plan discussed during the lake temptation. Most of the revelation of God's character takes place during that scene, but we will have to defer discussion of it until we analyze Saramago's testing narratives in chapter 6.

32. Frier, "O Evangelho," 370.

poured out in his name (330). Then, using the voice of the narrator and of other characters, Saramago judges his God according to humanitarian standards and finds him wanting for failing to show compassion to humanity.

None of the theodicies traditionally used to defend God are able to get Saramago's God off the hook in this *Gospel*. For example, a defense that offers heaven or some other type of recompense for earthly suffering is judged as an unsuitable justification for God's inhumanity now. Although God will occasionally compensate someone like Job for all that he has taken from him, the narrator charges that, by and large, God does nothing to repay the suffering of millions of others (105). While Saramago's God offers the hope, not the promise, of happiness in heaven in exchange for earthly suffering, Jesus says that this hope is not enough to make up for the misery that humans currently undergo (319).[33] What *Gospel's* humanitarian philosophy demands from God is not restitution for pain but the complete removal of it.

Similarly, a justification of recompense does not address the real problem of why suffering exists in the first place. It does not answer questions such as, if God knows the future, then why does he not prevent evil occurrences? Tragedies in Saramago's world raise many of the same questions that plague our own world, such as this question of divine foreknowledge and God's actions in light of it. After the slaughter of the innocents, Joseph is condemned because of his failure to rescue the children since he knew beforehand what was going to happen. The condemnation of Joseph functions in the novel as an implicit critique of God, who also knew about the event and surely had more power and time to stop it than Joseph did.

The incident also explores the question of God's goodness in light of his selectivity. Just as Joseph saved his own son while letting others perish, so too God rescues a few children like Isaac and Jesus while allowing many more to be slaughtered. Such a dereliction of duty to protect all the innocent children leads characters like the slave Salome to wonder whether God is so impotent that he cannot "come between the sword and little children" (180).

One typical response to such assaults on God's character is that God does not intervene in every case because such interference would destroy the free will of God's creatures. The free will defense, however, does not work in *Gospel's* world because Saramago's God has not given humans true freedom to do other than what God wills. *Gospel's* world is a fatalistic one (96) where God decides the fate (341). In this alternative universe, humans are "nothing but complete slaves of God's absolute will" (265) and are required to follow that will no matter what it is (150). As Jesus realizes, "[M]an

---

33. When told about all the deaths that God will cause, Matthew asks Jesus, "Will they receive eternal life?" Jesus responds, "Yes, but the condition should be less horrible" (368).

is a mere toy in the hands of God and forever subject to His will, whether he imagines himself to be obeying or disobeying Him" (181). Even covenants are illusionary because they make humans think that they have a choice when they really do not. The irony of being chosen by God is that it means humans have no choice (312–13). In fact, it appears that the only reason why humans have "freedom" in *Gospel's* world is so that God can punish them (171), and unfortunately for them, "God does not forgive the sins He makes [them] commit" (127).

In *Gospel*, Saramago dismantles these traditional defenses of God's character by changing the metaphysical nature of God himself. There is no reason for defending this God because he unashamedly admits to determining everything, from the slaughter of the innocents (155, 180) to the crucifixion of his son (311). The determinism of Saramago's world is basically a type of hyper-Calvinism, but unfortunately the divine dictator deciding the fate of humanity is not the loving God traditionally portrayed in Christianity. What Saramago presents is a version of Luther's "hidden God" who looks precisely like the sort of monster one would expect to find behind all of the evil in the world.

Because Saramago has inverted God's character, the "good news," that God is establishing his kingdom on earth, becomes extremely "bad news" for humanity.[34] Saramago's "kakaggelion"[35] functions as the ultimate satire on the gospel message, and this *Gospel* emerges as the most subversive of all the Gospel rewrites.

COMPLEMENTING OR COMPETING CHRISTOLOGICAL PORTRAIT?

Overview of Saramago's Jesus

Saramago's inversions of Satan and God change the entire playing field in the world of his novel and turn out to be the most significant factors influencing the depiction of Jesus. In this *Gospel*, Jesus learns at the feet of Satan rather than at those of his Father.[36] Because of the four years that they spend

34. Cousland, "Kakaggelion," 55.

35. Ibid.

36. Cousland makes a telling observation when he notes that one of the differences in *Gospel's* Christological portrait to those of the Gospels is that Saramago's Jesus is not a teacher. He preaches in public very little and only latterly in life after God commands him to offer the simple message of repenting of one's sins because God is getting ready to establish a new kingdom (334, 338). Instead, Pastor and Mary Magdalene function as Jesus' teachers (Ibid., 68).

together, it is no surprise that Jesus' character resembles the devil more than the deity. Tutored by his "Pastor," Jesus soon adopts his humanitarian brand of compassion and begins to imitate his master's mercy killings of the aged sheep (200) while refusing to sacrifice a young lamb to his Father at the temple (209, 211).

Jesus carries Pastor's humanitarian lessons into his own ministry so that when he multiplies the catches of the Galilean fishermen, he makes sure to keep moving from town to town to spread the wealth to everyone (275–76). Displaying an unselfishness that is admirable, Jesus refuses to set up his own fishing business but offers his miraculous powers freely to all (294). He castigates those who try to keep the price of fish artificially high by throwing some of the catch back and threatens to cease helping them if they do not share their blessings with others (280). With his other miracles, Jesus continues to display compassion on frail humanity by healing the sick, the deaf, lepers, and mutes. Rejecting his Father's habit of sparing only some while sacrificing the rest, Jesus refuses to be rescued while others around him perish. When caught in the midst of a storm, Jesus calms the sea so that all the fishermen return safely to shore with him (282).

Compassionate acts like these that relieve the suffering of others are probably what lead Bloom to proclaim, "The glory of Saramago's *Gospel* is Saramago's Jesus, who seems to me humanly and aesthetically more admirable than any other version of Jesus in the literature of the century now ending."[37] These deeds also help Jesus to pass *Gospel's* humanitarian standards and allow him to be classified as good, like Satan and unlike God.

Gospel's Portrait of Jesus in Comparison with the Gospel Portraits

In portraying Jesus as humane and compassionate, *Gospel's* portrait of Jesus is complementary to that of the Gospels. As with the Gospel plotline, Saramago again retains enough external features of the Gospel Jesus to keep his version from appearing as a blatant contrast. Christological attributes are cloned from the original version and transferred to the rewritten Jesus where they are then subtly twisted. In other words, Saramago's Jesus is to the Gospel Jesus what Bizarro is to Superman. Both doppelgangers resemble their originals in externals but do not retain their characters and often bungle many of the attempts to emulate their actions.

Saramago constructs his Jesus by preserving, at least nominally, many of the titles of Jesus, such as Son of God (262–63, 297) and Messiah (357). On this point, Saramago is markedly different from Ricci, who refuses to

---

37. Bloom, "One with the Beard," 162.

portray his Jesus in either of these traditional categories. Yet even though cast in these orthodox roles, Saramago's Jesus is far from successful in them. By observing what happens when this rewritten Jesus tries to fit into roles that were originally shaped by another, we again see Saramago's distorting process at work.

To begin with, Saramago's Jesus is a rather unaware and ill-prepared Messiah. He does not even know of his own identity as the Messiah until the very end of the novel when in a reversal of roles Jesus must ask John the Baptist to confirm his messianic identity and to give him advice for what he should do as the Messiah. John, quite rightly, tells him to figure it out for himself. When Jesus first hears a description of John, he comments that John better fits the part of the Messiah than he does, and the reader cannot help but agree with this assessment (354). The sole occasion when Jesus claims his messianic identity is during his trials, and there he does so only so that he may be sentenced to death as a false Messiah, a pretender to Israel's throne rather than as the Son of God (369, 372). Ironically, the only act performed by Saramago's Jesus that could be categorized as messianic is his dying. Like the Gospel Jesus, he intends his death to be a liberating act for his people; however, Saramago's Jesus hopes to free them from the clutches of God rather than from their sins (cf. Matt 1:21; 26:28).

As the Son of God, Saramago's Jesus is also unconvincing, partly because he does not resemble his power-hungry Father and partly because the reader is never entirely sure about Jesus' paternity. Although God himself informs Jesus of his divine identity (308), the reader does not know whether to trust God's word on this matter since God also reveals that in Saramago's world gods can lie (320). Jesus could, after all, simply be the son of Joseph who has been hoodwinked by God into fulfilling his purposes. Because God supposedly mixed his seed with Joseph's and since paternity tests are never completely conclusive on these matters, the reader is told that it would be hard to prove which one is Jesus' true father (262–63, 308; cf. 318). Jesus, to his credit, would prefer to be Joseph's son rather than God's (312).

To say that the Father and Son have a strained relationship in *Gospel* is putting it mildly. Unlike the Gospel Jesus, Saramago's Jesus and his God are anything but one (cf. John 10:30). Well-conditioned in Satan's humanism, Jesus questions the inhumanity of his Father's global domination plan, demanding to know why the one true God is unable to bring his purposes about without requiring the sacrifice of so many lives. Jesus, like Satan, believes that humans should be able to live and enjoy life on earth rather than renouncing their earthly existences so that they may have the chance of going to a heaven where none of life's joys await them (320).

In *Gospel*, Jesus "emerges in the novel not as the divine Son of God but as an unfortunate and deluded victim of a faulty religious impulse."[38] This Jesus is not a divine being in control of his destiny and the destinies of others but a pitiful figure "shanghaied by God, for God's own purposes of power."[39] When Jesus tries to renounce his Father and to rescind their covenant in order to help humanity, he is prevented from doing so because of the constraints of the fatalistic world that he inhabits where God forces everything and everyone to work according to his desires but not according to the good of humanity (315, 330, 369; cf. Romans 8:28). God takes control of even Jesus' words (340) and warns that if he refuses to perform miracles God will still make them happen (314–15). Even his final scheme to die as the "King of Jews" rather than as the Son of God is thwarted when God appears at the crucifixion announcing Jesus' identity as his Son (376).[40]

Ultimately, this rift between the Father and the Son undercuts the plausibility of Saramago's Jesus functioning as the "Son of God," but such disunion has to exist because of the radical transformation of God's character in *Gospel*. Because God is a selfish being only concerned with his own glory, he cannot work for the benefit and betterment of humanity. Whereas in the Gospels, the cross is seen as "the ultimate expression of God's compassion and mercy for humankind,"[41] in *Gospel*, the cross is the beginning of the genocide of humanity, starting with Jesus. Therefore, for Jesus to be considered good, he has to reject his Father. Saramago can complement the Gospel portrait of Jesus as compassionate and caring only by allowing him to fail in his role as the Son of God. Instead of resembling the obedient Son in the Gospels who is one with his Father in person and purpose, this Jesus opposes his Father in order to be merciful to humankind.

Aside from retaining the qualities of love and compassion for humanity, Saramago's Jesus manages to convey successfully only one other essential

38. Cousland, "Kakaggelion," 55.

39. Bloom, "One with the Beard," 162.

40. Jesus is not able to fully reject God's will even when he attempts to do so. Frier talks about the passive acceptance of authority throughout the novel, citing examples of Mary's acceptance of the patriarchal system, the laity's acceptance of the superior religious authority of the rabbis, the soldiers' acceptance of Herod's order to kill the children, and Joseph's acceptance of the slaughter of those children. Likewise, it is "Jesus himself who, even when he attempts to reject the law of the father, still implicitly recognizes it by attempting to outwit rather than defy that authority.... [I]n the end he makes a token gesture to fulfil the letter of God's Word (by dying as the Messiah of the Jewish people) rather than rejecting outright the creation of a tradition (that of orthodox Christianity) whose practical consequences he finds too appalling to contemplate. ... Jesus sees a lapse into fatalism and 'becoming one with his father-God' as preferable to a bid for independence" (Frier, "O Evangelho," 380–381).

41. Ben-Porat, "Saramago's *Gospel*," 102.

feature of the Gospel Jesus—his humanity. Like Boyd, one of Saramago's main concerns seems to be the humanizing of Jesus, which is no surprise given Saramago's humanist philosophy. Like the Gospels, Saramago emphasizes Jesus' kinship with Adam and thus with all of humanity, but "instead of making him a sinless second Adam as Paul does [cf. Rom 5:12–21], Saramago shows him to be fallible, ignorant, and sinful."[42]

Perhaps the most shocking aspect of Saramago's portrayal of Jesus' humanity is his sexuality. In *Gospel*, the reader meets a Jesus who desires to masturbate (227) and who, unlike Kazantkazis' Jesus, is not just tempted by sexual visions but actually fulfills them. Saramago's Jesus begins "living in sin with Mary Magdalene" (295) not long after he turns eighteen, and the two continue as lovers until his death.

Saramago's Jesus turns out to be fully human but not in the Chalcedonian sense. He is neither the prototype of what God intended humanity to be prior to the Fall nor the firstborn example of what resurrected humanity shall be. Instead, he is simply a reflection of what flawed humanity currently is—sinful, weak, scared, and confused. And yet he is also capable of love, compassion, and enjoyment of life. According to Saramgo's humanist philosophy, this Jesus is a success because he functions as the symbolic everyman. All of his imperfections are to be embraced and celebrated because they are part of his humanity. This Jesus is the prototypical tragic hero, who although destined to fail still chooses to strive against the oppressive forces, which in this case are God and religion. Saramago offers his Jesus as a noble example for the rest of humanity to emulate.

CONCLUSION

About halfway through the novel, the narrator informs us, "[T]his gospel was never meant to dismiss what others have written about Jesus or to contradict their accounts" (200), but if gods are capable of lying in *Gospel*'s world, then narrators are too. After discussing the various ways in which Saramago twists and transforms the Gospels' worldviews and characters, it should be clear that contradicting their accounts and the religious system based upon them is precisely what Saramago intends to do. While Ricci's work tries to convince us that faith is for the dim-witted and credulous and that miraculous events are illusionary and are only a result of rumors, misperceptions, and lies, Saramago makes no such claim and readily accepts their existence. Instead, his major aim is to demonstrate that Christianity is an oppressive regime whose claims and whose God need to be dismantled

42. Cousland, "Kakaggelion," 66.

in order to liberate humanity. Both authors offer competing narratives to those of the Gospels, but the problems that they have with the Gospels and their methods in targeting them are markedly different. Ricci's complaint with the Gospels is a historical one in which he questions the validity of any texts that claim absolute historical truth and of the testimony of the Gospels specifically. He makes assumptions as to the nature of reality and questions the historicity of the miraculous. Saramago's primary issue with the Gospels, on the other hand, appears to be more theological than historical as he asks what kind of God could be behind such a history.

In order to explore his concerns, Saramago constructs a counter-gospel, a *kakagelion*, as Cousland coins it, but his aim is certainly not only exploratory in nature but also persuasive in nature as he tries to convert not only Jesus but also his audience to his gospel of humanitarian compassion. In this attempt, he is only partially successful. Within his own narrative world, Saramago's new gospel succeeds in convincing Jesus although it is ultimately unsuccessful in overcoming a tyrannical God. Jesus, the student of Saramago's humanitarian compassion, functions as the character that critiques the hegemony of this divine dictator. Rather than accepting God's bribe of power and glory and the magical powers that come along with such an allegiance, Jesus tries to reject them. He determines that humans would do better on their own instead of relying on the divine deliverance of God. Judging matters from inside *Gospel*'s world, who would not agree with Saramago's critique of the God he has invented nor side with the humanitarian Pastor and his disciple Jesus in their efforts to overthrow such a dictator?

Saramago intends for his readers also to reject the hegemony of the Christian church and of its God in actuality just as Jesus rejects it in *Gospel*. Humanity does not need to be ruled by the majority religion. Instead, Saramago, along with other magic realists, calls us to celebrate, to perhaps even worship, the marvelousness of the ordinary. Instead of looking for divine deliverance, we are to deliver ourselves and to fight against oppressive tyranny wherever we find it, even if we find it in the so-called holy.

At the same time, Saramago undercuts his own persuasive rhetoric regarding the problem of evil and suffering with his presentation of God. As Paul Ricoeur once wrote, "Suffering is only a scandal for the person who understands God to be source of everything that is good in creation, including our indignation against evil, our courage to bear it, and our feeling of sympathy toward victims."[43] In the novel, suffering is only scandalous at first because Jesus and other characters believe God to be good. Once God's true character has been revealed, the puzzling problem of evil is solved, and the

43. Ricoeur, *Figuring*, 260.

tension between a good God and humanity's sufferings is resolved. The only one left scandalized is the reader who expects Saramago's God to match the character of the biblical God.

On one level, *Gospel* is ultimately unsuccessful in its critique of Christianity and will only serve to convince those who already hold a negative opinion of the faith and of its God. Its lack of success lies in its portrayal of God, which for all the novel's superficial fidelity to the Gospel narratives fails to take the claims of Christianity seriously. Because this fictional God does not resemble *any* monotheistic religion's traditional claims about God, let alone those of Christianity, *Gospel's* critiques of God, while landing within its own narrative world, mostly fall flat outside it. Christians reading the novel will likely see very little of their own beliefs about God in Saramago's creation and so will be able to dismiss not only this fictional portrayal of God but also its intended and extended critique of Christianity's God. Furthermore, there is something curiously duplicitous about Saramago's inversion of the Gospels' value system, since he seems to want to hold onto Christian values—which he hands often without any alteration to Satan—while at the same time wanting to denounce its heritage.

That being said, Saramago's God cannot and should not be entirely dismissed by thoughtful and careful readers of the Bible. While most would see Saramago's God as an inversion of the "biblical" God, Ben-Porat argues that even this maniacal version of the deity is a rewriting rather than a complete inversion because it "foregrounds elements that exist [in the biblical portrayal of God] but are largely ignored or explained away."[44] While Ben-Porat is correct in assuming that many would prefer to turn a blind eye to some of the less than favorable portrayals of God in the Bible, particularly some passages in the OT, there have certainly been many attempts to wrestle with these texts and to examine some of the more disturbing aspects of God's character and behavior narrated in the Bible.[45]

One of the best questions Saramago's narrative leads us to consider is how some of the traditional theories of atonement may negatively affect our view of God. For example, why is the violent death of Jesus necessary in order for God to draw all humanity to himself? Along with the midwife Salome, we may question whether or not God is so impotent or, worse, so sadistic that he cannot establish his kingdom without the shedding of his child's blood. Is God not great enough that he can offer forgiveness without founding it on violence? Such theological questions are important for Christians to consider

44. Ben-Porat, "Saramago's *Gospel*," 99.

45. E.g., Seibert, *Disturbing*; Gundry, *No Mercy*; Nelson-Pallmeyer, *Jesus Against Christianity*.

as we seek ways of explaining the atonement and of interpreting the meaning of Jesus' death, and Saramago does well to raise them.

Also important is Saramago's critique of religious violence and the atrocities committed in the name of God. As Longenecker concludes, "Saramago's genius is in linking the history of the Church directly with the problem of evil, as if they were virtually interchangeable phenomena."[46] Saramago's criticism, though hardly original, is an important reminder of how religion can be coopted and distorted for political agendas, and we can only hope that the violence he condemns most Christians would not condone. Most would agree with Saramago that the Crusades and the Inquisition were horrible periods in the Church's history and were unjustifiable. Unlike Saramago, however, they would not affirm these events as representative of Christianity but as perverse distortions of the faith. As Longenecker goes on to say, "[I]n making this link, Saramago also turns a blind eye to the countless counter-instances that testify to another dimension within the history of the Christian church: that is, the enactment of Christian communities as the locus for care among the needy and for the offsetting of hardship and injustice . . . Saramago's novel gains its dramatic poignancy only by conjuring up a popular but wholly one-sided portraiture of the Church."[47] Longenecker exposes Saramago's ploy and the deficiency of his portrayal of the Church. While Saramago is perfectly right in criticizing injustices committed by the Church and in the name of God, he is remiss in failing to tell the rest of the Church's story, of the countless ways in which it has shown compassion to humanity, fought against injustice, and succoured the suffering. In failing to do so, he weakens his own argument because he exposes it to charges of bias and distortion.

Ultimately, although Saramago's novel functions as a competing "gospel," it fails to convince because its narrative world, its characters, and its critiques of Christianity are neither fair nor normative representatives of Christianity. *Gospel* is a compelling read and literally superior to any of the other Jesus novels, but I must differ with Bloom's assessment that it offers the most humane fictional Jesus. In my opinion, that honor would be given to *The Hidden Years*. In fact, it is in Boyd's novel that we find a Jesus who responds to many of the criticisms that Saramago launches against God and Christianity's influence in the world. As we shall see in the second half of this monograph, to which we now turn, it is in Boyd's fictional Jesus that we discover what true compassion for humanity really looks like as we watch him undergoing his temptation in the wilderness.

---

46. Longenecker, "What God Wants, God Gets."
47. Ibid.

PART III

From New Texts Back
to the New Testament

6

The Temptation

From Gospel Sources to Gospel Rewrites

INTRODUCTION TO A HERMENEUTICAL CYCLE: GOSPEL WRITINGS, NOVEL REWRITINGS, AND A PREPOSTEROUS READING OF THE TEMPTATION

IN THE FIRST HALF of the book, we examined how Jesus novels transform the Gospels into new texts that relate to their progenitors in broadly competing or complementing ways. We have discussed techniques used in each of the four novels surveyed that ultimately serve to undermine or to support the canonical Gospels, and we have considered the Christological portraits offered in those novels.

In this section, we will revisit two of our competing and complementing examples—Boyd's *The Hidden Years* and Saramago's *Gospel*. This time, however, we will focus on their portrayals of one particular Gospel event—the Temptation. Boyd and Saramago, for all their differences in style and approach to fictionalizing Jesus' life, surprisingly have a great deal in common in their respective rewrites of the Temptation. For example, both authors present the testing of Jesus as the climax of their novels, giving prominence to an event that seems to be less than central in the plots of the Synoptic Gospels. If emplotment provides meaning, as Ricoeur has suggested,[1] then the placement of the testing scene as the climax of a Jesus novel certainly af-

1. Ricoeur, *Time and Narrative*, 61; Ricoeur, *Memory, History, Forgetting*, 251.

fects the meaning of the story being told. This placement is particularly significant given that in the Gospels the climax of Jesus' life is the Crucifixion, not the Temptation.[2]

As discussed in the prolegomenon, the intertextual relationship between the Gospels and these Gospel rewrites encourage the reading of these texts alongside one another. When readers actualize the reading pact, a cross-directional interpretation takes place as the novels are judged according to their progenitors and the Gospels are "preposterously" evaluated by taking into account the potential interpretive guidance offered by the rewrites. In order, therefore, to engage fully in this reading pact, after analyzing the novels' testing scenes, we will return to one of the original Gospel accounts of the Temptation and reexamine that passage within its own narrative setting and in light of questions raised by the rewrites.

By engaging in this cross-textual analysis, we will be able to offer an example of a hermeneutical circle that can arise when new texts come into contact with older texts and have the effect of sending the reader back to investigate those original texts afresh. Beginning with a short overview of standard interpretations of the Temptation in the Gospels, we will then move on to investigate the rewritten versions of that event and end in the next chapter with a reinterpretation of the original source material, specifically Matt 4:1–11.

NEW TESTAMENT SOURCES
FOR THE TEMPTATION AND INTERPRETATIVE ISSUES

The Synoptic Accounts

When rewriting the Temptation, novelists have several retellings upon which to draw because the event appears in all three Synoptic Gospels. Mark 1:12–13 presents the shortest version mentioning nothing about a fast and offering no explanation as to which type of tests Jesus undergoes or how he deals with them. Matthew 4:1–11 and Luke 4:1–13 follow another strand of the story, which source critics attribute to a common source other than Mark, such as Q (if Matthew and Luke have no literary relationship) or Matthew itself (if Luke used Matthew). It is this second strand that contains the descriptive material upon which most authors build when constructing their rewrites. According to this strand, Jesus goes into the Judean

---

2. Some might disagree and suggest that the Resurrection, not the Crucifixion, is the climax of action in the Gospels. I would argue that, at least in the Synoptics, the Resurrection is the resolution of the Crucifixion climax and not the climax itself.

wilderness, where he fasts for forty days and is tempted by Satan in three specific ways: to turn stone(s) into bread, to jump down from the temple pinnacle, and to worship Satan.

Even though Matthew and Luke include roughly the same material, they do diverge on a few points. The most notable difference between the two accounts is the order of the three tests. Both begin with the challenge of turning stone(s) to bread, but the challenge for Jesus to cast himself down from the temple and the enticement to worship Satan in exchange for earthly rule are reversed, with Matthew placing the worship challenge last and Luke placing it second.

Most interpreters when speaking collectively of the Temptation event reference Matthew more than Luke and follow Matthew's chronology. Likewise, novelists also predominantly follow Matthew's version,[3] and the Temptation scene in *The Hidden Years* is a prime example of this artistic preference. Because Boyd follows Matthew's ordering and complements that particular Gospel's version of the Temptation, we will continue our discussion on biblical source material by focusing mainly on the Matthean version.

The Matthean Version and Typology

Using typology, Matthew structures the Temptation in such a way that the setting of Jesus' forty-day fast on a mountain in the wilderness echoes the forty-day fast by Moses (and also Elijah) on a mountain in a wilderness setting.[4] Matthew especially heightens the connection by describing the fast

---

3. e.g., Dostoyevsky (*The Brothers Karamazov*), Mailer (*The Gospel according to the Son*), Boyd (*The Hidden Years*), and Barclay (*Jesus of Nazareth*). Milton (*Paradise Regained*) surprisingly prefers Luke's order; and Holmes (*Three From Galilee*) invents an entirely new order: temple, bread, and kingdom. Saramago (*Gospel*) and Crace (*Quarantine*) are revisionist accounts and unsurprisingly do not follow any of the Synoptic versions in particular but only borrow symbols and images from their narratives.

4. Commentators from early on, such as Tertullian, *Res.* 61 (ANF 3:593); Augustine, *Cons.* 2.4.9 (*NPNF* 6:105); John Chrysostom, *Hom. Matt.* 8:2 (*NPNF* 10:78); and Calvin, *Comm on Mat, Mar, Luk* Matt 4.1 (V1) have noted this typological portrayal. The pattern of a forty-day fast also captured the imagination of early Christians not only through the structure of the Lenten season but also in the early apocryphal literature (cf. *Life of Adam and Eve* 6.1; *Prot. Jas.* 1.4).

Warren Carter has also drawn attention to the use of *synkrisis* in Matthew whereby the reader is meant to compare Jesus with other characters, some of whom are outside Matthew's narrative. One of the major comparisons readers are meant to draw is between Jesus and Moses. Throughout Matthew—from Jesus' miraculous escape as a baby during the slaughter of the innocents (Matt 2:13; cf. Exod 1:22—22:10) to his giving of the law on a mountain (Matt 5–7; cf. Exod 19–31)—Jesus' life and ministry intentionally parallel that of Moses (Carter, *Matthew*, 179, 203–5; cf. Allison, *New Moses*).

as lasting for forty days and forty nights (Mark and Luke mention only forty days) so that Jesus further typifies Moses' unnatural feat of not breaking his fast at sundown and somehow still surviving.[5]

While Jesus' testing certainly recalls that of Moses, it also offers a striking allusion to that of the Israelites in the wilderness. Jesus, like his ancestors, goes into the wilderness where he wanders for forty days rather than forty years, and like them, he also experiences hunger during that period.[6] The similarities between Jesus' and Israel's wilderness experiences are further heightened by the content of the three temptations. Jesus' first temptation of bread recalls the Israelites' grumbling for food and their receiving manna from God (Exod 16). Likewise, when Jesus is asked to test God's protective promises by jumping off the temple peak, this potential trial of God reflects that of the Israelites at Massah when they demand water as proof of God's provision and presence (Exod 17). Finally, although there is debate over which specific OT story the third temptation represents, the typology points to Israel's pattern of betraying God by worshipping false idols. One specific example of this pattern occurs when the Israelites make and worship the golden calf (Exod 32).[7]

Whereas the tests follow a sequential reading of Exodus, Jesus' rebuttals to all three are drawn from Deuteronomy and are placed in Matthew in reverse order: 8:3—refers to manna; 6:16—refers to the Massah testing; 6:13—refers to worshipping God only. Deuteronomy 6–8 is set within Moses' address to the Israelites (5:1) prior to their crossing the Jordan and taking possession of the land (9:1). In his speech, Moses gives the Israelites instructions on how to succeed in the land by learning from and not repeating their previous failures in the wilderness. It is most pertinent for our discussion to note that these instructions from which Jesus quotes in his own forty-day wilderness temptation are set within an explanation of why the Israelites were tested in the wilderness for forty years (8:2). During that time God was testing them to see whether or not they would be obedient to God and faithful to their covenant.[8]

---

5. Beare, *Matthew*, 108; cf. Gundry, *Matthew*, 54. In Crace's *Quarantine*, other characters share Jesus' mountain refuge for those forty days. They observe a traditional fast, such as those still seen today during Muslim observances of Ramadan, beginning at sunrise and ending at sunset, but Crace's Jesus does not eat at all and subsequently dies after thirty days without food and water.

6. E.g., Tertullian, *Bapt.* 20 (*ANF* 3:679); Williamson, "Matthew 4:1–11," 51–55; and Hester, "Luke 4:1–13," 56. Having a holy experience on a mountain echoes the OT experiences at Sinai and Nebo (Deut 34:1–4; Num 27:12; cf. Taylor, "Temptation," 36).

7. Stegner, *Narrative Theology*, 4; Fenton, *Saint Matthew*, 63.

8. Donaldson, "Mockers," 8n1.

Matthew's Temptation, therefore, has rightly been called a "haggadic exegesis of Deuteronomy"[9] and an "early Christian midrash,"[10] in which Jesus functions as the archetypal obedient son who follows God's commands and succeeds in every area in which Israel failed.[11] Thus, the election of Israel and the testing of the Israelites in the wilderness are transferred to and isolated in one person—Jesus—highlighting his representative role.[12] Jesus is tempted not only for himself but also on behalf of the entire nation of Israel, and his victory serves as the reversal of Israel's defeat and its redemption.

What Is the Meaning of the Temptation and Its Three Tests?

Attempting to discern the meaning of the Temptation and particularly of each of the three tests has vexed interpreters for centuries and led to a variety of explanations. Luz has helpfully outlined four of the most typical interpretive positions of Matthew's Temptation for us.[13] Besides the typological view described above, he lists the parenetic, Christological, and messianic interpretations.

The first view, the parenetic, sees the Temptation as a simple story of Jesus overcoming typical temptations to evil. This interpretation, particularly popular among the early church and during the Reformation,[14] views the three tests as paradigmatic examples of resisting the sins of gluttony, vainglory, and greed. Jesus' victory is seen as a parenetic example meant

9. Taylor, "Temptation," 30.

10. Gerhardsson, *Testing*, 11.

11. E.g., Murphy-O'Connor, "Triumph," 39; Stegner, "Temptation," 11; Kingsbury, *Matthew*, 40.

12. Donaldson, *Jesus on the Mountain*, 92. Jesus' recapitulation of Israel's experiences is not isolated to the Temptation event. Indeed, it is a theme running throughout Matthew but particularly concentrated in the opening four chapters prior to the beginning of Jesus' ministry. It begins with his lineage from Abraham (1:1), continues through the slaughter of the innocents (2:16–18) and the exodus from Egypt (2:15), and culminates with the testing in the wilderness (4:1–11); (Donaldson, "Mockers," 11; cf. Hagner, who points out the same typology running throughout Matthew and comments, "For Matthew, all Israel's history finds its recapitulation in the life of Jesus" [Hagner, *Matthew*, 34; cf. France, *Gospel Matthew* 128]).

13. The following discussion is based on his summaries. For a fuller sketch of these positions and examples of commentators who hold these opinions, please see Luz, *Matthew 1–7*, 184–86.

14. E.g., Augustine, *Enarrat. Ps.* 8.13 (NPNF 8:32); *Tract. ep. Jo.* 3:14 (NPNF 7:475); and John Cassian, *Conferences* 5.6 (NPNF2 11:341–42). See also Lightfoot, *Talmud*, Matt 4:1–11; and Green, *Matthew*, 68.

to inspire and teach members of the Christian community how to conquer their own temptations.[15]

One problem with this interpretation is its assumption that "temptation" is always an enticement to evil or wrongdoing.[16] While this definition is reinforced by the linking of temptation (πειρασμός) with evil (πονηρός) in the Lord's prayer (Matt 6:13), such an understanding does not tell the full story of what temptation means either in the biblical narrative in general or specifically in Matthew's Temptation.

The Greek word πειράζω, translated as "tempted" in Matt 4:1, has several meanings but is most often used in the Bible to describe trying, testing, or tempting.[17] Typically, this testing is of "something or someone in order to determine or demonstrate worth or faithfulness."[18] The person performing the test can be anyone from Satan (e.g., Matt 4:1; 1 Thess 3:5) to Jesus (e.g., John 6:6) to humans (e.g., Exod 17:2; Isa 7:12; Heb 3:9). Even God is often depicted as the one doing the testing (e.g., Gen 22:1; Exod 20:20; Deut 8:2). In fact, in what are believed to be some of the earlier writings in the OT, testing is principally done by God and of God's people in order to prove their obedience, loyalty, and faith in God over a period of time (e.g., Gen 22:1–19; Exod 20:20).[19] It is thus problematic to define automatically πειράζω as an enticement to evil when we consider that God is the one doing much of the "temptation" in the Bible.

In a later tradition, Satan or other adversaries of God whose "purpose is to separate men from God" try to force humans to decide for or against God through a time of temptation (e.g., Job 7:1; 10:17).[20] Again, we see that temptation is fundamentally a loyalty test rather than an enticement to do

---

15. Similarly, a modern variant on the parenetic interpretation is that of the psychological interpretation, which equates Jesus' temptations with the universal temptations of materialism, thrill seeking, and a desire for power over the world.

16. This assumption is reflected in modern definitions of "temptation" (e.g., *The Shorter Oxford English Dictionary* says that it is "[t]he action of tempting or fact of being tempted, esp. to evil" [p. 2259]. *The Chambers Dictionary* calls it "enticement to do wrong" [p. 1706]).

17. Danker, "πειράζω," *Greek-English Lexicon*.

18. Twelftree, "Temptation of Jesus," 821.

19. Gerhardsson notes that in the OT this word typically occurs within the context of the covenant relationship between God and his people. Sometimes, it is used positively, describing the way in which God tests his people, but it is also used negatively, telling how those people tested God. The word implies that the testing is to see whether or not a covenant partner will hold up his or her end of the bargain (Gerhardsson, *Testing*, 26).

20. Seesemann, "πείρα," *TDNT* 6.23–36.

evil.[21] Of course, when failing that test means siding against God, then we could also define the temptation as an enticement to evil, if "evil" is simply defined as doing other than the will of God.

In sum, instead of automatically interpreting πειράζω as a temptation to evil, the term often refers more to testing where one's loyalties lie. Testing is the better translation for the word because it does not necessarily have the same pejorative connotation in English.[22] In Matthew's Temptation, although the aim of persuading Jesus to act against God's will is a negative one, the actions that Jesus is asked to do may not in themselves be wrong, such as Jesus placating hunger with bread. This distinction will turn out to be particularly important when analyzing the testing scenes in *The Hidden Years* and in *Gospel*.

The second alternative interpretation of the Temptation that Luz describes is known as the Christological interpretation. It suggests that the Temptation was written to identify who Jesus is and that the narrative's main agenda is to counter alternate identities attributed to him in antiquity. With the first two tests, Matthew shows that Jesus was not a magician or a Hellenistic miracle worker. With the final temptation, he rebuffs the notion that Jesus was a political Zealot. The meaning of the event under this interpretation is that Jesus proves himself to be the Son of God by rejecting these other identities.

While it is certainly true that the Temptation is a Christological passage and that part of its central meaning involves Jesus' identity as the Son of God, it does not seem likely that the pericope was constructed as an intentional counterargument to pictures of Jesus as a magician or a Jewish zealot. As Luz rightly concludes, "It is not possible to construct a unitary background against which our story polemicizes."[23]

Finally, the third view that Luz surveys is a messianic interpretation of the passage. It suggests that each of the three tests can be correlated with contemporary expectations for the Messiah. The three basic dimensions of messiahship according to this theory are prophetic, priestly, and royal. The Temptation becomes a test for Jesus to prove himself as the Messiah by fulfilling each of these expectations and also is a debate over how Jesus should

21. Again in the NT, we see that the principle use of πειράζω is not to describe a temptation to evil. The word occurs thirty-six times in the NT, but only three of these occurrences (Matt 6:13; 1 Cor 7:5; James 1:13–14) specifically refer to a temptation to wrongdoing.

22. France, *Matthew*, 96. France notes elsewhere that "tempt" always has negative connotations whereas the Greek πειράζω is more ambivalent (France, *Gospel Matthew*, 126).

23. Luz, *Matthew 1–7*, 185.

enact these particular roles. We will defer our response to the appropriateness of this view, however, until we analyze *The Hidden Years'* temptation.

With an understanding of these typical interpretations of the Temptation, we are now better prepared to analyze the rewrites of the Temptation.

THE TESTING SCENES
OF THE HIDDEN YEARS AND GOSPEL

The Temptation has long been a favorite story among fictionalizers, capturing the imaginations of many, from past literary giants, such as John Milton and Fyodor Dostoevsky, to modern novelists, such as Neil Boyd and José Saramago. Yet even though each artist begins with the same source material, they appropriate and manipulate it differently to create their own versions.

Boyd's account retains the Matthean structure for the event and appropriates its content for Jesus' test. The challenges to change stones to bread, to jump from the temple, and to worship Satan in exchange for the kingdoms of the world form the backbone of the scene. Only on top of these original elements does Boyd then go on to construct additional dialogue (over thirty pages of it!) so that his recounting becomes its own distinct narrative. Because his account retains a sufficient amount of the story's original features and clearly intends to function as another version of it, the testing scene in *The Hidden Years* can be classified as a prototypical rewrite of that Gospel event.

Gospel, in contrast, has not one but three testing scenes. All of these are better classified as global allusions to the Temptation than as rewrites because while they appropriate biblical motifs, the novel versions are very much their own literary creations and bear only a tangential resemblance to the Temptation in the Gospel accounts.[24]

Even with their vastly divergent relationships to their Gospel source material, both scenes serve as important examples of the reception history of Jesus' testing in modern literature. Beyond examining their relationships to their source material, we will also focus on the common characteristics of their climatic testing scenes: Boyd's wilderness temptation and Saramago's third and final testing scene, which takes place on the lake. As we shall see, both of the novels' climaxes draw together major themes woven throughout their narratives. While the novels are theologically diverse in their outlooks, both address similar challenges to the character of God and to Christianity, and in both, Jesus' fidelity not only to his Father but also to all of humanity is tested as the narratives present these dual loyalties as being in competition.

24. Ben-Porat offers Jim Crace's *Quarantine* (1997) as an example of a global allusion to Jesus' temptation (Ben-Porat, "Saramago's *Gospel*," 102–4).

THE HIDDEN YEARS' VERSION OF THE TEMPTATION

The Bread Test

The first test in *The Hidden Years*, which challenges Jesus to fulfill his own hunger with bread, is appropriately anticipated throughout the novel by descriptions of poverty and the precarious nature of life in first-century Palestine. The most pertinent scenes are those that depict a starving village of Nazareth, afflicted first by a locust invasion and then by an ensuing drought. During their suffering, the villagers accuse God of having abandoned them and ask what they have done to deserve such treatment. In these early chapters, Jesus' character is contextualized by the hunger and poverty he endures along with his village. He is presented as a man fully immersed in a world of destitution and as one who participates in the pain of his people. He "belonged to the brotherhood of want. He, Jesus of Nazareth, was one of the have-nots, the dispossessed" (100). Consistently throughout the novel, lines are drawn between Jesus' personal suffering, the suffering of Nazareth, that of the nation of Israel, and that of the entire world.[25] By the climax, the reader knows that this fully human Jesus participates in the suffering of all of humanity and knows from firsthand experience what it is like to hunger.

With such an emphasis on Jesus' empathy with humanity in the earlier chapters, it is no surprise that the bread test turns out to be not merely about satisfying Jesus' own hunger but also about relieving everyone's hunger. In this test, the bread functions as a synecdoche for food for all humanity, and turning stones into bread in the desert displays in miniature what Jesus can do on a global scale by solving the problem of world hunger. Subtle and sly, Boyd's Satan recognizes that humans are more often entrapped by an appeal to their best natures than to their worst, so he tempts Jesus by appealing to his compassion for humanity.[26]

Satan goes on to present his humanitarian appeal as the fulfillment of messianic expectations, and by doing so, Boyd's presentation of the first test coincides with the messianic interpretation of the Matthean Temptation. In Boyd's version, the common messianic expectation that Satan tries to

25. Some examples of these connections include the following: "Hunger was his [Jesus'] bond with home" (45); "It was his [Jesus'] share in the pain of his village" (151); Jesus was to "fulfill his own and his people's destiny" (176); "Was he [Jesus] not a circumcised Jew, a lover of the Law and Passover, a worshipper of the God who brought his people out of bondage? Was he not one with them in their joys and tribulations? One with them even in their guilt?" (200); "the quiet grief of the village and of all mankind" (56); and "Carpenter, you suffer when anyone is suffering" (116).

26. Again, we note the problem here of automatically translating πειράζω as an enticement to evil.

exploit is the "miraculous abundance of material goods" that many believed would accompany the Messiah and mirror the Mosaic manna.[27] With Satan's citation of the Mosaic precedent (212; cf. John 6:31–35), we see Boyd imitating Matthew's own use of typology in the Temptation. Only this time it is Satan who argues for Jesus to present himself as the new Moses and to fulfill these messianic expectations.

One of the main questions addressed in Boyd's version is what sort of Messiah Jesus would be. Satan asks Jesus to focus his ministry exclusively on social reform issues, such as the eradication of poverty and hunger. By actualizing the expected plentitude of the messianic age, he would radically reform society and deliver the world from evil since all sin is rooted in the lack of bread.[28]

Of course, while feeding the hungry is part of Jesus' messianic ministry,[29] it is not the whole of it. Boyd's Jesus refuses to be limited to being only the "bread king" and establishing an "everlasting brotherhood" that is rooted solely in bread.[30] Instead, he opts for God's larger plan. While the

27. Argyle, *Matthew*, 39–40; De Diétrich, *Saint Matthew*, 24; Williamson, "Matthew 4:1–11," 52; and Balmer, *Matthew*, 59.

Commentators who believe that this messianic expectation of a repetition of the manna-miracle of Israel's wilderness experience underlies the Matthean Temptation base their claims on texts like 2 Baruch 29:8, which states, "And it shall come to pass at that self-same time that the treasury of manna shall again descend from on high, and they will eat of it in those years, because these are they who have come to the consummation of time." Hagner, however, says that this expectation is from later rabbinic literature, such as Str-B 2:481–82 (*Matthew*, 65).

28. Wink, "Matthew 4:1–11," 393. Boyd may be following Dostoevsky, whose Grand Inquisitor in *The Brothers Karamazov* recounts and analyzes the Temptation scene in a similar fashion. He states, "Do You know that more centuries will pass and men of wisdom and learning will proclaim that there is no such thing as crime, that there is therefore no sin either, that there are only hungry people. 'Feed us first, then ask for virtue'" (Dostoevsky, *The Brothers Karamazov*, 337).

29. In neither Boyd's novel nor Matthew's Gospel does Jesus' rejection of Satan's plan imply that either the Matthean or the Boyd Jesus were opposed to alleviating poverty. In Matthew's account, Jesus goes on to multiply the loaves and fish for the masses. In Boyd's account, he hires himself out to earn milk for a starving child and gives his only fish away to a hungry prostitute.

30. Here Boyd follows Dostoevsky's description of the first test. According to the Grand Inquisitor, Satan's original challenge to Jesus was this: "Turn them into loaves of bread and men will follow You like cattle, grateful and docile" (Dostoevsky, *Brothers Karamazov*, 336). The Grand Inquisitor adds, "In bread, You were offered something that could have brought You indisputable loyalty: You would give man bread and man would bow down to You, because there is nothing more indisputable than bread" (339).

Interestingly, Eduard Schweizer cites Dostoevsky's Grand Inquisitor section as an excellent summary of the challenge given to Jesus during this test (Schweizer, *Matthew*, 65).

reader is never explicitly told just what that plan is, anyone familiar with the Gospels is able to catch the allusions to Jesus' future passion and death.[31]

While Boyd's temptation is a testing of messianic vocation, it is also, and more importantly, a temptation for Jesus to question the character of God. Within the question of hunger lies the great debate of theodicy, both in the novel and perhaps, as the novel leads us to consider, in the Matthean Temptation narrative itself. Boyd's Satan asks us to consider whether God still can be considered good in light of those who go hungry. He reminds Jesus of the Israelites starving in the wilderness and suggests that any God who would do that to his own people cannot be worthy of worship. Bringing the issue even closer to Jesus' home and heart, Satan points out that no manna came down from heaven to relieve the suffering of Nazareth when its bread ran out. Finally, the last challenge against God's goodness is Jesus' current situation. If God is really a good Father, then how can Jesus be starving in the wilderness now?

Satan's ultimate goal in having Jesus provide bread for himself is to have the Son deny the Father's goodness. Instead of learning the lesson of the Israelites and the manna—that man does not live by bread alone but by its source, God—Jesus would be replacing God and calling God untrustworthy and compassionless. Like most biblical tests, this one turns out be a testing of loyalty, and Boyd's Jesus chooses to remain faithful to his Father and to continue on the path he is currently following in obedience to God's will.

The Temple Test

With the second test, we again witness earlier themes being tied together during the temptation climax. For example, Satan's argument that religion can be problematic and even damaging in humanity's attempts to love God and to love others is not a new idea to Boyd's Jesus. In fact, it is an issue with which he struggles throughout the novel but particularly in the second part, beginning with his first visit to Capernaum and continuing with his pilgrimage to Jerusalem with Ezra. When Jesus first visits the Capernaum synagogue, he is bored by the dryness of the Rabbi's prayers and his endless discussion of purity laws. He is also taken aback by the pomp and pretense that he witnesses and wonders whether the formality of the building itself might not be responsible for the insincerity and showboating that he

31. For example, Satan's plan to feed the world is pitted against the "forlorn hope that mankind will feed off you [Jesus]" (214); the new paradise of bread becomes the alternative to the salvation of humans and the redemption of creation (215); and finally, the end of suffering is contrasted with Jesus' own participation in that suffering (216).

observes (118–23). All he witnesses at the synagogue is an effort at making people feel safe in their religion by reducing it to tedious regulations about cleaning cups and plates. Such discussions keep people from dealing with serious issues, such as unclean hearts (123–24). At the Jerusalem temple, Jesus witnesses even more problematic expressions of religion. Once again, he observes how the building itself encourages pageantry and thus leads people away from true worship. He also questions the necessity of animal sacrifice, a topic of general concern among both complementing and competing novels, and wonders whether God is really pleased with all of that blood. Jesus desires to see Jerusalem changed (176), and because he has opted for a prophetic rather than priestly ministry, he knows that one day he will have to confront the temple and the city (183–84).

When we arrive at the novel's temple test, we see that it retains the same verbal structure as the Matthean test. It too begins with Satan's invitation for Jesus to cast himself down, which Boyd's Satan also legitimizes with a quotation of Ps 91:11, and ends with Jesus' rebuttal, a quotation of Deut 6:16. As with the bread test, here too we see a messianic interpretation. When Boyd's Satan cites Ps 91:11, he refers to it as a messianic text, which he then challenges Jesus to fulfill (218–19). We are not told, however, why this psalm is viewed messianically or what expected messianic role Jesus would fulfill by embodying its description. We are simply told that by descending, Jesus would prove himself as the Messiah and gain everyone's attention.

In between the biblical challenge and the response that Boyd transfers into his narrative, he does a significant amount of gap filling with a theological discussion between Satan and Jesus that is far more intriguing than his rewriting of the imported material. Their discussion quickly shifts away from what Jesus is tempted to do—to cast himself down from the temple— and instead focuses on the building from which Jesus is tempted to jump. In Boyd's version, the act of Jesus casting himself down is not pictured as important in itself. It is only necessary because it will provide the validation of Jesus' messianic identity, which will also legitimize his authority to destroy the temple. The temple in turn functions as the symbolic starting point for a theological reflection upon the evils of institutional religion. As with his argument in the bread test, Satan again criticizes a system and asks Jesus to destroy and replace it with another better, more humane one.

During their conversation, Satan uses multiple arguments to try to convince Jesus that "religion is bad for mankind" (224). First, he reasons that religion promotes hypocrisy and misplaced trust. By obeying rules, people appear to be holy on the outside and believe that they are safe because they have performed their religious duties. Meanwhile, on the inside, they have never been cleaned nor have their hearts really changed. Their trust is misplaced because it rests in their ability to keep rules rather than in their God.

Second, Satan argues that religion misdirects and contorts worship. Institutionalized religion causes people to worship buildings and pageantry rather than God. Its designation of sacred spaces destroys the sacredness of the world and encourages people to forget that God is already present everywhere and can be worshipped wherever they are. Buildings like the temple also portray God as a pagan idol rather than as the wild and free Being whom the work of human hands cannot contain.

Third, Satan reminds Jesus of the pain and suffering that religion brings to many. According to Satan, religion preys upon the poor and uses their money to finance its elaborate pageantry and its ornate priestly costumes. It also causes physical pain to millions. From the endless blood of animal sacrifices to the future sacrifice of Jesus himself, religion decimates those in its path.

Not content to offer contemporary examples, Satan goes on to paint a vision of what a religion based on Jesus' death will look like when it becomes twisted by his followers. Temples, priests, and countless additional rules and regulations will arise once more to make people feel smug in their holiness without demanding a real change in their hearts and lives. Once more, the poor will be exploited, and their pennies will pay for new buildings, finery, and even statues of Jesus himself. Yet again, religion will be the cause of violence and suffering as Jesus' future followers will persecute Jews in retribution for his death and will launch crusades in order to regain Jesus' homeland. Rather than just hurting others, many of his followers also will inflict pain upon themselves by flaying their own bodies, depriving their own flesh, and closeting themselves away from the rest of the world. The "love of suffering for its own sake will be the new orthodoxy" because his followers will simply be following in his bloody footsteps (230). Satan prophesies to Jesus, "A religion based on you will be the worst the world has seen because it will be a perversion of the best" (226).

Satan's arguments affect Jesus deeply because they are basically the same ones that Jesus himself made earlier in the novel. Jesus too has witnessed these perversions, but the difference between Jesus and Satan is that Jesus believes them to be aberrations of religion and not the true nature of religion itself. When Jesus pulls himself away from Satan's perspective and starts to look through his own eyes, he sees that these distortions are neither the essence nor the totality of religion. Instead, he realizes that true religion is embodied in people like Rabbi Samuel and Rabbi Ezra. When he watches these saintly men embracing at the temple, Jesus thinks to himself that they stand for what is best in his religion (168–69). Now when tempted to sweep away religion completely, he is reminded by their examples of what is worth preserving and of why he has come to redeem the flawed system rather than destroy it.[32] While tempted to conform to Satan's plan, Jesus knows that he must continue to "walk the path my Father has mapped out for me" (223) by being loyal to God and by being prepared to suffer if necessary (224). As with the first test, this one too becomes a test of loyalty, and Jesus once again chooses to remain faithful to God and to continue on a path that will require suffering. He is willing to do this because Ezra, Israel, and even religion itself are worth redeeming.

The Kingdom Test

Unlike the first two tests, this final theological discussion does not revolve around any major theme already anticipated. It is simply the capstone to the first two tests because during it Satan reveals his real aim—not to save creation but ultimately to destroy it.

As in the first two tests, Boyd once again appropriates material from the Matthean Temptation. Mimicking his Gospel counterpart, Boyd's Satan offers Jesus the kingdoms of the world in exchange for Jesus' bowing down and worshipping him. In rejecting this bribe, Boyd's Jesus follows the Gospel Jesus in quoting from Deut 8:3 and banishing Satan. Aside from appropriating this material, Boyd's version of the kingdom test can only be connected immediately with Matthew's through the question that both raise of from whom Jesus will receive the kingdoms of the world. In both, he has the opportunity to follow Satan's way rather than God's, and in both, Jesus remains faithful to his Father.

Unlike the first two tests, however, we find no messianic interpretation. The lack of such an interpretation here is surprising given that most commentators who follow that view typically find the strongest support for their position in the kingdom test because it deals with the issue of kingly supremacy. Given that the Davidic Messiah was expected to be the ruler who inherits his forefathers' throne, the connections between a political messiahship and the kingdoms offered by Satan seem more obvious to commentators than the other messianic expectations supposedly rejected in the first two tests. Yet Boyd does not take advantage of this natural connection in order to continue his messianic interpretation of the Temptation. Instead,

---

32. As the reader is told earlier in the novel, "Jesus wanted to see Jerusalem changed. Not destroyed, as Nebuchadnezzar and Pompey had destroyed it. But transformed, purified, fulfilled. Jerusalem and all Israel had suffered far too much in keeping God's name alive for anything to be destroyed" (176).

Boyd again uses the biblical material to provide the framework for a much larger theological discussion.

One final time, Satan approaches Jesus as a true friend of humanity. He shows Jesus all the kingdoms of the world and comments on the evil he sees in them. Satan accepts responsibility for their condition and says that he has repented. While acknowledging his own culpability, he also blames God saying, "God has bungled, it is plain. He has made the world too easy a prey to my wiles and I am not happy with this. God has, without wanting it, made a monstrous error. He asked men for too much and is disappointed that they give him nothing" (233). Satan, the merciful one, longs for a better world for them and wants to turn the world over to Jesus so that Jesus might purify it and impose the order and justice needed to make creation good. He informs Jesus, "I can rid the world of evil once and for all, simply by going away. I am prepared to do this because I love mankind" (234). Once he has left, there will be nothing but goodness and love because humanity will no longer be tempted by evil. His only price for his withdrawal is that Jesus acknowledges that the world belongs to Satan.

Jesus' response to this final temptation is much longer than either of his first two as he explains in detail why he is rejecting Satan's offer. He recognizes that Satan's motivation has nothing to do with love of humanity and everything to do with triumphing over creation. Only if he were allowed to leave creation could Satan have any victory because with the possibility of doing evil removed from the world, the possibility of humanity demonstrating love would also be removed (235). While there would be no more sinners, there would also be no more saints. Jesus reasons that evil is allowed in the world not because it is as strong as goodness or because Satan is God's equal or even a serious rival. No, God allows evil to remain in order to redeem it. In fact, the "role of good is to suffer and absorb the evil and, by so doing, to redeem it" (234). Jesus recognizes the wisdom in his Father's plan and finally understands why his suffering is necessary. He also realizes that Satan's greatest punishment is in knowing not only that he will never have the final victory but that by remaining as a part of creation he will only contribute to the ultimate victory of good (235). Once more, Jesus rejects destroying the world and replacing it with a different creation. Instead he chooses to undergo the suffering that comes when one absorbs evil in order to redeem it and to redeem humanity.

GOSPEL'S VERSION OF THE TEMPTATION

Introduction: Gospel's Testing Scenes As Global Allusions

In Saramago's *Gospel*, we find a remarkably different approach to rewriting the Temptation. Rather than replicating the three tests in one temptation scene, as Boyd does, Saramago provides three distinct testing scenes, which are better classified as global allusions to the Temptation. These global allusions are: the four years Jesus spends with Pastor in the wilderness including the Passover test, Jesus' encounter with God in the desert, and Jesus' conversation with both God and Satan on the Galilee lake.

What Saramago does in each of these scenes is, in one sense, akin to Matthew's own usage of typology. Like Matthew, Saramago refers to earlier writings by appropriating themes, phrases, and symbols from them so that his new narrative is at once its own entity but also meant to be interpreted in light of the older stories. Yet these scenes are not just typological recastings of one character in another's story, as when Matthew presents Jesus as the new Moses, because the character in Saramago's scenes is still called Jesus and is related in a referential way to the Gospel Jesus.

In the following sections, we will explore Saramago's three testing scenes but give priority to the final one that functions not only as a revision of the Temptation but also as the climax of *Gospel*, which the first two testing scenes anticipate. As in the analysis of Boyd's temptation, we will again discuss how these temptations relate to their canonical predecessors. Since these are testing scenes, we will again be discussing the question of fidelity and how Jesus responds to these challenges of faithfulness to God and humanity. Similar to the portrayal in *The Hidden Years*, the lure to follow Satan and to reject God is based on a compassionate plea for humanity.

Jesus' Four Years With Pastor

The resemblance of the four years that Saramago's Jesus spends in the wilderness with Pastor (199–217) to that of the forty days that the Gospel Jesus passes in the wilderness with Satan is hardly lost on the astute reader. This period also resembles the biblical narrative because once more the test is primarily about loyalty.

From the moment Jesus asks to join his flock, Pastor endeavors to make Jesus one of his sheep (187). At the hands of his tutor, Jesus' education in the art of humanitarian compassion begins as Pastor tries to break Jesus out of his conservative mindset in which he blindly accepts whatever his Israelite religion has taught him about God and the world. In all of their theological conversations together, Pastor trains Jesus to analyze God's decrees and to decide for himself whether they are good and compassionate.

When the Passover festival arrives, Pastor tests Jesus to see if he has really learned anything regarding the value of life and whether he will follow God's sacrificial laws blindly without questioning their inherent cruelty. Pastor tells him, "[']Then pick yourself a clean lamb, Jesus, and take it to be sacrificed, since you Jews attach so much importance to such practices.['] Pastor was *putting him to the test*, to see if the boy could lead to its death a lamb from the flock they had worked so hard to maintain and protect" (204, italics mine).[33] On the way to the temple, Jesus, pondering the idea of animal sacrifice, wonders "why God could not be appeased with a cup of milk poured over His altar. . . or with a handful of wheat" (208). Suddenly, pity for the lamb stays his hand, and he refuses to sacrifice it.[34] Jesus realizes that he cannot willingly take part in such a slaughter and so rescues the lamb, preferring for it to die a natural death (211).

Jesus' refusal to take part in the sacrificial system functions as a denouncement of God's participation. With this salvific action, Saramago implicitly condemns God's inaction to deliver his own creatures.[35] Jesus' inability to slaughter this lamb is compared with God's ability to kill his own animals and, as we will later see, his own children. Seeing that Jesus has learned something under his tutelage and that Jesus has sided with him rather than God in this test, Pastor smiles when Jesus returns (216).

33. In his historical narrative cycle that began with *Levantado do Chão* and ended with *Gospel*, Saramago says that he was able to find his distinctive "narrative voice" that is a hallmark of his work (Klobucka, "Interview"). In *Gospel*, we see that all communication is mediated through this one narrative voice, and this is why there are no quotation marks or separate paragraphs to distinguish different speakers or to mark dialogue from narration. Technically speaking, there is no proper dialogue in the novel because it all has been taken up into the one "narrative voice." I have inserted single quotation marks here and in other places to help the reader who lacks the context to distinguish the speakers whose dialogue is being narrated by that one voice.

34. Saramago's novel is not the only fictional account that presents animal sacrifice as a troubling aspect of the Israelite religion (cf. Boyd, *The Hidden Years*, 176; Moore, *Lamb*, 281; Holmes, *Three from Galilee*, 82).

35. The narrator makes a similar point earlier in the novel when upon observing the sacrificial system in effect at the temple, he states, "Anyone witnessing this scene would have to be a saint to understand how God can approve of such appalling carnage if He is, as He claims, the father of all men and beasts" (73).

Jesus' Desert Test With God

Unfortunately, for both Pastor and the lamb, Jesus has neither absorbed Pastor's lessons completely nor sided with him fully. Three years after rescuing his lamb and passing Pastor's test, Jesus is once again tempted to sacrifice that same lamb.

In typical *Gospel* fashion, the traditional biblical roles of Satan and God are again reversed in this second testing scene when God, not Satan, offers Jesus a bribe of power and glory in exchange for Jesus' worship and obedience (220–221; cf. Matt 4:8–9). If Jesus had earlier displayed his allegiance to Pastor and Pastor's humanitarian compassion by depriving God of a sacrificial lamb, then now Jesus can affirm his allegiance to God and seal their covenant by offering the very lamb that he had rescued from the altar. Acquiescing to God's demand for them to be tied in "flesh and blood" (222), Jesus sorrowfully sacrifices his pet sheep and aligns himself this time with God rather than Pastor.

While this second testing scene refers to its biblical predecessors with its desert setting (218; cf. Matt 4:1) and the power and glory bribe (cf. Matt 4:8–9), it shares little else with the Synoptic versions. Ben-Porat, who also identifies this event as an allusion to the Temptation, describes it as "where innovation is much stronger than representation and disloyalty [to the original text] is stretched to the limit."[36]

Yet the Temptation is not the only biblical scene upon which this second testing is modeled. Cousland argues that it is a conflation of Jesus' own wilderness testing with that of Adam's Eden testing so that Saramago's Jesus recapitulates Adam's experience. The Adamic typology is clearly present when the narrator describes how Jesus "confronted the desert in his bare feet, like Adam expelled from Eden, and like Adam he hesitated before taking his first painful step across the tortured earth that beckoned him. But then, without asking himself why he did it, perhaps in memory of Adam, he dropped his pack and crook, and lifting his tunic by the hem pulled it over his head to stand as naked as Adam himself" (219). In the final analysis, Saramago's Jesus resembles Adam much more than the Gospel Jesus because he fails the temptation and yields to the bribe of power and glory.[37]

When Pastor hears what Jesus has done, he is disgusted and angrily says, "You've learned nothing, begone with you" (222). Contrary to Matthew's Gospel, it is the Satan characer who banishes Jesus from his presence and not the other way around (cf. Matt 4:10). Even though Jesus lives in a

36. Ben-Porat, "Saramago's *Gospel*," 100.
37. Cousland, "Kakaggelion," 66–67.

deterministic world in which his fighting may ultimately be futile, Pastor still wants him to fight against that world's inhumanity and therefore against the God who stands behind it.[38] With this banishment, Saramago's Jesus, similar to Adam before him, is cast out of a *pastor*-al Eden, and his moment of weakness makes certain his now evitable death. As Cousland writes, "By bowing to the authority of God and agreeing to sacrifice the lost sheep, he guarantees his own upcoming role as a sacrificial victim."[39]

Jesus' Lake Test With God and Pastor

Saramago, once again true to his revisionist methodology, sets this final forty-day testing scene on a lake rather than in the desert wilderness, where the first two testing scenes and those in the Gospels occur. Even this watery setting, however, is not as unconnected to its dry counterpart as it would first appear. As Saramago's God notes while in the midst of the lake's mist, being there is not unlike being in the desert (311). Simon too likens Jesus' forty days on the lake to the experience of searching for God in the desert (335).

As promised at their last meeting in the desert, God reappears to Jesus when God is ready to fill Jesus in on the fine print of their contract. Their discussion revolves around Jesus' identity as the Son of God and what his future mission will be (307). God explains that he is dissatisfied with being only the God of the Jews (311) and has a territorial expansion scheme for becoming the God of the entire world. In order to gain this wider market share, however, God needs his son to be crucified as a martyr because apparently martyrdom is the best public relations scheme for marketing and expanding a new religion. When Jesus asks why he cannot simply preach the kingdom or call people to repentance as the prophets did, God says that the people need "stronger medicine, shock treatment," and the crucifixion of God's son will provide precisely that jolt (316).

This time around, Jesus is not afraid to question either God's plans or his character. Jesus, now more familiar with God's character, predicts that God will gobble up those who follow him (313). Having now fully adopted Pastor's philosophy of humanitarian compassion, Jesus wants to make sure before he helps set in motion God's global domination plan that the lives of his followers will be better and happier in this life as a consequence of his martyrdom (317). Unfortunately, Jesus' first suspicion is confirmed with

38. Referring to Pastor's dismissal of Jesus, Frier comments, "What Jesus needs to learn is that merely perceiving the inevitability of an event does not make that situation *ipso facto* one that should readily be accepted" (Frier, "O Evangelho," 375).

39. Cousland, "Kakaggelion," 67.

God's answer of a list of martyrs, the Crusades, and the Inquisition that will result because of Jesus' death. In the middle of the long list of martyrs, God pauses to ask Jesus if he has had enough yet, and Jesus retorts, "That's something You should ask Yourself" (324). Horrified, Jesus discovers that his followers' earthly lives will not be better but worse because of his death. But the "good news," at least in God's opinion, is that "they will have the hope of achieving happiness up in heaven" (319). Upon hearing this distressing news, Jesus laments his role as God's son and tries to break their covenant by refusing God's bribe. Jesus cries, "Father, take from me this cup. . . . I don't want the glory." Unfortunately, God responds, "But I want the power" (330).

Pastor, ever the humanitarian, is moved by the suffering that will be inflicted upon Jesus and upon all of humanity under God's scheme, so he tempts God with a proposal that is not unlike what Boyd's Satan suggests to Boyd's Jesus during the kingdom test. To prevent all of that future anguish, Pastor will sacrifice himself and his earthly kingdom. He reasons that with his removal from the earth, evil itself will disappear. Because God's power would be ultimate already, his global domination plan would be redundant and Jesus' death unnecessary (330–331). God, however, disagrees and does not succumb to the temptation. He replies to Pastor, "I much prefer you as you are, and were it possible, I'd have you be even worse. . . . Because the good I represent cannot exist without the evil you represent, if you were to end, so would I, unless the devil is the devil, God cannot be God" (331). In return, "Pastor shrugged and said to Jesus, [']Never let it be said the devil didn't *tempt* God[']" (331; italics mine). Even though Pastor knows that there is probably nothing to be done to stop this megalomaniac's plan, he still tries to tempt God. The question remaining is whether Jesus will follow his Pastoral example.

At the end of the boat temptation, all hope seems lost because Jesus appears to be acquiescing to God's demands. It is not until the end of the novel, however, when Jesus tries to die as the "King of the Jews" rather than as the "Son of God" in order to thwart God's plans (369) that we discover Jesus' true allegiance is with Satan and with humanity. Although he may not be able (and as it turns out, is not able) to oppose God's will, he decides to at least try (369), and in so doing, he proves himself to be a true disciple of Saramago's humanitarian compassion and to be aligned with the devil rather than with God.

The Lake Testing As the Climax

As in *The Hidden Years*, the final testing scene in *Gospel* serves as the novel's climax. In this scene, *Gospel's* discordance with the Gospels becomes fully unmasked, allowing us to observe the extent to which Saramago's bad news competes with the Gospels' good news. Throughout the novel we can observe Saramago's criticisms of the Christian religion and of its God through several recurring motifs that converge into one massive conversation between God, Jesus, and Satan on the lake. There, Saramago's humanitarian philosophy finally conflicts openly with his caricature of Christianity and of the God he creates to stand behind the religion. Some of the foremost issues against which Saramago rails in this scene include the problem of innocent suffering, the guilt caused by that suffering, the distortion of life and its natural joys, and the problem of religious violence in general along with the particular case of a Father's cruelty to his own son. All of these themes, in one way or another address the problem of the devaluation of human life.[40]

First, let us begin by reviewing the innocent suffering motif. Earlier this problem was presented through events like the Bethlehem slaughter, the mistaken crucifixion of Joseph, and the sacrifices of birds and beasts at the temple. Now on the lake, this unsettling issue is focalized in the future suffering and martyrdom of Jesus' innocent and unsuspecting followers. By recounting name upon name of those sacrificed to the Christian religion, the narrator prompts the reader to question whether a system built upon and inclined to produce so much suffering can be good for humanity. The reader, along with Jesus, is also led to consider the goodness of a God who can recite "in the monotonous tone of one who chooses to suppress compassion" the names of so many victims (321).

Second, when faced with the suffering of innocent victims, most of the novel's characters respond with a profound sense of guilt whether or not they bear responsibility for that suffering.[41] *Gospel* draws an implicit but very intentional comparison between these characters and God, who as we learn during the climax, "feels no remorse" (329). The juxtaposition of these characters and their reactions to the innocent suffering of others leads the reader to ask why it is that these characters, who are far less responsible

---

40. Cf. Cousland who says that Saramago believes that an "implicit disregard for human life" is central to Christianity (ibid., 65).

41. For example, Joseph, who is only guilty of the sin of omission rather than one of commission, carries the burden of the deaths of the slaughtered innocents in Bethlehem for the rest of his life (95–96). Similarly, although Jesus is in no way complicit for their deaths, he inherits his father's guilt and his nightmares and spends a lifetime afflicted by the knowledge of that atrocity (144).

for such suffering, are capable of feeling guilt and remorse, yet God, who ordained these events, feels nothing. Jesus' reaction to learning about his heavenly Father's lack of remorse and inability to feel guilt over such suffering is remarkably similar to his earlier response when he learns about his earthly father's complicity in the Bethlehem slaughter. As he did before with Joseph, Jesus once again assumes his Father's guilt when he tells God, "Well, since I'm already bearing this burden of having to die for You, I can also endure the remorse that ought to be Yours" (329). This act makes Jesus both a truly humane and tragic figure and presents him as the foil to God, whose truly inhumane and uncompassionate character is fully revealed.

Third, as in the first testing scene, one of Saramago's main issues with religion is that it offers a distorted view of the body and prevents people from enjoying the natural pleasures of life. In the desert, the example provided is sexuality.[42] On the lake, the supporting illustration is the renunciation of life by Jesus' future disciples, many of whom will cloister themselves away from society and beat their own bodies to prevent themselves from indulging their natural desires. As Pastor points out to Jesus, this renunciation is a second way that Jesus' disciples will part with their lives, the first being the martyrdoms mentioned above (325–27). Jesus realizes that God and this new Christian religion he intends to found have nothing to do with enjoying life but will destroy humanity's experiences of natural happiness.

Fourth and finally, another theme reemerging throughout the novel and climaxing in the lake testing is the problem of religious violence. During the first four-year testing period, the problem of violence committed in the name of religion is embodied in animal sacrifice.[43] As we see in the climax, violence inflicted upon innocent sufferers is not only found in the sacrificial system but also in wars promulgated by religious beliefs.[44] Here, Saramago's God forecasts atrocities, such as the Crusades and the Inquisi-

42. Pastor accosts Jesus' view of sexuality by arguing that no part of his body is inherently shameful. He suggests that there is something wrong with a god who cares more about prohibiting the enjoyment derived from fulfilling "natural" sexual desires than about protecting his creatures from neglect, oppression, and slaughter (196–97).

43. Similar to the way that God's care for children is judged against a father's provision for his son in the Gospels (Matt 7:9–11), Pastor prompts Jesus to consider whether God's concern for his creatures should not at least parallel that of the creatures' concern for one another. If an ewe would be horrified to learn that her lambs were being slaughtered in the temple (193), then how can God not be horrified?

44. Saramago made plain his own feelings towards religion and the violence it engenders during his Nobel Prize lecture. There, in discussing the writing of one of his other novels, he tells how with only the light of his own reason he had to "penetrate the obscure labyrinth of religious beliefs, the beliefs that so easily make human beings kill and be killed" (Saramago, "1998 Nobel Lecture").

tion, which will be committed by Christians crying, "God wills it" as they kill others (328).[45] At the end of hearing about so much "good news" that God will bring to humanity, Pastor comments, "One has to be God to countenance so much blood" (330).

Unfortunately, all of this violence will be brought about by one act, the most atrocious of any that we have yet mentioned—Jesus' crucifixion. What makes this act so heinous is that it is committed by a father against his very own son. Of course, we have been prepared for this revelation all along with the symbolic nature of the nightmares in which Joseph rides to kill his own son and the narrator's comments about the dreadful death of being killed by the very father who gave him life (91).[46] We know very well what Saramago thinks of such a father and what we are to make of this God, but the key question is what Jesus himself will make of such a God. In this climactic scene, Saramago forces his Jesus character to come face to face with each of these problems afflicting humanity and to question the God who is responsible for them. Jesus' real test is whether he will still align himself with such a monster and allow such a system to be founded in his name.

As are most versions of Jesus to some extent, this one also is created in his author's image for he reflects the horror and repugnance that Saramago feels when facing such a God and such a religion. While it takes him time to garner the courage, Saramago's Jesus, like Saramago, chooses to rebel against this "good news" and endeavors to prevent God from founding his kingdom on the blood of his creatures.

CRITIQUING THE HIDDEN YEARS AND GOSPEL'S TESTING SCENES TOGETHER

From their typological portrayals of Jesus to their characterizations of Satan to their challenges to God's character, the testing scenes of *The Hidden Years* and *Gospel* complement one another even though they ultimately

45. Earlier in the novel, the narrator makes the telling observation that those fighting under the initials INRI will not be that different from those who bore the insignia SPQR (118–19). Both symbols represent systems of power that preach peace and freedom but that deliver destruction and enslavement.

46. Ben-Porat comments on this matter: "Knowing that this plan involves the crucifixion of God's son, even a reader who can be satisfied with the inevitable Freudian explanation of the homicidal aspect of father-son relations cannot but muster this knowledge of the planned sacrifice of Jesus to explain why Joseph sees himself in his dream as a soldier coming to kill his son rather than as the father who tries to save him. For a discerning reader this strange reversal of roles between a protective father and his son's murderer becomes another strong link between the novel and the Gospels" (Ben-Porat, "Saramago's *Gospel*," 101).

offer conflicting answers to the issues they raise. The surprising congruence of these two narratives, especially given their novels' divergent theological positions and relationships to their Gospel source material, is what has prompted us to use them as dialogical partners for examining the reception of the Temptation event in Jesus novels. In this section, we will highlight their similarities in order to explore their divergent responses. Within these responses, we will once again see why *The Hidden Years* functions as a complementing narrative to the Gospels while *Gospel* serves as a competing one.

Humanitarian Compassion

In writing on the Temptation, one scholar wisely has observed, "To live is to choose, to decide between good and evil alternatives,"[47] but sometimes the choice is not between good and evil at all. Both *The Hidden Years* and *Gospel* picture Satan tempting Jesus not with something that is evil or wicked but with something that is good—to have compassion for humanity. Both Satan characters promote an agenda focused on relieving and eliminating the systemic causes of humanity's suffering. They view physical, earthly happiness as being of primary importance and denounce anyone or any system that devalues human life. Both Satan characters present themselves as compassionate humanitarians who for the benefit of humanity are willing to sacrifice their own positions of power and remove themselves from the earth if by their removal sin and suffering will cease.

The Satan characters of both novels also share the idea that humans do not need to be saved so much from themselves as from the structures that afflict them. In *The Hidden Years*, Satan presents the two greatest causes of human misery as hunger and religion, and he blames God for both of these flawed systems. Boyd's Satan reasons that, if Jesus were to eliminate these systems, then humans would naturally be good and sin would be no more. In *Gospel*, Pastor hints to Jesus that religion, and its dogmatic beliefs, might be the greatest structure oppressing humans and keeping them from enjoying life. More precisely, he thinks that God is the one great structure, the one dominating and oppressive system, that needs to be challenged and changed. In *Gospel*'s narrative world, if humans are evil, it is because these systems have distorted their natural goodness.

---

47. Filson, *Matthew*, 69.

The Problem of a Good God and Human Suffering

In the opinion of both Satans, God should be judged according to humanitarian standards that measure a person's goodness by the amount of benefit or harm that person brings to the world. Based on this criterion, both condemn God because not only has God failed to show compassion by relieving suffering, but also, according to them, God is the one ultimately behind the dysfunctional systems that oppress humanity.

Both Satans want Jesus to join in their condemnation of God and of the flawed systems that God supports. In a very biblical sense, Jesus' fidelity to God is *tested* when God's character is attacked and Jesus is asked to join the assault. One of the main differences between the two novels is in the way that their Jesuses respond to these loyalty tests and the answers they offer to the question regarding God's goodness raised by the evil and suffering that exist in the world. In the end, both Jesus characters make the correct choices within their narrative worlds, but only one of those narrative worlds complements that of the Gospels.

The Response of Gospel: Condemnation and Futile Opposition

Saramago's Jesus answers this question by agreeing with Satan's very accurate assessment of God's character. Abandoning his identity as the Son of God, this Jesus prefers to side with humanity against the "Ultimate Structure" oppressing them. Given the two options he faces of siding with a maniacal God planning world domination or joining with a compassionate Satan who offers to sacrifice his position in order to relieve human suffering, Saramago's Jesus makes the better choice available to him within Saramago's fictional world.

As we have seen before, Saramago's characterization of God and the different metaphysical nature of his fictional world create a contradictory Jesus character who, unlike his Gospel counterpart, sides with Satan when tested rather than with God. Saramago's novel offers an answer that distorts the original premise of the question and blocks us from returning to it. Because of this reformulation of the given propositions, Saramago's narrative does not contribute to solving the problem of God's goodness in light of suffering. On that topic, his novel does not converse but only condemns. According to *Gospel's* worldview, there is no question of how a good God can allow suffering to exist. Its answer is simply that if there is a God, then that God cannot be good.

The Response of The Hidden Years: Redemption and True Compassion

Boyd's Jesus, however, recognizes that Satan's portrayal of God's character and his feigned compassion for humanity are false. Realizing that God really does have humanity's best interests at heart, Boyd's Jesus remains faithful to his Father and his Father's proposed redemptive plan for the world.

Boyd's God, in one sense, turns out to be the true humanitarian for whom Saramago is searching. This God and the Jesus who represents him are so much in love with creation, flawed though it may be, that God refuses to destroy any part of it. Instead, his mission plan is one of redemption, and it is embodied in Jesus' statement: "The role of good is to suffer and absorb evil and, by doing so, to redeem it" (235).

The Hidden Years' main response to the problem of evil and suffering is not an explanation of why it exists in the first place but rather a picture of what a good God is doing about it now. Once, when the disciples-to-be complain about the suffering they endure under Roman occupation and ask why God has left them in exile in their own land, Jesus does not try to explain why they are suffering but answers by telling where God is during that suffering. According to Jesus, "God is with us. . . If we are exiled in our own land, so is he. He can be found anywhere, so if it is his will that we witness to him in suffering and want, so be it" (133). This statement encapsulates the novel's understanding of how God reacts to suffering in the world—by joining in it and by joining with his people.

In the novel, God provides this incarnational response most clearly through the character of Jesus whom Boyd depicts as the one through whom "God came to the Lake of Galilee" (144). Just as Matthew makes plain from the beginning of his Gospel that Jesus is Emmanuel—God *with* us (1:23), so too Boyd powerfully and artistically displays this theological theme throughout his novel. Through his portrayal of Jesus, Boyd offers a truly compassionate response to the problem of suffering because he shows a Jesus who does not just relieve suffering but willingly *suffers with* humanity by sharing its pain.

Strangely enough, the greatest response to the problem of suffering and the best display of compassion according to *The Hidden Years'* theology is not pictured in the novel but only foreshadowed. The novel's temptation scene clearly points towards the cross as the path of humble obedience on which Jesus chooses to remain.[48] His joining with the people in suffering

---

48. Boyd's point, like Matthew's, is clear: "[I]n the Temptation Jesus began to move along a path of humble obedience to the Father which, if continued, would lead inexorably to the cross" (Donaldson, *Jesus on the Mountain*, 100).

throughout the novel and particularly in the testing scene prefigures the way that Jesus will finally take up all of that suffering on the cross and redeem it (cf. Matt 8:17).[49] The "co-"passion, finally seen in Jesus' own Passion, is interpreted in Boyd's testing as the true embodiment of compassion—*suffering with* humanity by living among sinful humans under sinful structures and dying in order to redeem both. This version of compassion emerges as true humanitarianism because it destroys nothing and redeems everything.

Conversely, in *Gospel*, compassion for humanity and Jesus' passion are pitted against one another. Even so, Saramago ironically and perhaps inadvertently joins the two together when his Jesus decides to suffer as the King of the Jews in order to prevent the future suffering of many. Saramago's version at this point partially coincides with the biblical accounts as Jesus experiences his own passion on behalf of humanity. The real difference between Saramago's account and the view portrayed in Boyd's work is that in the former Jesus' passion is meant to rescue humanity *from* God whereas in the latter Jesus' passion will redeem humanity to be *with* God.

Is Humanitarian Compassion Enough?

The Response of Gospel

Saramago's celebration of humanism suggests that human nature and human desires are innately good and should be indulged. If only all the structures oppressing humanity could be removed, then there would be no further suffering. As we learn in the tale in the novel about Satan's parallel world, Satan would deny humans nothing and place no dogmatic belief structures on them, and therefore, there would be no problem of original sin, suffering, or punishment.

Yet *Gospel* undercuts its own evangel with Jesus' miraculous fishing ministry. When Jesus enacts Saramago's humanistic vision of compassion by eliminating hunger in a small sector of Galilee and providing an Eden of fish, the results are less than stellar. What Boyd's Jesus had predicted would happen if he were to give humans abundant bread (that is, when he says, "Would he not even destroy his neighbour's bread to starve him into submission" [216–17]) comes true in Saramago's novel. Instead of destroying bread to starve others into submission, the fishermen, following the principle of supply and demand, throw back part of their miraculous catches in order to regulate prices by keeping the price of fish artificially high (280).

---

49. De Diétrich, *Saint Matthew*, 25.

While both Boyd and Saramago are adept at pointing out the systemic problems facing humanity and both question God's culpability for those systems, only one of them addresses the human factor contributing to societal ills. *Gospel* simplistically blames the entire problem on God and despairingly tells us that nothing can be done so long as humans are under such a monster's thumb and continue to be brainwashed by his propaganda. Episodes like the miraculous fishing ministry, however, give us glimpses that perhaps all would not be well even in *Gospel*'s world were the divine tyrant removed and all the oppressive systems overturned. Perhaps there would still be a further factor contributing to the problem of evil and suffering, the human one, that Saramago fails to address and for which he does not offer a solution.

The Response of The Hidden Years

In Boyd's version, the inherent sinfulness of humanity, not God, is the real problem that needs correcting. His Jesus recognizes that, even if he were to provide a perfect structure, humans would still find a way to sin just as the first couple in the garden did. Without different humans, a different structure will never eliminate all of their woes. Only a different sort of human will ever be satisfied with Paradise, and only if humans themselves are changed, will they then change the structures. For humans to choose to love God and to choose to love and care for one another is what Boyd's Jesus sees as the ultimate good, and it also happens to be what Matthew's Jesus sees as the two greatest commandments (22:37–39).[50]

Even though Boyd's Jesus fights hunger by providing food for the starving and challenges the beliefs and guardians of the traditional religious system, Boyd's Jesus refuses to limit his ministry to just a humanistic one. He sees the solution to humanity's suffering lying not simply in dismantling unjust structures but in redeeming the people within those structures and thereby by redeeming those same structures through the efforts of the now-redeemed people. He encompasses their needs within a larger nature change when he tells Satan, "Peace. . . love, generosity. These are important, these come first" (214). By aligning himself with God rather than Satan, Boyd's Jesus plans to make a nature change possible for humanity.

---

50. For in the narrative world of *The Hidden Years*, humans have the freedom that they lack in *Gospel*'s world. God does not force obedience nor irrevocably determine anyone's destiny, including Jesus'. Because humans have this freedom, they can do something about transforming the inhumane structures that affect them.

Boyd's criticism of unjust systems, unlike Saramago's, turns out to be constructive because it aims at correcting the aberrations of those systems in order to build them up rather than to destroy them completely. Because *The Hidden Years* has a deep and firm belief in the power of redemption, it also has the freedom, not often displayed in complementing narratives, to critique even Christianity. The novel does not fear to point out problems because, unlike *Gospel*, it believes that there are solutions to them. Whereas Saramago's *Gospel* is a tragedy of epic proportions, Boyd's *The Hidden Years* turns out to be a hopeful narrative pointing towards the end of suffering and the ultimate redemption of all creation.

CONCLUSION OR ANOTHER BEGINNING?

Having now analyzed and compared the testing scenes in two Jesus novels, we can see that rather than settle issues of interpretation, they merely raise more for us. The novels function in their own right as commentaries on the biblical texts, but more than that, they transform the texts and defamiliarize them so that we are sent back to them with many novel questions. The novels prompt us to "preposterously" return to examine the Matthean Temptation narrative in light of these subsidiary narratives. In preparing to do so, we find that there are many new and exciting questions to be explored.

The intriguing priority of place given by these novels to their temptation scenes raises the question of importance of the Temptation within the overall Matthean narrative. In both novels, the testing of Jesus functions as the climatic conflict tying together central themes woven throughout their narratives. Since *The Hidden Years* focuses on introducing Jesus' person during the final years of his life prior to his public ministry, it makes sense that the temptation would be the climax of that novel. In contrast, *Gospel* spans Jesus' entire life, yet Jesus' temptation on the lake functions as the climax of that novel as well. Jesus' subsequent short-lived ministry and martyrdom serve only as the resolution of his conversation on the lake with God and Pastor. In Matthew's Gospel, however, the Crucifixion, not the Temptation, functions as the climactic conflict between Jesus and the "satanic characters" of that Gospel. The Temptation appears towards the beginning of Matthew's Gospel, and at first glance, it does not seem to function in as important a capacity as the novels would suggest. Perhaps though there are more connections between the Temptation, which the novels appropriate and present as the climax of their own "gospels," and the Crucifixion, which Matthew presents as the climax of his Gospel, than first meets the eye. Therefore, one of our main questions when reexamining Matthew's Temptation will be to ask how it functions narratively within that Gospel and if it serves as some sort of pre-climatic event, perhaps somehow tied to the true climax of Matthew's Gospel—the Crucifixion.

Another important issue raised by the novels is that of typology. Saramago links Jesus' own testing back to that of Adam whereas Boyd, following a well-established point in Matthean scholarship, demonstrates how Jesus' experience in the wilderness is tied to that of ancient Israel's. Yet the novels not only gaze backwards on these intertextual allusions to the OT, but they also look forward to Jesus' later crucifixion. Such a connection was subtly suggested in Boyd's novel and more explicitly shown in Saramago's work, where the debate during the lake temptation centered on whether or not Jesus would obey his Father by dying on the cross. They demonstrate how a scene can be tied both typologically backwards to previous narratives and characters and also forwards. The novels' own linkage between these scenes leads us to reconsider whether Matthew, who we know was fond of intertextual allusions, may have also placed intratextual allusions to his own work within the Temptation narrative.

The theme of compassion inherent in both of the novels' temptations leads us to examine if and how this theme can be seen in Matthew's Gospel. The novels present two dueling notions of compassion and offer the Jesus characters of each a falsely dichotomous choice of deciding for one at the expense of the other. This observation causes us as readers to once again pause and consider whether or not Jesus' own passion was also anticipated in Matthew's Temptation narrative.

Finally, the temptations in both novels are not solely tests of whether or not Jesus will side with Satan or God and with their competing kingdom visions; they are also invitations for Jesus to question God's character and thus to "test" God. Theodicy is a major theme of both narratives as they call into question God's goodness in light of the problem of human suffering. Such a dominant theme in both novels provokes us to reexamine Matthew's Temptation to see if there is any questioning or "testing" of God in light of the problem of universal suffering.

As this chapter draws to a close, we see that the "preposterous" interpretation process is just beginning. Reading rewrites can be a dangerous experience because they challenge us to think and to open up new avenues of exploration. They provoke us to reconsider texts whose interpretations we may have already considered a settled matter. Rewrites breathe new life into our tired eyes and cause us to read familiar texts anew. In the next chapter, we will continue that journey.

7

A Preposterous Reading of the Temptation and its Narrative Role in Matthew's Gospel

INTRODUCTION

As we return to Matt 4:1–11 to examine it "preposterously," we are aware of several pertinent issues that the rewrites have uncovered, perhaps unknowingly, regarding Jesus' testing. The main hypothesis with which we will begin our exploration is as follows: In addition to being couched in OT typology and serving as an intertextual allusion to Israel's experience in the wilderness, Jesus' testing in Matthew's Gospel functions as a pre-climax to the final climax of Jesus' passion and as an intentional intratextual allusion to that scene.

We will examine how the Temptation anticipates the Passion narrative, specifically mirroring the first half (vv. 31–44) of the Crucifixion pericope in 27:31–56. We will argue that the implied reader, who is an informed reader and one who would reread Matthew's Gospel and so know it very well,[1] is intended to juxtapose the Temptation with the Crucifixion and in so doing

1. Noting the effort required by readers in order to identify allusions, Allison reminds us that Matthew was composed with some sort of liturgical, and possibly catechetical, end in mind so that it would have been read and heard over and over again. The first evangelist would expect the repeated usage of similar words and images to evoke connections within the readers' minds between different passages. As Allison states, "Matthew did not write for bad or casual readers; he wrote for good and attentive listeners" (Allison, "Anticipating the Passion," 712–13).

interpret Jesus' passion through the theological lenses that the Temptation provides. After analyzing these narratives and arguing the case for the intratextual allusions between them, we will then reread these texts within their own narrative context and discuss Matthew's theological understanding of Jesus' passion and death as it becomes clearer through the pairing of the Temptation and Crucifixion pericopes. Secondary issues that will be kept in mind as we pursue the primary hypothesis include the invitation to "test" God's character in light of the problem of suffering and the dichotomous choice between compassion for humanity and Jesus' own passion, issues that were prominent in the Gospel rewrites by Boyd and Saramago.

MATTHEW 4:1–11 AS A "SCENE OF ANTICIPATION" FOR THE PASSION, SPECIFICALLY 27:31–44 OF THE CRUCIFIXION NARRATIVE

Scenes of Anticipation

Our first step in reexamining Matt 4:1–11 in light of the "preposterous" hypothesis we have constructed involves an examination of current Matthean scholarship. Within the stacks of articles and monographs dedicated to the Gospel of Matthew, we find a 1994 article written by Dale Allison entitled "Anticipating the Passion," which was later revised and included in his 2005 book *Studies in Matthew*. In it, Allison develops a new category for Matthean texts that foreshadow the Passion and names them "scenes of anticipation."[2] He defines these passages as those "in which the end of Jesus is foreshadowed by both event and language."[3] Typically, these scenes share with the Passion rhetorical strategies, recurrent structures, common terminology, or similar events.[4]

2. Ibid. He discusses four types of texts, which he calls explicit predictions, implicit predictions, "growing conflict" scenes that move the plot towards the Passion, and "scenes of anticipation."

In the article, Allison refers to the Passion narrative as Matt 26:47—27:56. Kingsbury has described it more broadly as Matt 26–28 (Kingsbury, *Story*, 84). Brown in his two-volume opus on the four Passion narratives deals with Matthew's Passion narrative as beginning with Gethsemane (26:30) and ending with Jesus' burial (27:66; Brown, *Death*). When I refer to the Passion narrative, I follow Brown in understanding it as Matt 26:30—27:66.

3. Allison, "Anticipating the Passion," 712.

4. The texts that he identifies are the "turning the other cheek" passage (5:38–42), the predictions of afflictions his disciples will undergo (10:17–23), the Transfiguration (17:1–8), and the request of James and John for places of honor (20:21). In his 2005 work, he adds John the Baptist's death (14:1–12) to the list. John Paul Heil in his

Allison notes that most of these scenes have gone unnoticed in commentaries for two reasons. The first is that, unlike explicit Matthean predictions that often directly reference or quote their source material, these scenes of anticipation are allusions and as such are not obviously stated.[5] In fact, the implicit nature of allusions is one of their defining characteristics.[6] The second reason is that when searching for allusions most commentators tend to focus on inter- and not intratextual allusions. These intertextual allusions have been well documented,[7] and they provide a lens through which Matthew intends his readers to interpret Jesus' life and specifically the theological significance of his passion and death. As Allison suggests though, Matthew has provided even further interpretive guidance through intratextual allusions placed throughout his own narrative.[8] Allison's very fine thesis, however, involves

---

narrative-critical study on Matt 26–28 also discusses earlier texts that anticipate Jesus' passion and resurrection. He focuses on the infancy narratives (1–2); John the Baptist's passion and death; scenes of conflict with Israel's leaders; predictions of his passion, death, and resurrection; and earlier resurrection miracles and discussions of Jesus' resurrection powers. Like Allison, he omits the Temptation narrative from his discussion (Heil, *Death*, 7–21).

5. As Susan Lochrie Graham has pointed out in her work on the OT intertextuality in Matt 27:39–44, within the Crucifixion narrative Matthew is typically given more to allusions than to direct quotations ("A Strange Salvation," 504).

6. Cuddon, "Allusion," 31. Unfortunately, allusions are often dismissed as only existing in the minds of the readers because they can occur without overt authorial prompting to which readers can point in order to defend their existence. Establishing an allusion thus consists of pointing towards the use of common words, phrases, themes, structures, and images that prompt readers to draw connections between two previously disconnected passages. Their identification is more an art than a science (Hays, *Conversion*, 30).

7. The standard intertextual allusions found in Matt 27:31–44 are the following:

- The first offer of wine mingled with gall (χολή) (27:34; cf. Ps 69:21 [LXX 68:22]; also, the second offer of sour wine (ὄξος) found in 27:48 alludes to Ps 69:21)
- The division of and casting lots for Jesus' clothing (27:35; cf. Ps 22:18 [LXX 21:19])
- The association with criminals in death (27:38; cf. Isa 53:12)
- The mockery and the "wagging of the head" by those passing by (27:39; cf. Ps 22:7, 9 [LXX 21:8, 10]; other passages that employ this motion as an expression of derision include 2 Kgs 19:2; Job 16:4; Jer 18:16; Lam 2:15; and Sir 12:18; 13:7)
- The mockery and taunts of "Save yourself!" and "He trusts in God; let God deliver him now, if he wants to" (27:40, 43; cf. Ps 22:7, 8 [LXX 21:8, 9]; Wis 2:18–20)
- The mockery (27:44; cf. Ps 22:9; 69:9)

Brown also suggests that Jer 48:27 (LXX 31:27) may be behind the Passion narrative (Brown, *Death*, 989).

8. Allison, "Anticipating the Passion," 711–12.

one conspicuous omission. Nowhere does it acknowledge the Temptation as a scene of anticipation for Jesus' passion and death.

State of the Research

Even though Allison fails to acknowledge the Temptation as a scene of anticipation for the Passion, other commentators have noticed various connections between these two passages though none have linked them as closely as we will in this chapter. In what follows, we will review their scholarly observations and divide them into three categories: verbal, thematic, and structural parallels.

Main Verbal Allusion: The "Son of God" Statements

The main verbal allusion between the two pericopes is the well-documented "Son of God" terminology.[9] Identical verbal agreement occurs in 4:3; 4:6; and 27:40 with the phrase "If you are the Son of God" (εἰ υἱὸς εἶ τοῦ θεοῦ) and a parallel occurs in 27:43 with "I am the Son of God" (θεοῦ εἰμι υἱός).[10] Redaction criticism alerts us to the particular importance of this "Son of God" terminology within Matthew's Crucifixion because in both cases (27:40, 43) the phrases are Matthean additions to the Markan Crucifixion material.[11] That this phraseology parallels the Temptation narrative can hardly be seen as coincidental especially when we consider that Matthew's redaction (4:1–11) of the very sparse Markan Temptation narrative (1:12–13) also includes two additions of the "Son of God" title.

9. E.g., Carter, *Matthew*, 214; Davies and Allison, *Matthew 19–28*, 127, 1070.

10. So strong is the bond forged between these narratives by the use of this title that it has led Ulrich Luz to argue that the Baptism and Temptation stories form an inclusio with the Passion story in Matthew's Gospel (Luz, *Matthew 21–28*, 538).

11. Redaction criticism has alerted us not only to the importance of Jesus' divine sonship within the Passion narrative but also to its importance throughout the entire Gospel of Matthew. Mark has eight occurrences of "Son (of God)" and four instances in which God is referred to as Jesus' "Father." Matthew retains most of these and adds to them ten additional references to Jesus as Son (of God) and forty references to God as Father (Bauer, "Son of God," 772–73).

Thematic Allusions

THEMES CONNECTED WITH JESUS' IDENTITY as THE SON OF GOD

The "Son of God" connection is not a matter of shared terminology only. The phrase also links themes common to both passages, which include suffering, divine protection, kingly sovereignty, trust, and obedience. Throughout this chapter, we will discuss in turn each of these themes and the commentators who have noticed them.

TEMPTATION THEME

It is also widely noted by commentators that both passages involve some sort of testing or temptation of Jesus.[12] While the theme of testing in the Temptation narrative is obvious and requires no defense, the same is not true of the Crucifixion narrative, which lacks the Greek word πειράζω (testing).[13] Often only the mocking nature of the actions done to Jesus and the comments hurled at him are emphasized while the underlying temptation for Jesus to give in and to do precisely what the mockers have said or to accept what the soldiers have offered is missed. An exception to this oversight is the fact that several commentators have seen the challenge for Jesus to come down from the cross as not merely a taunt but also as a temptation.[14] Certainly, if we focus on the nature of the actions in both narratives rather than demanding strict verbal parallelization, then it is easier to see that the theme of testing is shared by both passages.

Some scholars have even viewed the Crucifixion as Jesus' last temptation much as Kazantzakis once did in his novel and as Scorsese did in his cinematic adaptation of it.[15] Hultgren, for one, calls the Passion Jesus' "supreme temptation" and finds it odd that it is rarely discussed when commentators speculate on which of the other "temptation" narratives in Mat-

---

12. E.g., Gerhardsson, "Gottes Sohn," 96–103; Hagner, *Matthew* 14–28, 837; Senior, *Passion*, 132.

13. Although πειράζω cannot be found in the Crucifixion pericope, πειρασμός does occur at the start of the Passion narrative itself in the Garden of Gethsemane (26:41). Precisely at the beginning of Jesus' own time of trial, he encourages his disciples to watch and pray so that they may avoid such testing. Thus, if one considers the Crucifixion pericope within its larger Passion context, "testing" language is present and certainly sets the tone of the narrative that follows.

14. Green, *Matthew*, 222; de Diétrich, *Saint Matthew* , 146.

15. Hagner, *Matthew*, 837.

thew's Gospel may have influenced the composition of 4:1–11. He asserts that the Passion narrative "was arguably the single most important factor that went into the creation of the Temptation narrative."[16]

CONFLICT WITH SATAN (SATAN'S REPRESENTATIVES) THEME

Finally, in both pericopes we find the theme of conflict between Jesus and "satanic characters."[17] Once again, this theme is obviously stated in the Temptation where Jesus faces the devil directly. In the Crucifixion, it is more subtlety nuanced. There, we find Satan's role reprised by the passers-by and the religious representatives who, like Satan in the Temptation narrative, tempt Jesus with the same taunting challenge of "If you are the Son of God" to do other than what his Father desires.[18]

Structural Parallels

TRIADIC MODELS

While commentators frequently notice the verbal or thematic allusions, it is rarer to see anyone proposing structural parallels between the Temptation

---

16. Hultgren, *Narrative*, 101.

17. Luz, *Matthew 21–28*, 538; Donaldson, "Mockers," 7, 10, 15; Graham, "A Strange Salvation," 506.

18. One commentator even passed over acknowledging the representatives themselves and simply stated, "Once more Satan tempts Jesus" at the crucifixion (de Diétrich, *Saint Matthew*, 146). Graham has rightly noted that the allusion to the Temptation found in the conflict at the cross serves to characterize further Jesus' opponents as "satanic and bestial" ("A Strange Salvation," 506). Warren Carter has aptly demonstrated that throughout Matthew Jesus' opponents are often connected with Satan:

> The audience uses two particular words to identify the religious leaders as the devil's agents: (1) In 4:3 the devil is called 'the tempter' (ὁ πειράζω, ho peiradzōn), the one who tempts or tests Jesus (4:1). The same verb, "to tempt" or "to test," indicates the purpose of the religious leaders towards Jesus (16:1; 19:3; 22:18, 34–35). Like Satan, they oppose God's purposes by trying to divert Jesus from doing and teaching the will of God. (2) The devil is also described as 'the evil one' (13:19, 38; ὁ πονηρός, ho ponēros). The same adjective describes the religious leaders and their actions as 'evil' (9:4; 12:34, 39, 45b; 16:4; 22:18). Disciples pray to be delivered from 'evil/the evil one' (6:13b). Satan's temptation of Jesus (4:1–11) is paradigmatic for the behavior of the religious leaders in other ways. Like Satan, the religious leaders challenge God's evaluation of Jesus. They deny that God acts in Jesus (9:3), ironically ascribing God's actions to Satan (9:34; 12:22–32). They join passers-by to reject God's evaluation of Jesus as God's Son (27:39–44; 26:62–64). In calling for Jesus to come down from the cross, they resist God's will (27:40; cf. 16:21) (*Matthew*, 145).

and Crucifixion pericopes. A few comparisons of triads found in the narratives, however, have been offered. Birger Gerhardsson suggests that Israel's Shema (Deut 6:5)—the triadic command to love the Lord with all one's heart, soul, and might—forms the underlying structure for both passages.[19] Raymond Brown argues that in Matt 4 Jesus endures a triad of tests at the hands of Satan and that in Matt 27 he suffers a triad of mockings by the passers-by, the Jewish leaders, and the two thieves.[20] Finally, Hans Kammler takes a less direct approach than Gerhardsson and Brown in comparing the Temptation's structure with that of the entire Passion narrative. Instead of arguing for a triadic model in the Crucifixion pericope, he suggests that the Temptation draws upon various portions from chs. 26–28 to form its triadic structure.[21]

---

19. He connects loving God with a whole heart with Jesus' starvation in the wilderness (4:2–4) and with Jesus' thirst at the cross (27:33–34). In both cases, Gerhardsson sees Jesus as being tested to murmur and grumble against God rather than to continue loving him with an undivided heart. He then links loving God with one's whole soul with the temple temptation (4:5–7) and with the overall experience of being abandoned by God and being delivered up to death on the cross (27:38–50). Just as in the Temptation, Jesus on the cross is now required to accept God's will and to continue loving him even if God does not deliver him from death and requires his soul. Finally, Gerhardsson connects loving God with one's whole might with the kingdom temptation (4:8–10) and with Jesus' loss of all his worldly possessions symbolized by his loss of clothes at the cross (27:35–37). In both cases, he chooses to love God rather than to cling to earthly mammon (Gerhardsson, "Judéo-Christianisme," 28–30).

The above is a summary of Gerhardsson's position based on three of his works. In *The Testing of God's Son*, he first argues that the Temptation is a haggadic narrative based on Deut 6:5. In footnote 29 on page 80, he indicates that the threefold Shema schema lies behind other accounts and that the most important of those is the Crucifixion narrative in Matt 27:33–50. In his later article, "Gottes Sohn als Diener Gottes," Gerhardsson briefly mentions how he sees the Shema underlying the Crucifixion narrative. In "Du Judéo-Christianisme a Jésus par la Shema," he explicitly connects the Temptation and Passion narratives based upon their shared structure centered on Jesus enacting the Shema (Gerhardsson, *Testing*, 76–79; Gerhardsson, "Gottes Sohn," 102; Gerhardsson, "Judéo-Christianisme," 28–30).

20. Brown, *Death*, 983–84n1, 996; cf. Davies and Allison, *Matthew* 19–28, 618. The strongest connection between these two triads is found between the second temptation ("If you are the Son of God . . . throw yourself down [from the pinnacle of the temple]" [4:6]) and with what Brown labels as the first mocking performed by the passers-by ("If you are the Son of God . . . come down from the cross" [27:40]).

21. He equates Jesus' dying of hunger in 4:3 with his dying upon the cross in 27:42, 40b. Jesus' refusal to take advantage of his sonship by calling upon an angelic rescue in 4:6 is connected with his Gethsemane statement in 26:53 and the taunt in 27:43 for God to come and save him. Finally, he sees a parallel between the final temptation on a mountain in 4:8 where Jesus refuses the kingdoms of the world and the final scene in Matthew (28:16–20), which again takes place on a mountain, where God gives Jesus all of the power in heaven and on earth (Kammler, "Sohn Gottes," 176–80).

The Three Tests: Parallels Between the Temptation Tests and the Crucifixion Tests

I agree with the above assessments that there are triadic structures in both narratives, but I disagree as to what that structure looks like in the Crucifixion pericope. The following is a summary of the triads that I have noticed in each of the narratives:

First, the rejection of bread in the Temptation narrative (4:2–4) mirrors the rejection of wine in the Crucifixion narrative (27:34). Second, the challenge for Jesus to cast himself down from the temple (4:5–7) anticipates both of the later challenges for him to come down from the cross (27:39–40; 27:41–43). The first time the mockers taunt him to come down from the cross, they connect his inability to do so with the temple charge at his trial. The second time, his coming down from the cross is associated with divine intervention. Both of these themes are drawn together in the second test at the Temptation. Third, the issue of Jesus' kingship is raised in both pericopes (4:8–10; 27:42–43; cf. 37) with Jesus being tempted to receive it through an easier route that involves his doing precisely the opposite of what God desires (worship Satan, come down from the cross).

Below is a chart of the triads in both narratives:

The Temptation (Matt 4:1–11)	The Crucifixion (Matt 27:31–44)
Test by and refusal of bread (Matt 4:2–4)	Test by and refusal of wine (Matt 27:33)
Test to cast himself down from the temple and rely on divine protection (Matt 4:5–7)	Test to come down from cross connected with the temple (Matt 27:39–40)
Test of receiving kingdom (Matt 4:8–10)	Test to come down from the cross connected with his kingship and with divine protection (Matt 27:41–43; cf. 27:37)

Although there is a structural parallel between the triads, there is not a perfect one-to-one correlation. The themes that are presented concisely in each of the three Temptation tests are interwoven throughout the Crucifixion narrative and are not isolated to only one of the tests on the cross. For example, in the Temptation account, the references to Jesus as the Son of God occur in the first and second tests, but at the Crucifixion, they occur in the second and third tests. Also, one of the themes found in both narratives is the assumption that if Jesus is indeed affiliated with God, then God will rescue Jesus from harm, either by angels (4:6) or by God himself (27:43).

This theme occurs in the second Temptation test but in the third Crucifixion test. I also agree with Kammler's assessment that the Temptation alludes to a wider range of Matthean passages than just those found within ch. 27. Throughout the rest of this chapter, we will see how themes found throughout Matthew are drawn together in the Temptation.

Thus, while there is a shared triadic structure between the Temptation and the Crucifixion pericopes, the significance of this structure lies not in building a direct correlation between the two triads but in developing the Temptation as a scene of anticipation for Jesus' passion and death. The structure leads the reader to connect the two stories in order to illuminate part of the theological significance of the Crucifixion by reading it with the Temptation narrative.

THE BREAD TEST IN COMPARISON WITH THE PASSION

Introduction

Both narratives begin with Jesus being "led" to the place of testing. In the Temptation narrative, Jesus is "led up" (ἀνάγω) to the wilderness (4:1). In the Passion narrative, he is "led away" (ἀπάγω) to be crucified (27:31).[22]

After arriving at the specified destination (the wilderness in 4:1; Golgotha in 27:33), Jesus faces his first test that in both cases has to do with items that provide bodily sustenance. In the desert, he is tested with bread (4:2–4) to ease his hunger. At the cross, he is tested with wine to ease his pain (27:34).[23] There is a dramatic parallel of beginning Jesus' testing in the wilderness and his testing on the cross with these refusals of dietary items.

More importantly, these items are not just any type of food and drink but ones that carry theological significance in Matthew's narrative. At the Passover meal (26:26–28), Matthew links the two items refused in each

22. Aside from the trial and Passion material (chs. 26–27), where it is natural to find Jesus being "led away" (ἀπάγω; 26:57; 27:2, 31) or "taken" (παραλαμβάνω; 27:27) around by his captors, the only time Matthew has the adult Jesus being led by someone else is in the Temptation narrative, where he is "led up" by the Spirit (ἀνάγω; 4:1) and "taken" by the devil (παραλαμβάνω; 4:5, 8). As a child, Jesus along with Mary is "taken" (παραλαμβάνω; 2:14, 21) by Joseph to and from Egypt.

23. Gerhardsson and Kingsbury, who follows him, are alone out of the commentators I surveyed in connecting these two events (4:2–4 with 27:33–34), but Gerhardsson comments only fleetingly that just as in the original test when Jesus suffered hunger, he now suffers thirst at the cross. Gerhardsson thinks that the point of the test in both cases is to see if Jesus will resist the urge to complain and rebel against God ("Judeo-christianisme," 29 [23–36]; cf. Kingsbury, *Story*, 89).

story—bread (ἄρτος; 4:3) and wine (οἶνος; 27:34)—when Jesus breaks the bread (ἄρτος; 26:26) and shares the cup [of wine] (ποτήριον; 26:27–28)[24] with his disciples. These items symbolize the new covenant that he will establish through his own body and blood, another allusion to his upcoming passion. Thus, both refusals are of items that in Matthew's Gospel are symbolically tied to Jesus' sufferings, and in both cases, had Jesus accepted them, they would have relieved his own pain but at the cost of following God.

Why Was the Wine Refused?

While we know that Jesus refuses the wine, the Crucifixion leaves a narrative gap by failing to tell us *why* Jesus rejects it. Most commentators who focus on the mocking intent in the soldiers' offer of the wine explain Jesus' refusal as simply a rejection of either their mockery or the bitter taste of the wine.[25]

24. In none of the Synoptic Gospels is the word "οἶνος" specifically used during the Passover meal. Instead, wine is the substance assumed to be in the cup (ποτήριον; 26:27) that he gives his disciples to drink, telling them that it (the wine) is his blood poured out for them. Because he then goes on to say that he will never again drink from "this fruit of the vine" (τούτου τοῦ γεννήματος τῆς ἀμπέλου; 26:29), referring to the substance that they had just drunk, the reader understands that wine was what they consumed.

In addition, we know that wine (four cups according to Pes. 10.1) was traditionally drunk at the Passover meal where the blessing pronounced over it was: "Blessed art thou, O Lord our God, king of the universe, creator of the fruit of the vine" (m. Ber. 6.1, italics added). Although there is no wine specifically mentioned at the Passover meal, I think that it is safe to assume along with most commentators (e.g., Davies and Allison, *Matthew 19–28*, 469; Joachim Jeremias, *The Eucharistic Words of Jesus*, 50–53) and with most of Christian tradition that wine was the substance that symbolized Christ's blood (see Jeremias for a discussion of how it was most likely red wine and thus the comparison with blood was more obviously made [Jeremias, *The Eucharistic Words of Jesus*, 53]).

It is reasonable to assume that even without a direct verbal link between the cup [of wine] at the Passover and the wine at the cross, the implied reader is still able to make the connection between the two and is even expected to do so given the implications of suffering made when Jesus symbolically connects the Passover wine with his own blood that soon will be spilt. This prediction finds fulfillment on the cross where the second reference to wine takes place. It is hard to imagine that the implied reader would not at least ponder the significance of any references to wine within the Passion narrative given the obvious connection between Jesus' own passion and his words at the Passover.

25. For example, Gundry writes that the Matthean redaction of having Jesus taste the wine before refusing it gives the reader the reason for his refusal: the gall's bitter taste. He believes that this answer is bolstered by the Ps 69 allusion, a Matthean redaction (Gundry, *Matthew*, 569).

To this reasoning, I would respond by asking why the Matthean redaction could not give us the simpler and more obvious reason for Jesus' refusal of the wine: he rejected it after tasting it simply because it was wine and not some other drink like water. Thus, the tasting performs the narratival function of assuring the reader that Jesus understood precisely what it was he was rejecting.

Intriguingly, Brown believes that Jesus' refusal of the wine in Mark is a rejection of numbing his pain, but he says that the same reason is not apparent in Matthew's version, where the author inserts a new explanation for the refusal by stating that Jesus tasted the wine before rejecting it. This added detail suggests to Brown that after tasting the gall within the wine, Jesus recognizes the mocking intent and rejects the wine because of the mockery behind the offer.[26] To my mind, this explanation does not make sense narratively. Even with acknowledging the soldiers' intention as one of mockery, *their* intention does provide the reason for *Jesus'* refusal of the wine. Though he knew of their mocking intent, Jesus does not protest against any of the soldiers' previous mockeries when they "hold court" with him as king, dress him with a scarlet robe and a crown of thorns, place a reed as a scepter in his hand, and hail him as "King of the Jews" (27:27–30). We are also not told that he rejects their second offer of vinegary wine to drink (27:48; cf. Mark 15:36; Luke 23:36; and John 19:29–30),[27] and if we are to understand both of these gestures in terms of the Ps 69:21 allusion underlying both of them, then this second offer of wine would have been just as much a mockery as the first and even more so if one considers the Lukan parallel (23:36), which states explicitly that the soldiers were mocking Jesus with the offer. Why then are we not told that he refuses this second offer? What difference is there between the first and second offers so that Matthew feels the need to tell us that he rejects the first one?

Jesus' first refusal of the wine needs to be explained in some other way than as a rejection of mockery, which Jesus consistently does not reject throughout the Passion, including the second offer of vinegary wine. The best explanation appears to be one that multiple commentators have offered: Jesus refuses the wine because he recognizes it as a narcotic that would have reduced or altogether ended the pain of his crucifixion, and he prefers to endure it fully and consciously.[28]

John Paul Heil's narrative-critical reading of Jesus' death and resurrection connects his rejection of the wine with his acceptance in Gethsemane of drinking God's cup (26:39). Heil explains, "Jesus thus declines the drugged

---

One also needs to consider the possibility that perhaps this Matthean redaction preserved an authentic piece of history—that Jesus actually did taste the wine before refusing it. Perhaps the redaction needs no further explanation than this.

26. Brown, *Death*, 943. Another common reason for Jesus' refusal is that it accords with his vow of abstinence in 26:29, but this is even less persuasive than the rejection of mockery explanation.

27. In the Synoptics, we are not told that he receives the wine either. Only in John is Jesus pictured as actively taking the wine.

28. E.g., France, *Matthew*, 395; Morris, *Matthew*, 715; and Heil, *Death*, 79.

wine in order to 'drink' and fully experience the 'cup' of suffering and death willed for him by God (26:39, 42; 20:22–23)."[29]

His rejection of the wine plays the important narrative role of setting the tone for the entire Crucifixion narrative by showing Jesus' determination to experience the suffering his Father has allowed.[30] Perhaps a parallel rejection of the wine at the second offer was not necessary because at that point Jesus had finished drinking his Father's cup to the full and all that was left for him to do was to breathe his last breath (27:50). The two offerings of wine provide bookends to Jesus' suffering on the cross, but only the rejection of the first needs to be stated in order to set the scene of Jesus' consistent refusal to escape pain and his willingness to drink the cup of suffering.

Intertextual Allusions Helping to Explain the Intratextual Theological Questions

Now we turn to explore how Jesus' refusal of the bread in the wilderness anticipates his refusal of the wine at Golgotha and the narrative and theological connections between the two pericopes. One of the main ways in which these two passages are connected is through the shared theological questions raised by the similar situations in which Jesus finds himself and by the way in which the significance and meaning of these situations are explained through the OT intertextual allusions underlying them.[31]

---

29. Heil, *Death*, 79. cf. France, who says, "Jesus' refusal of the laced wine might be simply because it was, as in the psalm, an unpleasant drink offered in spite. But if, as is more likely, it was intended to dull the pain, Matthew may have mentioned Jesus' refusal in order to show his determination to go through the ordeal in full consciousness. He has chosen to drink the cup which his Father has given him (26:39–42) and will not be deflected by any human potion, however well meaning" (France, *Gospel Matthew*, 1067). The connection between the "cup" and Jesus' suffering within the Matthean narrative is further strengthened by its use in 20:20–23. There, Jesus asks James and John if they can drink the cup that he is to drink.

30. Green lists the refusal of the wine as an example of the way in which Jesus accepts his fate (Green, *Death*, 315–16).

31. Graham's research supports the above statement. In assessing the intertextuality of 27:39–44, she has already noted, "On the surface, then, Matthew has drawn on two complexes of terms and images, one related to the language of impious mockery, and the other to the Son of God title. This vocabulary, found also in the Wisdom of Solomon, echoes the language of the Psalms, Lamentations, 2 Kings, Exodus, and Deuteronomy, both by direct allusion and by allusion to other Matthean passages, especially the Temptation narrative. By making use of this language, Matthew, no doubt intentionally, has created an interpretive context for the pericope which would be readily recognizable to those Greek-speaking readers and hearers of his gospel who were familiar with Jewish scriptures" ("A Strange Salvation," 507).

Matthew 4:2–4; Exodus 16; and Deuteronomy 8:2–3

As we have already seen, it is commonly accepted among scholars that Matt 4:1–11 is an example of OT typology in which Jesus relives the experiences of Israel in the wilderness described in Exod 16, 17, and 32. In each of the three tests that Jesus undergoes, he responds to Satan with quotations from Moses' speech in Deut 6–8 in which Moses recounts those wilderness experiences and highlights the Israelites' failures within them.

The particular experience that Jesus "relives" in the first temptation, which we will refer to as the bread test, is described in Exod 16 where the Israelites complain because they are starving in the wilderness. The theological question raised by the Israelites during that experience is why God would let his people die from hunger. The Israelites accuse God by saying that he has brought them there "to kill this whole assembly with hunger" (ἀποκτεῖναι πᾶσαν τὴν συναγωγὴν ταύτην ἐν λιμῷ; 16:3).

In Moses' review of that experience in Deut 8:2–3, which Jesus quotes from in Matt 4:4, he explains why the Israelites were allowed to starve in the wilderness. Moses says that God led (ἄγω)[32] them into the wilderness (ἔρημος) to test (ἐκπειράζω) them.[33] In the LXX, God is said to have mistreated or done evil (κακόω) to them and caused them to go hungry (λιμαγχονέω)[34] in order to teach them "that man does not live by bread alone, but man lives by everything that proceeds out of the mouth of the Lord." When the Israelites face this theological dilemma, instead of continuing to trust in God's provision, their response in Exod 16:3 is first to long for the good old days in Egypt when they could get their own bread and meat and second to wish for death rather than starvation.[35]

Once again in another wilderness, the same theological question is raised as to whether or not God will let his righteous one, his own Son, die from hunger. Unlike the Israelites, Jesus refuses to complain against God and does not prefer to return to a place where bread can be gained by his

32. Note both the connection with ἀνάγω in 4:1 and with ἀπάγω in 27:31.

33. The words ἔρημος and πειράζω also occur in Matt 4:1.

34. Interestingly, this is the only occurrence of λιμαγχονέω in either the LXX or the NT, but there is one example of a similar word λιμοκτονέω, which means "to let go hungry" or "to let starve to death" occurring in Prov 10:3a. There it says, "The Lord will not allow the righteous to hunger [λιμοκτονέω]" (NAS). It is not surprising that the Israelites might question why they were starving if they thought that God did not let such things happen to the righteous.

35. As we see with the allusion to Deut 8:2–3, Boyd's Satan may have biblical precedent for his critique of God's treatment of Israel. Causing someone to hunger certainly is not a "good" action and is even considered "evil" according to the LXX version of these verses, and it calls into question the character of God.

own strength. Instead, as the Son of God, Jesus trusts in God and waits for his provision.[36]

Jesus and the Path of Suffering

In this way the test of bread in the wilderness is a scene that anticipates the wilderness that Jesus will again experience on the cross when he, like the Israelites before him, felt very much abandoned by God (note the cry of dereliction later in 27:46). Once again by taking a substance that is offered to him, Jesus will have the chance to alleviate his pain, if not altogether end it through an early death, if we accept the suicide theory regarding the gall additive to the wine,[37] much as the Israelites had once wished.

Throughout Matthew, Jesus, unlike the Israelites, consistently chooses to accept the path of suffering and never opts for an early end or an easing of his suffering. Just as Jesus says no to the bread that would have ended his painful fast (4:2–4), no to Simon Peter when he tries to deter him from a path of suffering (16:21–23), no to calling on angels to deliver him from the soldiers (26:53–54), no to avoiding the pain of his Father's cup in Gethsemane (26:39, 42, 44), Jesus now says no to drinking the wine that would have alleviated his pain on the cross (27:34). Instead of taking matters into his own hands by providing bread for himself in the wilderness or by drinking the wine at the cross, Jesus chooses to undergo the test given to him until God himself sees fit to provide relief.

Matthew 27:34; Psalm 69:21

This question of whether or not God will let his righteous one, his own Son, die resurfaces and is presented most strongly at the Crucifixion. Although not caused by hunger this time, the death of God's child is still very much the theological dilemma at hand. Once again, as with the OT allusions underlying the bread temptation (Exod 16, Deut 8:3), the question is tied to another OT allusion, Ps 69:21. This verse is part of a larger psalm that is

36. This interpretation of the underlying theological questions posed by the OT intertextual allusions in both Matt 4:2–4 and 27:34 is similar to Gerhardsson's. Just as Israel once was tempted to do, Jesus is now tempted to doubt the goodness of God because of the human afflictions of hunger and thirst that he undergoes. Yet Jesus, unlike Israel, offers the perfect example of Shema obedience. He chooses to love God with his whole, undivided heart and refuses to doubt God's goodness even in the face of these trials (Gerhardsson, *Testing*, 76–79; "Gottes Sohn," 102; "Judéo-Christianisme," 28–30).

37. Harrington, *Matthew*, 395; cf. Davies and Allison, *Matthew 19–28*, 613.

the cry of a righteous sufferer. The psalmist describes the ways in which his enemies afflict him and also how they are afflicting the one whom God has struck down and wounded (69:26). Thus, not unlike the OT background to the bread test, we find in this OT allusion that God is at the heart of the affliction that Jesus endures as the righteous sufferer, an identification that will grow throughout the Crucifixion as Matthew draws on other intertextual allusions depicting the suffering of a righteous one, including Ps 22, Is 53, and Wis 2.[38] By rejecting the relief that could have been his through the bread and the wine offered at the beginning of each experience, Jesus continues on the path of suffering laid out for him by his Father and continues the testing in both the Temptation and Crucifixion narratives.

The Son of God and Suffering

At this point, we are moving beyond the connections between specifically the bread and wine tests to discuss briefly how a theme raised in the bread test anticipates one that occurs throughout the wider Crucifixion narrative. That theme is the connection between the Son of God title and suffering.

At the Crucifixion, Jesus suffers not just as a righteous man but also as the Son of God. As Terrence Donaldson has already noticed, during the Temptation narrative Satan portrays certain assumptions of what it means to be the Son of God, and these same assumptions appear on the lips of the mockers during the Crucifixion. The first occurs during the bread temptation, and it is the "satanic" assumption that Jesus' sonship implies the absence of suffering.[39]

It is intriguing that this assumption reoccurs at least three times in Matthew's narrative. Each time, the "satanic" character represents the more traditional position that God would never let his Son suffer, and each time Jesus subverts this notion by showing that sonship entails suffering.

Jesus' testing in the wilderness follows on the heels of the baptismal scene during which Jesus is declared to be the beloved Son (ὁ υἱός μου ὁ ἀγαπητός, 3:17) by a voice from heaven, presumably God's. In the wilderness, the tempter twice suggests that *if* Jesus is the Son of God (εἰ υἱός εἶ τοῦ θεοῦ,

---

38. Senior has also noted the connection between 27:42, Wis. 2, and Ps. 22 that shows Jesus as the righteous sufferer and has argued that v. 42 particularly displays the "theme of the testing and mocking of the righteous man" (*Passion Narrative*, 289).

39. Donaldson in his brief exploration of the connection between the assumptions of Satan and those of the mockers regarding what Jesus' Sonship meant very astutely noted three themes in the Temptation that recur in the Crucifixion: 1. Sonship is equated with the absence of suffering (4:3); 2. Sonship implies divine protection (4:5–6); and 3. Sonship means universal sovereignty (4:8–9; Donaldson, "Mockers," 8–9).

4:3, 6) then he should not suffer. First, he is encouraged to end his painful fast (4:3), and later Satan says that God would not allow even one of his Son's feet to be harmed were he to fall from the temple (4:6). Jesus' response to this assumption is not only to continue steadfastly in his fast until God relieves him (4:11, he sends angels to care for him) but also to banish the one tempting him with ὕπαγε, σατανᾶ (4:10), a phrase unique to Matthew.[40]

The second time this assumption occurs follows a pronouncement of Jesus as God's Son (ὁ υἱός τοῦ θεοῦ, 16:16), but this time Simon Peter makes the declaration. On this occasion, Jesus explicitly states that suffering is his path (16:21). When Simon Peter tries to turn him from that path assuming that such a thing could never happen to the Son of God, he is lumped together with the first character in Matthew's narrative who tempted the Son of God to avoid suffering as Jesus tells Simon Peter to ὕπαγε ὀπίσω μου, σατανᾶ (16:23).

One last time at the cross, satanic characters try to deter Jesus, albeit not sincerely, from his path of suffering, and this scene again follows after another one containing a "Son of God" (ὁ υἱός τοῦ θεοῦ) pronouncement, albeit it is "pronounced" as an accusation at Jesus' trial (26:63). At Jesus' execution after his trials, twice the satanic characters suggest that *if* he is the Son of God (εἰ υἱός εἶ τοῦ θεοῦ, 27:40, cf., θεοῦ εἰμι υἱός, 27:43), then he should be able to avoid suffering and come down from the cross (27:40, 43).[41] The fact that he does not (the mockers would say cannot) serves only to prove in their minds that he is not the Son of God because, of course, God would not allow his Son, his righteous one, to suffer.

Donaldson has pointed out that all of these "Son of God" statements are Matthean redactions (with the exception of 3:17) and that these redactions suggest that the relation between the Son of God and suffering was a particular concern of Matthew. Donaldson even goes so far as to say, "Matthew's prime concern in the Passion Narrative was to show that the path of Sonship into which Jesus was called at baptism led inevitably to the cross."[42]

---

40. Also at the Transfiguration, there is an acknowledgement of Jesus as God's beloved son. Shortly after, Jesus again speaks about his upcoming passion. Perhaps with having the idea of Jesus as "Son of God" and his suffering in such close narrative proximity, we are again witnessing Matthew's concern with tying these two concepts together to show that Jesus' identity as the Son of God implies suffering.

41. France notes, "[H]ere again Jesus must have felt the force of the temptation to exploit his special relationship with God in order to escape physical suffering" (France, Gospel Matthew, 1070).

42. Donaldson, *Jesus on the Mountain*, 99. He cites Senior's redactional work on Matthew's Passion narrative (Senior, *Passion Narrative*, 323).

Conclusion to the Bread and Wine Tests

The Gospel rewrites first suggested to us that one of the main issues underlying the Temptation might be a question of theodicy. Can God be considered good in light of the problem of human suffering? In both novels, Jesus is tempted by Satan to "test" and question the goodness of God's character in light of suffering.

While there is no discussion of the global problem of suffering, we can now see that the particular theological dilemma of the suffering of the Son of God is certainly a question underlying both the Temptation and the Crucifixion. We see this on one level through the bodily pain that Jesus undergoes once through hunger and once through crucifixion, two very slow and agonizing ways to die that would have been some of the most dreaded means of death during the Roman Empire.[43]

We have also witnessed that Matthew recognizes the challenge to God's own character based on Jesus' suffering. Through the use of the OT intertextual allusions he places to under gird both of the bread and wine tests, he wrestles precisely with the problem of righteous suffering and God's role in it. The assumption in both OT allusions is that God takes care of his people, those who trust in him, and the claim that Jesus trusted in God, was God's Son, and yet suffered is a perplexing problem that Matthew continues to address throughout both narratives.

The bread test functions as a scene of anticipation for the Crucifixion where Jesus is tested again to blaspheme the God who has brought him there and to take matters into his own hands in order to relieve his suffering. In both scenes, Jesus is tempted to ease his pain with a dietary item, and both times he refuses. These refusals function as preludes to the entire passages and set the tone for both pericopes by introducing how Jesus will consistently reject the temptation to avoid suffering and remain steadfast throughout his tests. In the end, both rejections offer a sophisticated and significant theological point: by refusing to accept the bread and the wine that would have eased his pain, Jesus is able to offer his own bread—his body—and his own wine—his blood—for the world. Instead of drinking the wine, Jesus chooses to drink to the dregs the cup his Father has given him.

43. cf. Kammler, "Sohn Gottes," 178.

THE TEMPLE TEST IN COMPARISON
WITH THE CRUCIFIXION

Introduction

Following the bread test, Satan once again tempts Jesus in a manner that anticipates his later trials during the Passion. As noted in the discussion of the triadic structure of both narratives, there is not a one-to-one correlation between the second test at the Temptation and the second one at the Crucifixion. Instead, the temple test weaves together pieces scattered throughout the Crucifixion narrative.

We will begin this section by exploring the terminology common to both narratives starting with the famous "If you are the Son of God" challenge found in both of the second tests. As the most prominent connection between these passages, it has received the greatest amount of attention, but it is not their only connection. The phrase functions as the tip of an intratextual iceberg. Like any iceberg tip, its presence alerts us to the fact that there is much more just below the surface.

By examining these connections, we will see how themes that are consolidated into a tightly woven structure in the temple test appear at various points in the Crucifixion narrative, particularly clustering around the second and third tests. Such an analysis should give us more insight into the way in which Matthew has taken several key issues from the Crucifixion pericope and intentionally constructed the Temptation narrative as a prelude to the Passion.

When discussing the themes that dominate both narratives, we will explore how OT allusions support the rhetorical strategy of the satanic characters who tie the "Son of God" title to an assumption of divine protection. In effect, their arguments are one and the same: Jesus can prove his identity by calling upon or provoking God to rescue him either personally or through angelic intermediaries. We will see how Jesus' reactions to both the temple test and the Crucifixion tests subvert the "satanic" assumptions as to what substantiates a sonship claim. At both events, Jesus demonstrates that a true Son proves his identity not through divine deliverance but through a trust that does not require proof from his Father.

Verbal Allusions

During the temple test, the devil taunts Jesus saying, "If you are the Son of God" (εἰ υἱός εἶ τοῦ θεοῦ, 4:6), then "cast yourself down" (βάλε σεαυτὸν κάτω; 4:6) from the temple (τοῦ ἱεροῦ; 4:5). Satan reminds Jesus that there is no need for him to worry about coming to harm because God has promised to care for his Son by sending "angels" (τοῖς ἀγγέλοις, 4:6) to rescue him. As we shall see below, each of these highlighted phrases—"If you are the Son of God," "cast yourself down," "temple," and "angels"—echo the Passion narrative and contribute to helping the Temptation function as a scene of anticipation for Jesus' passion.

"If You Are the Son of God"

As we have already noted, the phrase "If you are the Son of God" (εἰ υἱός εἶ τοῦ θεοῦ) is the key verbal link between the Temptation and Crucifixion narratives. There is verbatim agreement between 4:3, 4:6, and 27:40, and a verbal parallel occurs in 27:43.

The most sustained comparison between the phrase in both narratives is found in Hultgren's chapter entitled "The Obedient Son of God: The Temptation and the Passion (Matt 4.1–11//Luke 4.1–13)."[44] There he focuses on the connections between specifically the temple test and various parts of the Passion rather than examining all three Temptation tests. His discussion begins his comparison by linking Jesus' trial charges with the challenging taunts hurled at him upon the cross.[45] After establishing the "If you are the Son of God" phrase as a likely reference to the trial charge (Matt 26:63), he discusses how it probably formed an integral part of the original Passion narrative and was not a Matthean insertion reminiscent of the earlier Temptation story. He argues that the Son of God phrase alerts us instead to the Temptation's dependence on the Passion passage where the phrase is already embedded in the narrative.

"Casting" and "Coming" Down

While only the second Crucifixion test begins with the phrase "If you are the Son of God," both the second and third tests at the Crucifixion share with the temple test the challenge for Jesus to "cast" or "come" down from a significant higher point. At the Temptation, Satan tells Jesus: "[C]ast yourself down" (βάλε σεαυτὸν κάτω; 4:6) from the temple (τοῦ ἱεροῦ; 4:5). At the Crucifixion, passers-by and the temple authorities mockingly tell Jesus to

---

44. Hultgren, *Narrative Elements*, 95–127. What follows is a summary of some of his arguments from that chapter.

45. Ibid., 107–8.

"come down from the cross" (κατάβηθι ἀπο τοῦ σταυροῦ; 27:40; καταβάτω νῦν ἀπο τοῦ σταυροῦ; 27:42).

Hultgren again assists us by noticing that the connection between these two passages extends beyond the conditional statement regarding Jesus' sonship and continues to the shared imagery of downward motion. The "verbal parallels are the vehicle for conceptual parallels"[46] for in the downward motion seen in each event, Jesus could have set into motion a scenario that would test God's divine protection. Perhaps even in the descending direction, we see a symbol for the ironic nature of these temptations. In "coming down," Jesus would not have raised himself up or have proven his sonship. Instead, he would have cast himself down from his exalted position as the Son of God by giving into satanic demands that led him away from God's will as his obedient Son.

Temple Connection

Next, we notice that the Temptation and the Crucifixion share another verbal allusion through references to the temple in both narratives. While the Greek is not the same—the Temptation narrative uses τὸ ἱερὸν (4:5) whereas the Crucifixion narrative uses τὸ ναός (27:40)—the referent for both terms is the Jerusalem temple.[47]

At the cross, the passers-by begin their taunting test by saying, "You who would destroy the temple and build it in three days, save yourself!" (27:40). The most likely explanation for this temple allusion is that it is a reference to Jesus' trial since, like the "Son of God" phrase, the temple reference links the Crucifixion pericope with Caiaphas' trial where Jesus was accused of claiming that he could destroy and rebuild the temple (τὸ ναός) in three days (26:60–61). Both the temple and the "Son of God" charges have led to Jesus' current predicament of hanging on a cross,[48] so it is not surprising that allusions would be made to both while punishment for those "crimes" was being executed.

Although the combination of temple and sonship language in the Crucifixion scene can be explained as an allusion to Jesus' trial charges,

46. Ibid., 109–10.

47. According to Michel, the NT uses τὸ ἱερὸν and τὸ ναός with little distinction between these words (Michel, "ναός," TDNT 4:880–90). Schrenk, in discussing the use of τὸ ἱερὸν, notes that it can be used more generally for the entire temple complex whereas τὸ ναός often refers more specifically to the inner shrine, but he also notes that in the NT both words are used interchangeably for the Jerusalem temple (Schrenk, "ἱερὸς, τὸ ἱερὸν, κτλ," TDNT 3:221–83).

48. Senior, *Passion Narrative*, 283.

such an obvious answer cannot clarify why another temple reference combined with the "Son of God" phrase appears at the Temptation. Hultgren offers us an answer for these verbal parallels: "If the Temptation narrative was written under the direct influence of the passion narrative, this close connection of temple and Sonship might explain (at least partially) why the second temptation (the third in Luke), in which Jesus' Sonship is challenged and in which Jesus is challenged to tempt God to save him from death, occurs precisely at the temple."[49] When we come to discuss the thematic allusions between the two narratives below, we will explore another reason for the connection between temple and sonship language in the Temptation narrative.

Angels

The final verbal allusion to the Passion found in the temple test occurs when Satan tells Jesus that his Father "will command his angels (τοῖς ἀγγέλοις, 4:6) concerning you." Admittedly, there is no reference to angels within the part of the Crucifixion narrative upon which we are focusing (27:31–44), and so this allusion does not tie these two particular pericopes together except for the fact that no divine assistance arrives in either narrative so long as the testing continues. The 4:6 angelic allusion, however, does have parallels within the wider Passion narrative. At Jesus' arrest in 26:53, Jesus asks, "Do you think that I cannot appeal to my Father, and he will at once send me more than twelve legions of angels (ἀγγέλων)?" The similarity between this idea and Satan's reference to Ps 91:11 is striking: If Jesus is in danger, he can call upon his Father who will send angels to rescue him.[50]

Neither a legion of angels nor the Lord of hosts appears to rescue Jesus from his testing either in the wilderness or at the cross. Intriguingly, it is only after Jesus has withstood all of the tests and shown himself to be the true Son of God that angelic assistance arrives to minister to him in the Temptation narrative (4:11). Likewise, it is only after Jesus has finished being tested on the cross and suffered death itself that an angel again appears as a character in Matthew's narrative (28:2–7). Given the pervasiveness of angels in Matthew's introduction (1:20, 24; 2:13, 19; 4:11), their absence as characters throughout the rest of the Gospel prior to the Resurrection is

49. Hultgren, *Narrative Elements*, 109.

50. France and Hultgren are the only two commentators that I surveyed to have noticed this connection (France, *Gospel Matthew*, 127; Hultgren, *Narrative Elements*, 109–11).

striking. Perhaps the long silence between the Temptation (4:11) and Resurrection appearances (28:2–7) serves only to connect further these two passages as vindications of Jesus' true sonship after overcoming his tests. It may be that the reappearance of angels after Jesus' completion of his Temptation tests is meant to function as a prolepsis of the later angelic appearance at Jesus' resurrection.

Thematic Allusions

The Son of God and Divine Protection

At the cross, however, Jesus' tempters assert that it is not angels but God himself who should be ready to rescue his Son (27:43). Interestingly, in both pericopes the belief that divine rescue will occur for a true Son is placed on the lips of the satanic characters. At the Temptation, it is the devil himself who speaks (4:5), and at the Crucifixion, it is those who reprise his role—the chief priests, scribes, and elders (27:41). In the sections that follow below, we will explore their assumption that sonship implies divine protection and the grounds upon which that assumption is based.

Intertextual Allusions Helping to Explain the Intratextual Theological Questions

With the bread and wine tests, we saw how the intratextual theological question that dealt with the issue of the Son of God and suffering was interwoven with intertextual OT allusions. Matthew again uses this rhetorical strategy when dealing with the belief that the Son of God will be divinely protected. In Matt 4:6, the devil quotes directly from Ps 91:11–12, and in Matt 27:43, the temple officials allude to Ps 22:8 (and perhaps to Wis 2:18–20).[51] Interestingly, both times these satanic characters find biblical support

---

51. These allusions are prime examples of the difference between the way OT texts are handled in the Passion narrative and the way they are handled in the Temptation narrative. In the former, we find very few direct quotations from the OT and almost no introductory phrases alerting us to their existence. Even without these verbal prompts, the informed reader is able to recognize that the narrative is brimming with OT echoes just beneath the surface.

In the latter, we find a more typical Matthean way of introducing OT references although none of the Temptation examples fall into the category of formula quotations (i.e., 1:22–23; 2:15; 2:17–18; 2:23; 4:14–16; 8:17; 12:17–21; 13:35; 21:4–5; 27:9), which are uttered by the narrator rather than by the characters and have longer introductory phrases. Four times (vv. 4, 6, 7, and 10) in the eleven short verses of the Temptation narrative, we find quoted scriptures introduced by the phrase "it is written"

for their positions in psalms that speak of God's deliverance of those who trust in him. These psalms undergird the satanic characters' argument that if God cared for Jesus, then God would save him and vindicate his identity as the Son of God through an act of divine intervention. The theology found in these psalms not only helps to explain both narratives but also ties them even closer together.

MATTHEW 4:6 AND PSALM 91:11–12

"For it is written" begins the devil's citation of Ps 91:11–12 in Matt 4:6. He quotes directly from the LXX, leaving out only one phrase in between the two cited sections: "He will command his angels concerning you," and "On their hands they will bear you up, so that you will not dash your foot against a stone." These lines belong to a psalm that speaks about the Lord's protection over those who live in his shelter and abide in his shadow (v. 1), in short about those who trust (ἐλπίζω, v. 2; cf. πείθω, Matt 27:43) in the Lord. Throughout Ps 91, the psalmist pictures how God will rescue the one who loves and calls upon God (vv. 14–15). He describes how the Lord will not allow any harm whether it comes by pestilence (vv. 3, 6), humans (vv. 3, 5), or animals (v. 13) to befall the one who trusts in the Lord. Satan has only to reference part of this psalm to provoke an entire web of protective images descriptive of how the Lord cares for the one who seeks that shelter. Although in the psalm itself protection is not linked directly with sonship, the tempter makes this connection by tying the "Son of God" title to these verses.

Of course, divine protection for God's Son is not a novel idea invented by Satan but a concept that reoccurs throughout the OT. In analyzing the temple test, Gerhardsson discusses other passages that speak about God's protection for his covenant sons.[52] He notes that it is not uncommon to find an angel executing that protection over God's covenant children, the Israelites. Particularly important is the fact that many of these references occur during

---

(γέγραπται). These introductory phrases, however, occur on the lips of Jesus or Satan rather than on those of the narrator.

52. While there are multiple examples, some of the most pertinent ones to our discussion are those in which God is pictured as a "shepherd," "watchman," or "protector" of Israel especially during their wilderness wandering years (e.g., Ps 28:9; 77:21; 78:52; 79:13; 95:7; 100:3; Is 63:11). In Exod 19:4, God describes how he bore Israel up on eagles' wings, and in Deut 32:10, he tells how he "sustained him in a desert land, in a howling wilderness waste; he shielded him, cared for him, guarded him as the apple of his eye." Gerhardsson shows how God's care for Israel is frequently compared to that of a parent's (e.g., Num 11:12; Is 46:3; Hos 11:3). For further discussion of OT passages depicting God's protection of his covenant son Israel, see Gerhardsson, *Testing*, 54–56.

the wilderness years (e.g. Ex 23:20, 23; 14:19; 32:34; 33:2),[53] a setting that we have already noted forms much of the typological basis for Jesus' own wilderness test. Gerhardsson also demonstrates how Ps 91 shares many images with other psalms describing protection in the temple (e.g., Ps 36:8f; 61:5). He argues that rabbinic interpretation understood this psalm as a temple psalm and associated it with Israel's desert wandering (e.g., Midr Teh 91). He concludes by saying, "Protection during the wilderness period and protection in the temple were portrayed with the same imagery. Innumerable associations link these two themes together, principally of course the basic theme: the covenant son is assured of protection against all dangers."[54]

Psalm 91 could be applied to any faithful Israelite and covenant son. That it is applied to *the* Son of God serves only to strengthen Matthew's typological picture of Jesus as the faithful representative of Israel succeeding where Israel failed in the wilderness.[55]

After observing the connections between Ps. 91 and the second temptation raised by Gerhardsson, Hultgren concludes: "Thus when the devil places Jesus on the πτερύγιον of the temple, challenges Jesus to throw himself down, and quotes Ps 91, he is calling upon Jesus to test God's faithfulness. Will God protect his Son and deliver him from death?"[56]

MATTHEW 27:43; PSALM 22:8; AND WISDOM 2:18

This question is precisely the same one underlying Matt 27:43's allusion to Ps 22:8. Perhaps on one level we see Matthew trying to answer for his readers the theological dilemma raised by the death of God's Son. If Jesus was truly the Son of God, then why did God not rescue him?

On the surface level, we see this question ironically posed by the mockers who believe that God's lack of protection for this supposed Son proves his illegitimacy because they assume, as their satanic forbearer had, that

---

53. Ibid., 55–56.

54. Ibid., 58. Gerhardsson goes on to make one further connection between the temple test and Ps 91. He explains that Jesus' placement on the pinnacle or wing (πτερύγιον) of the temple recalls the theme of divine protection, especially the idea of God protecting his children under the shadow of his wings found throughout the psalms (e.g., Ps 17:8; 57:2; 61:5). Even Ps 91 speaks about divine protection for those who abide in the "shadow of the Almighty" (v. 1) and describes how they will be covered with his pinions and find refuge under his wings (πτέρυγας; v. 4; Gerhardsson, *Testing*, 56–61).

55. Hagner, *Matthew*, 67.

56. Hultgren, *Narrative Elements*, 111.

sonship implies divine protection. Also like the devil, their assumptions are undergirded by an OT allusion strategically placed on their lips by Matthew.

In v. 43, Matthew once again draws upon Ps 22 as he has at various points throughout this pericope. As in the psalm itself (22:7), Matthew has the mockers utter the taunting challenge to let God come and save this righteous sufferer. There is striking agreement between the situations described in Ps 22, where the one who "trusted" (חטב, MT 22:5, 10; cf. "hoped" [ἐλπίζω], LXX 21:5, 9) in the Lord is mistreated and mocked, and in Matt 27:31–44, where Jesus who "trusts" in God (27:43) is crucified and mocked. The verbal agreement, however, is not exact between the two passages even though the logic behind the taunting challenges is similar: if you really trust in God, then let God save you now.

As multiple commentators have noticed, Matthew rephrases Ps 22:8 and uses it in a similar way to its appropriation in Wis 2:18. Some believe that Wis 2 may have even influenced Matthew's writing directly.[57] In Wis 2, we find oppressors testing (πειράζω; 2:17) the identity of a righteous man at the end of his life and waiting to witness divine deliverance as proof specifically of his sonship and not solely of his righteousness or trust in God. Those afflicting him argue that "if the righteous man is God's child, he will help him, and will deliver him from the hand of his adversaries." In Wis 2:18, we find the similar conditional phrase "if" (εἰ) seen in Matt 27:40 that raises the question of the sufferer's true identity. We also see a "test" of that identity that demands divine intervention as proof because once again the assumption is that if someone is really God's child, then God will rescue him.

In Matt 27:43, the lack of divine intervention discredits Jesus' sonship claims, and the use of Ps 22:8, and perhaps of Wis 2:18, bolsters the mockers' view that Jesus' death serves as a complete disavowal by his "Father" God.[58] For Matthews's readers though, Jesus' refusal to demand divine intervention from God functions instead as a complete avowal of Jesus' identity as God's Son.

The Testing of Divine Protection

At both the Temptation and the Crucifixion, Jesus is asked to test God by provoking God to act on his behalf. Regarding the temple test, Hagner says that Jesus is challenged to put himself in danger in order to force God to

---

57. E.g., Senior, *Passion Narrative*, 287–89; Gundry, *Matthew*, 571; and Garland, *Matthew*, 264.

58. Filson, *Matthew*, 296.

save him. He calls the test a "jump to safety" rather than a jump to destruction.[59] In the Crucifixion narrative, Jesus' life is already in jeopardy. There too he is asked to "jump" into God's saving arms and off the cross.

Hultgren has already noted that this theme of calling upon divine aid reverberates throughout the Passion narrative and is not located solely within the dual demands of the passers-by and the temple officials for Jesus to "come down from the cross" (Matt 27:40, 42).[60] Beginning in Gethsemane with the twelve legions of angels ready to save Jesus (26:53), continuing with the mockers who sardonically await God's deliverance of his "Son" (27:43), and ending with the observers who mistake Jesus' cry of dereliction for an appeal to Elijah for rescue (27:49), there is always the possibility, be it ever so slight, that Jesus could choose to opt out of this path of suffering and appropriate the divine assistance that is his to command.

Although in one sense Jesus' faithfulness never really seems to be in doubt, tension is created throughout the narrative for the reader who waits to see if an angel or some other divine being will swoop in and take Jesus off the cross. Perhaps the reader is to ask why Jesus did not call upon that aid. Why instead is the only cry heard on Jesus' lips one of abandonment—"My God, my God, why have you forsaken me?" (27:49)—rather than of deliverance? The reader, unlike the onlookers at the cross, has more of an omniscient perspective on the matter and knows that Jesus need not have made that cry of forsakenness and easily could have cried out instead for the deliverance that God would have provided.

The answer to these questions is provided by Matthew, who by developing the Temptation as a scene of anticipation for the Crucifixion has already given the reader theological tools to interpret Jesus' refusal to call upon God to deliver him. At the temple temptation, we discover that it is not just a test of Jesus but also a test of God himself. Had Jesus "cast himself down," he would have tested God's promises of divine protection to see if they would hold true. Understanding the temple challenge in this light explains Jesus' cryptic quotation of Deut 6:16: "'You shall not put the Lord your God to the test'" and his refusal to "jump to safety."

It also partially explains why Jesus does not call on God's deliverance at the cross. At the Temptation, Matthew ties the issue of divine deliverance with the suggestion that the Son of God should test God, and by doing so, he also frames the mockers' challenge at the cross in a negative light. The ironic undercurrent to both narratives is that such an obvious proof of sonship as

59. Hagner, *Matthew*, 67.

60. Hultgren, *Narrative Elements*, 109–10, 111.

requested by the satanic characters would have carried with it an implicit denial of that very identity because it would require Jesus to test his Father's protection, something that a true Son would never do.

Gerhardsson discusses at length how the testing of God by his covenant sons is considered the ultimate sign of "discontent, distrust and unbelief and therefore [is] itself a radical breach of the covenant."[61] At Massah, it is a test of whether or not God would fulfill the thirst of his people in the desert. At the Temptation, it is to see if he would protect his Son from danger. Finally, at the cross, it was to see if he would deliver that same Son from death.

The Son of God and Trust in God

In both narratives, Matthew links the idea of not testing God with trusting God. At the temple test, Jesus displays a trust in God's provision that does not require proof. The level of Jesus' trust is magnified by the comparison drawn between Jesus' testing and that of the Israelites in the wilderness.[62] At Massah, they doubted rather than trusted God's character and his ability to uphold his covenant (Exod 17:1–7). Their lack of trust in his protection led them to test God requiring him to prove his ability to provide (Deut 6:16).

The trust displayed by the Son of God on that temple wing, however, points not only back to the wilderness wanderings but also forward to the cross. As a prelude to the Crucifixion, we see at the Temptation that Jesus is ready to trust God even unto death.[63] In answering the question as to why the temple test is dominated by the theme of endangering one's life, Gerhardsson notes, "[T]he narrator wants us to see not merely that Jesus is reluctant to tempt God, but also that he is ready, in obedience to God, to lose his life."[64] His refusal to "come down" when tempted to do so again displays his trust in God,[65] which Carter says is a specific trust in God's power to raise him up after he died (cf. 16:21; 17:23; 20:19; 26:32).[66]

Further linking these two narratives together is the Son of God title, which, according to Graham, is "associated in this [G]ospel with trust and obedience under testing, which may well include suffering."[67] While this connection takes place first in the Temptation and then in Jesus' denounce-

61. Gerhardsson, *Testing*, 60.

62. Donaldson, "Mockers," 8–9.

63. Hultgren, *Narrative Elements*, 103, 111; cf. Donaldson, "Mockers," 10–11.

64. Gerhardsson, *Testing*, 61.

65. Hagner, *Matthew*, 67; Kingsbury, *Matthew: Structure*, 76.

66. Carter, *Matthew*, 214.

67. Graham, "Strange Salvation," 506–7.

ment of Peter as Satan (16:21–22), the moment when these ideas crystallize together is at the Crucifixion. There, Jesus' trust in God is highlighted by the Matthean interpolation in v. 43 that specifically links the Son of God title with trust while he suffers upon the cross.[68]

Conclusion

The satanic assumption of the first set of temptations is that sonship cannot involve suffering, but Jesus rejects that notion showing that suffering is precisely the path of the Son. Similarly, in the second temptation and the material to which it alludes in the Crucifixion narrative, another satanic assumption appears: that sonship can be proven by an act of divine intervention. Contrary to popular "satanic" opinion, however, the Son of God would never prove his identity by invoking divine protection even if his life were to depend upon it precisely because a true covenant son trusts God and does not test his faithfulness. Just as with the bread and wine tests, Jesus proves his sonship both at the Temptation and at the Crucifixion by rejecting what he is being tempted to do in order to confirm the presuppositions of others as to what it means to be the Son of God.

In light of these connections between the temple test and the Crucifixion narrative, it appears that the second Temptation test functions as a prelude to Jesus' death on the cross.[69] Although he could have called upon God or angels to lift him up, Jesus at the cross displays true sonship foreshadowed in the Temptation by trusting that after passing the test God himself will raise him up and angels will once again appear.[70]

THE KINGDOM TEST IN COMPARISON WITH THE CRUCIFIXION

Introduction

After successfully passing the bread and temple tests, Jesus undergoes one final test at the Temptation that, like the first two, functions as an anticipatory test of what he will face at the cross. Like them also, this third test deals with theological questions raised by the death of God's Son, who also happens to be presented in Matthew as the Messiah, the King of Israel and

68. Kingsbury, *Matthew: Structure*, 75.

69. Hultgren, *Narrative Elements*, 113.

70. Carter, *Matthew*, 214.

the world. While there are connections between the third tests (4:8–10 and 27:41–43), Matthew foreshadows material throughout the wider Passion narrative in the final Temptation test, which we will call the kingdom test.

Verbal Allusions: Kings and Kingdoms

As in each of the Temptation tests, we find Matthew making intratextual allusions to the Passion by introducing language and concepts that parallel those found in the Crucifixion. At the kingdom test, Satan offers to give Jesus the "kingdoms of the world" (βασιλείας τοῦ κόσμου) if only Jesus will fall down and worship Satan (4:8–9). At the third Crucifixion test, satanic characters promise to believe in Jesus as the "King of Israel" (Βασιλεὺς Ἰσραήλ) if only he will prove himself by coming down from the cross (27:42). Similarly, in 27:37 the Roman government "honors" Jesus with the title "King of the Jews" (ὁ βασιλεὺς τῶν Ἰουδαίων). We will discuss each of these "kingly" references in turn.

"King of the Jews" and the "King of Israel"

According to 27:37, the charge against Jesus was inscribed above his head: "This is Jesus, the King of the Jews" (οὗτός ἐστιν Ἰησοῦς ὁ βασιλεὺς τῶν Ἰουδαίων). This accusation is the same one brought against Jesus during his Roman trial. When Jesus stands before Pilate, the only question Pilate asks of him to ascertain his innocence or guilt is "Are you the King of the Jews?" (σὺ εἶ ὁ βασιλεὺς τῶν Ἰουδαίων; 27:11).[71] After the governor hands Jesus over to be crucified, his soldiers mock him as the "King of the Jews" (βασιλεῦ τῶν Ἰουδαίων; 27:29) before leading him away to crucify him.

The "King of the Jews" title plays a prominent role throughout the Passion narrative along with its parallel title "King of Israel," which appears only in 27:42. In the NT, which of the two titles is used depends upon the ethnicity of the speaker.[72] Only Israelites use the title "King of Israel" (cf.

---

71. He also asks Jesus if he is not hearing the many accusations made against him by the chief priests and elders because Pilate is amazed that Jesus does not reply to their charges (27:12–14).

72. As Elliot has demonstrated, the use of the term "Jews" versus "Israelites" reflects an in-group and out-group differentiation. Israelites always self-identified as Israelites and used that designation to refer to one another. Outsiders often mistakenly referred to all Israelites by the geographic designation "Jews" whether or not they were from Judea. Thus, Jesus is called the "King of the Jews" by Gentiles, such as Pilate and his soldiers, even though he was raised in Nazareth and most of his ministry, according to the Synoptics, took place in Galilee (Elliott, "Jesus the Israelite," 119–54).

Matt 27:43; Mark 15:32; John 1:49; 12:13) whereas Gentiles prefer the term "King of the Jews" (cf. Matt 2:2; 27:11, 29, 37; Mark 15:2, 9, 12, 18, 26; Luke 23:3, 37; John 18:33, 39; 19:3, 19, 21).

In Matthew, the "King of the Jews" and the "King of Israel" titles are closely associated with "Christ" (Messiah).[73] We see "King of the Jews" and "Christ" used interchangeably in the magi story (2:2, 4). Then again at the trial, Pilate uses both terms. When addressing Jesus directly, he asks whether or not he is the "King of the Jews" (27:11). When addressing the crowd, he refers to Jesus as "the one called Christ" (27:17, 22), there using the Israelite terminology for their "King." In Matthew, the "Christ" is the "King of Israel" for the Israelites, but Gentiles refer him to as the "King of the Jews."[74]

After observing this kingly terminology, we see how all three of Jesus' trial charges—a claim of destroying and rebuilding the temple (26:60–61), a claim of being the Son of God (26:63), and a claim of being the King of the Jews (27:11)—resurface in the Crucifixion. What is more surprising is that these same themes also appear in the Temptation narrative long before Jesus' trials!

"Kingdoms of the World"

At the Temptation, "king" language occurs during the third test when the devil offers to give Jesus "all the kingdoms of the world" (πάσας τὰς βασιλείας τοῦ κόσμου; 4:8) in exchange for his worship. The implicit offer is to make Jesus the king of the world by giving him all of the kingdoms.

While there is certainly royal terminology used at both the Temptation and the Crucifixion, it might be questioned whether the difference between gaining the "kingdoms of the world" and being called the "King of the Jews" and the "King of Israel" is too great for 4:8 to serve as an allusion to the Crucifixion. When we look at Matthew's understanding regarding whom the "King of the Jews" was expected to be, we see that the king was to rule over not only Israel but also over all of the kingdoms of the world. There is a

73. In discussing the use of the title "King of the Jews" throughout Matt 27 (vv. 11, 29, 37), Davies and Allison use the term interchangeably with "Christ" and note that "the words convey that Jesus' claim to be the Christ (cf. 26.64) involves kingship (cf. 21.5; 25.34, 40)" (Davies and Allison, *Matthew 19–28*, 233, 581).

74. In both statements to the crowd, Matthew redacts Mark, who in the same scene calls Jesus the "King of the Jews" (15:9, 12). When the temple officials mockingly suggest that Jesus should come down from the cross, Mark 15:32 has them refer to Jesus as "the Christ, the King of Israel." Matthew again redacts Mark by dropping "the Christ" part of the title, apparently viewing it as redundant (Ibid., 620). Perhaps these Matthean redactions provide us with a further glimpse into the way in which Matthew views these terms as interchangeable.

universal flavor to Matthew's kingly theology, as we shall see below, so that when we keep this theology in mind, the allusion seems an obvious one.

Thematic Allusions

The Son of God and Kingly Sovereignty

In the third test at the Crucifixion, the mockers equate the "Son of God" with the "King of Israel." Pointing to the parallelism of these terms seen in 27:42 and 27:43, Donaldson suggests that there is a theme running throughout both the Passion and the Temptation of linking the Son of God with universal sovereignty. Like the mockers, the devil assumes that a claim to sonship is also a claim to royalty.[75] This statement may be surprising, since the term "Son of God" does not appear in the third temptation. Even though the term is absent there, it is still clear that Jesus is being tested as the Son of God throughout the entire Temptation narrative and that this identity is at stake, perhaps more so in the third test than in either of the other two tests, should Jesus fail.[76]

INTERTEXTUAL ALLUSIONS AND OTHER MATTHEAN PASSAGES HELPING TO EXPLAIN THE INTRATEXTUAL THEOLOGICAL QUESTIONS

According to Evald Lövestam, the "Son of God" title is already implicitly present at the third temptation. The OT background to the term "Son of God" found in Ps 2 ties the ideas of Son of God and ruler of the nations together.[77] The final challenge is simply an outflow from the typical understanding of what it means to be the Son of God.

Lövestam also is not alone in thinking that the title's OT background already links it with the notion of universal sovereignty. Bauer notes that there are other OT references to the king as the son of God (e.g., 2 Sam 7:14; Ps 89:26–27) but that it is in Ps 2 where "the king in his capacity as son of God exercises authority over both the people of Israel and the nations."[78]

---

75. Donaldson, "Mockers," 7–9.

76. Cf. Kingsbury who argues that in all three tests Jesus is clearly tempted in his capacity as Son of God (Kingsbury, Matthew: Structure, 51).

77. Lövestam, *Son and Saviour*, 100; cf. Donaldson, *Jesus on the Mountain*, 91, 94.

78. Bauer, "Son of God," 771; cf. Donaldson discusses the universal sovereignty promised to the Son in Ps 2 (Donaldson, "Mockers," 10–11). Also of interest is the fact

In analyzing the *Sitz im Leben* of Ps 2, Kingsbury suggests that it could have been used during a coronation ceremony of Israelite kings descended from David. He says, "In the course of each such coronation, the new king asserted in the name of Jahweh that he reigned over all the nations (cf. Ps 2:7–8)."[79]

That this psalm is one of the most important OT passages giving substance to the "Son of God" title in Matthew is confirmed by the use of Ps 2:7 at both the Baptism and the Transfiguration. In both scenes, Jesus is declared to be the Son by a divine voice from heaven—"This is my Son, the Beloved, with whom I am well pleased" (Οὗτός ἐστιν ὁ υἱός μου ὁ ἀγαπητός, ἐν ᾧ εὐδόκησα; 3:17; 17:5).

In other passages where Jesus is called the Son in Matthew's Gospel, sonship is also tied to kingship. For example, the Temptation concludes Matthew's introductory presentation in which Jesus is called the Son of God (cf. 2:15) and is presented as the king ("son of David" [1:1] and "King of the Jews" [2:1–12]).[80]

Kingsbury has argued that in Matthew's theology the term "Son of God" encompasses other titles and messianic expectations so that the Son fulfills expectations related particularly to David and to Abraham, of whom he is also the "son" (1:1).[81] Matthew finds precedent in the OT for subsuming these titles and their expectations under the larger notion of the Son of God. In several passages (e.g., 2 Sam 7:14; Ps 2:7–18; 89:26–27; 1 Chr. 17:12–13; 22:10), the one known as God's son or his first-born is also the king from David's household and the one who will rule over Israel and the nations. Kingsbury concludes, "Matthew's basic understanding of Jesus Messiah is as

---

that in Ps 2, God promises divine protection to the king, his son. Once again, we see how certain themes related to sonship in Matthew are interconnected and reoccurring throughout the Gospel and its OT allusions.

79. Kingsbury, *Matthew: Structure*, 49.

80. Donaldson, "Mockers," 8–9.

81. In his introduction, Matthew alludes to Jesus' Davidic sonship and its roles with the obvious titles, such as "son of David," (1:1) "Messiah," (2:4) and "King of the Jews" (2:2), and with less obvious references, such as Jesus' birth in Bethlehem (2:1–2, 5–6). He also includes the idea that Davidic sonship involves ruling and shepherding God's chosen people Israel (2:6).

Kingsbury suggests that Matthew alludes to Jesus' Abrahamic sonship and its universal implications through the Gentile Magi who journey to worship Jesus (2:1–2, 11). Abrahamic typology and its implications are an important part of Jesus' kingly sonship because it was Abraham, after all, through whom the nations of the earth would be blessed (cf. Gen 12:3; 18:18; 22:18; 26:4). He concludes his argument by stating, "[I]t is evident that what Matthew does in ch. 2 is to attribute to Jesus exactly as the Son of God messianic expectations otherwise more narrowly associated with him as the Son of David or the Son of Abraham (Kingsbury, *Matthew: Structure*, 46–47).

the Son of God, a concept that, again, not only does not discount messianic expectations associated with either David (Israel) or Abraham (nations), but is expansive enough to embrace them."[82]

Thus, we see that the tempters at both the Temptation and the Crucifixion are not wrong in their assumption that sonship implies kingly sovereignty. They are simply falling in line with Matthew's own theology that he has developed by interweaving throughout his narrative the OT concept of understanding the King of Israel as God's Son, who is destined for universal sovereignty.

How to Gain a Kingdom, According to Satanic Characters

These satanic characters, however, provide a sharp counterpoint to Matthew's theology regarding the issue of *how* the Son of God will gain that kingdom. Twice in Matthew, Satan and those who reprise his role offer the kingdom to Jesus via another route than God's. The first time, he can gain the kingdom by being unfaithful to God, by worshipping another, and by choosing to follow the tempter's way rather than God's.[83] The second time, he can obtain the kingdom by being unfaithful to God and not drinking the cup that God has given Jesus to drink. In each narrative, the choice is between following God's will or the will of those tempting him.

Both times, Jesus is tempted to take easier routes to the kingdom by either falling down and worshipping Satan or coming down from the cross. Jesus can follow them, or he can continue on the harder road, the path of suffering, by following his Father's will.

Interestingly, both of the satanic offers of the kingdom also involve irony with the tempters offering things that already belong to God's Son or that will eventually be given to him after he passes these tests (cf. 28:18). The devil's offer is a parody of God's promise to the messianic king to "make the nations your heritage, and the ends of the earth your possession" (Ps 2:8; cf. Ps 72:8; Rev 11:15).[84] The temple officials mockingly offer to recognize his identity as the King of Israel. Ironically, it is the Israelite leaders who do not recognize Jesus' kingship while the leaders of other nations (e.g., the magi; 2:1–12) have already bowed down and worshipped him as the King of the Jews.

---

82. Ibid., 47.

83. Hagner, *Matthew*, 68.

84. Ibid.

The Son of God and Filial Obedience

If Jesus were to give in and follow the satanic characters rather than God, he might have gained a kingdom, but in what sense could he still have been called the Son of God since one of the main characteristics of sonship is filial obedience? This theme of obedience is in fact one of the main threads connecting the Temptation and Passion narratives together.[85]

At the Temptation, Jesus functions as humble and obedient "Israel" and shows how a true covenant son obeys the Father.[86] At the cross, Jesus' final act is obedience to God even unto death. The question that remains is whether or not Jesus has lost the kingdom by being obedient. The reader, like the mockers, knows that the Son of God is meant to be the King of Israel and of the nations, but how could the cross ever lead to that glory? Typically, a king is not crucified but is the one doing the crucifying. As it seems to the mockers and to Peter before them (16:22–23), the way of the cross appears to be incongruous with the way of gaining a kingdom. Yet throughout the Gospel, Matthew makes it clear that the cross is the obedient Son's destiny (cf. 16:21; 17:23; 20:19, 22–23; 26:39, 42) and shows Jesus rebuking those who try to deter him from that suffering (4:10; 16:23).[87]

Two notions that Satan and the mockers play off against one another are two roles that belong to the Son of God. Like Kingsbury before him, Donaldson points out how the Temptation concludes Matthew's introduction where Jesus is presented as the Son of God (cf. 2:15). According to him, the two particular roles highlighted in that introduction for the Son of God are that of king (1:1; 2:1–12) and of humble and persecuted "Israel" (2:13–18).[88] Jesus accepts this dual role at his baptism (3:13–17). The devil pits these roles against each other in the Temptation (4:1–11), and the

---

85. E.g., Graham, "A. Strange Salvation," 506–7; Gerhardsson, *Testing*, 61; and Carter, *Matthew*, 214.

86. Hagner, *Matthew*, 67.

87. Green in his concluding analysis of the primitive passion narrative lying behind those of the four Gospels discusses how that narrative makes clear that Jesus anticipates multiple aspects of his passion and death and how he willingly accepts his fate. The narrative also shows that Jesus' death is the result of "divine causation" and that the cross was God's will (Green, *Death*, 315–16).

88. Donaldson, "Mockers," 8–9. He goes on to state, "In the opening chapters of the Gospel, Jesus is presented as God's Son who has come to save (1.21) and to shepherd (2.6) God's people Israel. But this presentation incorporates two distinct Old Testament models of Sonship: God's Son the enthroned king, victorious over his enemies and exercising universal authority (Ps. 2; 2 Sam. 7.14); and God's Son Israel, called to a life of humble obedience to God's will (Exod. 4.22–23; Deut. 8.5; Hos. 11.1)" ("Mockers," 11).

"diabolical pressure" to abandon one in order to gain the other continues all the way to the cross. Donaldson explains:

> The suspense experienced by the reader is not so much whether Jesus will succumb to temptation; this is not really in doubt, even in Gethsemane (26.26–44). Instead, the suspense arises from the reader's concern as to how, if Jesus' resistance to temptation leads to his death, he will then be able to achieve his calling as enthroned Son and saviour. The terms within which Jesus' mission is to be carried out seem to contain an inner contradiction, threatening to make the mission itself impossible to achieve.[89]

In other words, how can Jesus be both the obedient Son embodying Israel and also the glorious king? The tempters implicitly pit these two concepts against one another and present Jesus with a falsely dichotomous choice.

Matthew's Jesus, however, opts for a third way. As he has done before with the previous tests, Jesus again subverts the tempters' assumptions of what it means to be the Son of God. He shows that he can indeed be both the King of Israel and the obedient Son embodying Israel because the kingdom is gained by obediently enduring the cross and is given on the other side of it (cf. 28:18). At the cross, Jesus ironically finds his kingship by losing it. According to Matthew's theology, by drinking his Father's cup, which involves remaining on the cross and not coming down as the tempters suggest, he gains the nations and redeems the world (20:28; 26:28)."[90]

Conclusion

It has become increasingly clear that the Temptation functions as an anticipatory scene for Jesus' passion and death and particularly for the Crucifixion scene. In the final Temptation test, we once again see how Matthew presents "satanic" assumptions only to subvert them. When Satan pits the dual roles of obedient Son and king of the nations against one another and asks Jesus to reject the first in order to gain the latter, Jesus refuses the choice, banishes Satan, and proceeds to demonstrate by going to the cross precisely how obedience leads to kingship.

---

89. Ibid., 11–12.

90. Davies and Allison, *Matthew 19–28*, 619, 620. When talking about 20:20–28, Allison says that James and John's request also brings together the ideas of the Kingdom of God and Jesus' passion: "The implied lesson is that the way to the one is the way to the other, that entrance into the kingdom cannot come without first drinking the cup of suffering and judgment" (Allison, *Foreshadowing*, 230).

At the Crucifixion, we again encounter this false dichotomy where Jesus is again asked to choose between being obedient to his Father's will and receiving the kingdom via an easier route. The Son of God, however, has shown himself to be steadfastly committed to his Father and to his Father's path, and the habits of obedience developed earlier in the narrative come to full fruition during this final test. In Matthew's Gospel, Jesus dies refusing to renounce his Father's plan and trusts that he will receive the kingdom on the other side of the cross.

CONCLUSION TO THE PREPOSTEROUS READING: DID THE REWRITES GET IT RIGHT?

The Temptation's Function As a Pre-Climax Or "Scene of Anticipation" for the Passion

After examining Matthew's Temptation narrative within its own literary context, we are now in a better position to judge whether the themes suggested by the Boyd and Saramago accounts of Jesus' testings and the questions that they led us to ask of Matthew's Temptation were well-founded. The priority of place given to their testing scenes as the climaxes of the novels led us to wonder whether the Temptation functioned as some type of "pre-climax" to the true climax in Matthew's Gospel, the Crucifixion. We noticed that in addition to complementing Matthew's own use of typology and tying Jesus' experiences back to those of OT characters, the novels also linked Jesus' testing forward with his own upcoming passion and death. Because of this connection, we hypothesized that Matthew might be doing something similar, though less overtly, through structural, verbal, and thematic allusions.

After thoroughly exegeting these passages, we see that the Temptation does indeed serve as what Allison calls a "scene of anticipation" for the Passion, and, in particular, the Crucifixion. In a different way than that of the novels, Matthew has given the Temptation a priority of place by situating it at the culminating point of his introductory presentation of the person of Jesus.[91] In Matthew, the position of an event points to its importance. Especially significant in Matthew are the opening chapters, which "establish the point of view from which the whole story is told and the values by which

91. Cf. Kingsbury, whose structure of Matthew divides into three main sections: the person of Jesus Messiah (1:1—4:16); the proclamation of Jesus Messiah (4:17—16:20); and the suffering, death, and resurrection of Jesus Messiah (16:21—28:20); (Kingsbury, *Story*).

the audience must evaluate subsequent events, sayings, and characters."[92] By situating the Temptation in this key narrative position, Matthew has placed it as a lens through which much of the rest of his theological portrait of Jesus is to be viewed. By doing this, he produces what literary scholars have called the "primacy effect," a term that refers to how information introduced at the beginning of a message affects the audience's direction of interpretation throughout the rest of a text.[93]

Through the lessons learned at the Temptation, Matthew gives his readers guidance in understanding Jesus' determination to continue on his Father's path rather than avoiding the suffering of the cross by showing that obedience to and trust in his Father are essential characteristics of the Son of God. Matthew reinforces this "primacy effect" by reiterating throughout the Gospel the continued struggle between the Son of God, who tries to fulfill his Father's will, and those satanic characters who try to deter him from doing it.[94] By repeating these confrontations and Jesus' refusals, Matthew emphasizes that Jesus has opportunities to avoid the suffering of the cross but chooses not to do so.[95] Also, by connecting Israel's lessons of covenant faithfulness typologically relived at the Temptation with Jesus' tests at the Crucifixion, Matthew uses the Temptation to teach his readers what an obedient covenant son acts like and how the cross is consistent with rather than a nullification of Jesus' identity as that true Son of God.

By reading the Temptation and Crucifixion pericopes together, we are given important insights into the theological significance of Jesus' death. We begin to understand why the Son of God refuses to avoid his passion and what the implications of his steadfastness are. Jesus' refusals of the highly symbolic bread and the wine allow him to continue as the obedient covenant Son drinking his Father's cup and offering his own bread and pouring out his own wine for the forgiveness of sins (26:26–28). His refusals to call upon God to save his life mean that he can offer his life as a ransom for many (20:28). Finally, his refusals to gain the kingdom by any other means than his Father's allow him to gain all authority in heaven and on earth on the other side of the cross (28:18). In the final summation, we see, beginning

---

92. Carter, *Matthew*, 104.

93. Perry, "Literary Dynamics," 53.

94. Perry explains that for the primacy effect to achieve its desired result, it needs to be reinforced throughout the text by material that rephrases the primary text's point of view (ibid., 57).

95. Carter in discussing what the results of redaction criticism reveal regarding Matthew's theology notes that Matthew presents a more exalted view of Jesus in which his human qualities, especially those of limitations and ignorance, are decreased but in which his control over circumstances are increased (Carter, *Matthew*, 58–59).

with the Temptation, that Jesus has multiple opportunities to avoid the cross but that he refuses each of them, remains faithful to his Father's path, and proves by his death that he is truly the Son of God.

We are indebted to both Boyd and Saramago for alerting us to the narrative importance of the Temptation and its connection with the Passion. Certainly the purposes behind the allusions and explicit references to Jesus' passion found within the novels are not the same as those of Matthew, but the foreshadowing of the cross within their temptation events does complement the anticipation of the Crucifixion in Matthew's Temptation.

The "Testing" of God's Character in Light of the Problem of Suffering

The secondary issues in our "preposterous" hypothesis were partially correct and partially incorrect. One of the themes presented in both novels that first led us to reexamine Matthew's Temptation was that of theodicy. The Satan characters in both novels question God's character in light of the problem of human suffering and tempt Jesus to question God's character as well.

Here, we see an excellent example of modern concerns being written back into Jesus' story. To answer the question of "what would Jesus do," novelists can simply place their Jesus characters in situations that provoke this question and narrate how they think Jesus would respond. The novels use their testing scenes to have Jesus deal with several modern queries, one of which is the issue of theodicy. In the novels, Jesus' personal suffering is not the focus but merely the catalyst for a larger discussion of suffering in general and why God allows it to take place.

Matthew too deals with the problem of suffering, but unlike the novels, he focuses on the particular problem of Jesus' suffering. Along with Paul, Matthew recognizes that Jesus' crucifixion is a stumbling block for Israelites who look for signs of God's power and instead see God's "weakness" at the cross (1 Cor 1:22–25). The theological dilemma of the suffering of God's Son is precisely the question with which Matthew wrestles for his audience and which he attempts to answer through the Crucifixion narrative and the Temptation narrative that anticipates it. Matthew explains by showing that Jesus could have avoided any suffering, be it that of hunger or of death, but that he consistently chose not to do so. Instead, he continued in obedience to his Father's will, and according to Matthew, that obedience rather than any absence of suffering is the true "sign" of a Son of God.

Something else that the narratives do share is the underlying challenge for Jesus to call his Father's character into question. The only difference is that Matthew's Jesus is asked to do so in light of the problem of his own suffering whereas the Boyd and Saramago Jesuses are asked to do so in light of the problem of global suffering. The response of Matthew's Jesus to the implied questioning of God's character matches that of Boyd's Jesus but not of Saramago's Jesus. Because God's character is judged as good in both Matthew's Gospel and Boyd's novel, their Jesuses remain with God and with God's way of bringing about the kingdom through Jesus' suffering. Saramago's Jesus, however, willingly questions God's character and agrees with Satan that God's blood-thirsty desire for sacrifices—those of Passover lambs, that of Jesus' life, and those of the lives of Jesus' followers—is extremely problematic. Of course, such rebellion is understandable within *Gospel*'s narrative world, where the character of God does not at all resemble the person of God described in Matthew's Gospel.[96]

---

96. This leads us to ask what Matthew's portrait of God looks like. Like most NT writers, Matthew assumes more than he explains about God. Matthew's God is assumed to be the God of the OT, of the patriarchs and the prophets (e.g., 1:22; 2:15; 3:9; 22:32). We are told that all things are possible for God (19:26) who is powerful (22:29) and opposed to Satan (12:28). God is pictured as someone to be loved (22:37) and worshipped (4:9). There is the assumption that God is someone people would want to see (5:8) and whose children they would want to be (5:9). God is said to provide for those children even better than for creatures (6:30). God is not only Jesus' Father (7:21; 10:32–33; 11:25–27; 12:50; 15:13; 16:17; 16:27; 18:10; 18:19; 18:35; 20:23; 26:39; 26:42; 26:53) but also the heavenly Father of many other children (5:16; 5:45; 5:48; 6:1–9; 6:14–18; 6:26; 6:32; 10:20; 10:29; 13:43; 18:14; 23:9). Also in Matthew's Gospel, we are led to infer certain characteristics about God based on descriptions of what God's kingdom is like. In it, God receives tax collectors and prostitutes while some religious leaders (21:31–45) and the rich may be excluded (19:24). God accepts those who produce good fruits (21:43), who do God's will (7:21), and who minister to the marginalized and the suffering in society but rejects those who do not minister to them (25:31–46).

The most direct statement dealing with God's character is perhaps found in 7:9–11, where God's blessing of God's children is compared to that of earthly parents. Inasmuch as "evil" parents still know how to bless their children, so much more so does God know how to bless those who are God's children.

Perhaps most important is the way in which God's character is tied to Jesus himself in Matthew. In this Gospel, Jesus is presented from the beginning as Emmanuel, "God with us" (1:23), so that as we read about Jesus' character and actions throughout the narrative, we are meant to understand them as revealing something about God's interactions with humanity. The Son of God is intricately linked with his Father throughout the Gospel so that inasmuch as Jesus receives a favorable portrayal, so too does his Father, who is reflected in Jesus and who receives the credit for Jesus' good works (9:8; 15:31).

Compassion for Humanity Vs. Jesus' Own Passion: Competing Ideas of Bringing About the Kingdom

Both novels pit Satan's plea of compassion for humanity against God's plan for Jesus' own passion and present them as competing ideologies of how to bring the kingdom about. Yet, we must question whether or not these novels have helped us to reach the heart of the Temptation of Matthew's Gospel at this point.

Like the novels, Matthew also presents seemingly conflicting options between which Jesus is asked to choose. One way represents a path of obedience to God while the other is Satan's by-path. Matthew shows through repetition that Jesus consistently was offered a way out of suffering and chose to reject it each time. It appears important to Matthew that Jesus consciously chose to obediently follow his Father's will and that he had the option to do otherwise.

Like Boyd's novel and unlike Saramago's, Matthew combines many seemingly diametrically opposed options and brings them together in a new synergistic way. Jesus can be both God's obedient covenant son and also suffer and die. In fact, that suffering is what will ironically lead to his receiving power and glory after his death (312) and will pave the way to establishing God's kingdom, but Matthew does not focus on how Jesus' own passion in turn displays compassion for the world. Surprising to discover is the fact that the novels' emphasis on the implications of Jesus' death for humanity is not one of the major themes of Matthew's Gospel. Through our own analysis of the Temptation and Crucifixion, we can see that Matthew's main theological concern in the narratives is not soteriological. He does not explain *what* effect Jesus' suffering has on humanity or develop any sort of detailed atonement theology.[97] Instead, Matthew focuses on answering *why* the Son of God suffers. His answer is because God wills it and because Jesus as the true covenant Son of God obeys God's will.[98] Ironically, Saramago's novel, the competing one, agrees with Matthew's answer and stresses that the reason for Jesus' death was simply because God wills it.

---

97. In fact, the only places in Matthew where we see any hint of how Jesus' sufferings function in an atoning capacity are in the ransom statement (20:28), in his explanation of the new covenant symbolism of the bread and the wine as his own body and blood offered for the forgiveness of sins (26:26–28), and possibly, as Green suggests, in the substitution of Jesus for Barabbas (27:15–23) and the crowd's ironic response of accepting Jesus' blood on themselves and their children (27:25); (Green, *Death*, 319).

98. Cf. Green who says, "According to the passion account, why did Jesus die? Because God willed it! It was necessary in God's salvific plan. This is the most significant theme around which all others are related and from which they draw their significance" (ibid., 315).

Of course, Matthew does not answer why it was God's will.[99] Narrative gaps like these are where fictionalized accounts of Jesus' life flourish. Typical to its genre, Saramago's narrative attempts to give us an answer as to why God wills Jesus' death, but unfortunately, the novel's answer bears no "good news" for humanity.

Summation

Unsurprisingly, we find that the rewrites sometimes "got Matthew right" with their presentations while at other times their depictions were more novel than right. Even though some aspects of their testing scenes turned out to be more competing than complementing, we can agree that they were always stimulating and provoked the important function of sending us back to the original source, in this case Matthew. I believe that the above results stand on their own as an important contribution to Matthean scholarship. At the same time, this "preposterous" exegesis also serves as an example of how Gospel rewrites can positively contribute to biblical scholarship. Although Jesus novels are perhaps primarily a part of the reception history of the Gospels, they can also turn the flow of interpretation around and assist in helping us to better understand the original texts.

---

99. That is unless we take Jesus' statement at the Last Supper about his death leading to the forgiveness of sins (26:26–28) as God's answer.

Conclusion

INTRODUCTION

JESUS NOVELS PROVIDE AN array of areas for investigation. Serving as important examples of reception history of the Gospels, they reflect a myriad of modern conceptions of Jesus and his story. The multiplicity of factors affecting their composition could have led us down a number of roads. In our now concluding quest, we have chosen to focus more on the texts themselves than on the factors behind their creation, although we have certainly done some examination of those influences as well. By directing our attention at the textual level and by activating the reading pacts imbedded within the novels, we have been able to analyze not only their fictional Jesus characters but also the novels themselves and their function as Gospel rewrites. Through this process, we have discovered that our literary analysis is not confined only to the rewrites themselves. Instead of ending with the novels, our quest circled back to the Gospels as we "preposterously" interpreted these sources in light of questions raised and views presented in these fictional accounts of Jesus' life.

As we reflect on our journey through these literary landscapes, we will begin by assessing how useful our categories of complementing and competing were in understanding the relationship between the rewrites and their progenitors and in evaluating the Christological portraits they created. Then we will discuss the value of "preposterous" interpretation particularly in relation to biblical studies. Finally, we will offer further avenues of exploration in the field of Jesus novels before concluding.

COMPLEMENTARY AND COMPETING REWRITES

One of the principal guiding assumptions of this study has been that while all Jesus novels function as Gospel rewrites, their relationships with the canonical Gospels can be extremely varied. We divided the rewrites into two broad but heuristically useful categories and surveyed several techniques used by the novels in order to achieve their aims of either complementing or competing with the Gospels. Not surprisingly, the particular novels we discussed both conformed to these categorical expectations and often subverted them. Sometimes the very techniques used to compete with the Gospels turned out to produce portraits of Jesus that at points were quite complementary. The reverse was also the case with the complementing novels.

As we have seen with Rice's *Out of Egypt*, some of the most theologically conservative works can end up competing with the Gospels. Rice in her comments about the novel is explicit in her desire to produce an orthodox Jesus character, one that matches the depictions seen in the Gospels, yet her determination to remain faithful to the traditions handed on to her by her church leads her to produce a seven-year-old Jesus whose picture occasionally conflicts with the Christological portrayals of the Gospels. For example, Rice's concern to affirm the miraculous worldview of the Gospels and Jesus' ability to perform mighty works backfires to some extent. By tying Jesus' powers to his divinity rather than to an indwelling of God's Spirit, she affirms his miracles at the cost of portraying a fully human Jesus. *Out of Egypt* exemplifies a common feature of complementary novels: in their rush to testify to Jesus' divinity, such works often compete with the Synoptic Gospels' style of much slower revelations of Jesus' identity and sometimes less explicit declarations of divinity. In this way, they can potentially compromise the fully human portrayal of Jesus that the Gospels give. In conclusion, we saw that Rice's novel more closely complements ancient childhood biographies and the non-canonical infancy gospels than the Gospels themselves. The former focus on displaying an unchanging character and a continuation of fantastic abilities from childhood into adulthood. The latter, particularly the Synoptic Gospels, first display Jesus' miracles after his baptism and after his time of fasting in the wilderness.

Contrary to many other complementary novels, Boyd's *Hidden Years* does not strive to match the higher Christologies of the later Church creeds, so it is better able to complement the Gospels themselves. Yet even this most faithful and engaging rendition was capable of competing with the canonical sources, as it did with its less supportive stance regarding the incursion of the miraculous into the natural world. As we can see from these examples, complementary novels rarely agree with the Gospels on every matter addressed in their narratives. Still they display enough of a resemblance to and an intention to rewrite the Gospels in a faithful manner so that *complementary* remains the best description of the novels.

Conversely, competing novels do not contradict their canonical sources at every turn of the page. In Ricci's *Testament*, one of the central plot devices designed to undermine the Gospel presentation of Jesus' person ironically functions to create a complementary depiction of Jesus' ministry. Jesus' illegitimate conception and his subsequent bastard status in *Testament* are instrumental in influencing his theology on the inclusive nature of the kingdom of God and his ministry to societal outcasts. Also, although Jesus' death is in no way considered a sacrifice or ransom for the sins of many as it is in the Gospels, there is a salvific element to it in *Testament* when Ricci's Jesus provokes his own death in order to prevent the deaths of his co-prisoners.

Likewise, the death of Saramago's Jesus also contains a salvific aspect. By having his Jesus fail in his role as the Son of God, Saramago creates a somewhat complementary portrait of a compassionate and caring Jesus, although this one tries to die in order to save current and future followers from a manipulative God, whose world domination plan will ultimately lead to pain and destruction for many. Furthermore, the ultimate answer as to why Jesus suffers in Saramago's novel mirrors that of Matthew's own explanation—because God wills it—even though Saramago develops a God character who is fundamentally different from the one in Matthew's presentation.

Not surprisingly, we find that the categories of "competing" and "complementing" are an oversimplification of the complex relationship between each Gospel rewrite and its Gospel sources. Indeed, one of the most enjoyable aspects of working with Jesus novels is their ability to defy strict categorization and their sometimes playful, often overt, and occasionally unwitting ability to subvert even their own competing or complementing intentions. While they provide a beneficial place from which to begin our examination of the intertextual nature of these texts, they are by no means the final word on their Christological portraits or on their stances towards the historicity, theology, or worldviews found in the Gospels. It is on account of the questions and complications that such an approach unearths that the thesis involves a further "reflexive" step in its consideration of Jesus fiction.

"PREPOSTEROUS" INTERPRETATION

Our study found that some of the central roles of Gospel rewrites are those of filling in the gaps left by the canonical versions of Jesus' life and of proposing answers to some of the many questions regarding the actual Jesus. Instead of satisfying our curiosity and resolving unanswered mysteries though, these retellings can raise even more issues and send us back to the original texts with more questions than we previously had.

As readers return to the Gospels and interpret them preposterously, they are able to test theories proposed in the rewrites against the original texts. While some may find such anachronistic interpretation ultimately unhelpful and perhaps even harmful, Mieke Bal reminds us that all exegesis is in one sense "preposterous" in that we always interpret texts *after* they have been written and bring to them our own cultural and personal presuppositions. Bal actively engages with the ideas presented in later texts and argues that they too should be allowed a voice within the interpretative act. In this thesis, we have drawn on Bal's theory and suggested that such willful anachronistic interpretation may aid in understanding the original texts themselves better. Our own test-case "preposterous" examination of Matthew's Temptation and Crucifixion narratives—which was provoked by issues raised in two Gospel rewrites—demonstrates how later texts can positively inform our exegesis of their predecessors.

Of course, it should be noted that while responding to later texts, any responsible exegesis will not be guided solely by them or unduly influenced by their rewritings of the original. Exegesis that is balanced and beneficial should combine multiple critical tools and listen to the expertise and ideas of many voices. The rewrites proposed illuminating novel ideas for us and helped us to form our questions regarding how the Temptation functions in Matthew's Gospel and relates to the Passion narrative. However, after constructing an initial hypothesis, we then tested it by using the tools of other forms of criticism—such as narrative, source, and redaction—and by comparing it against the findings of various scholars. As a result, our novel thesis was strengthened as some elements were confirmed through our investigation of Matthew's Gospel and secondary sources while the purely preposterous suggestions that lacked confirmation within the original text were not supported. Such a refining process is essential for any rigorous study as it continues to be sharpened, qualified, and corroborated by being tested against different theories and through the accumulation of further knowledge.

What is perhaps most intriguing to witness is that this "preposterous" method of interpretation is by no means one-directional. We do not simply develop a hypothesis based on the posterior texts—which prompts us to travel back to investigate the original texts—and stop there. Instead, our investigation of the prior texts and our now more informed understanding of them leads us to reexamine the rewrites once again. We are thus moved to ask, as we did in the conclusion of chapter 7, whether or not the rewrites are accurate and why, if at all, such accuracy matters. As we can see, then, the intertextuality of these works creates a hermeneutical circle that continues as long as readers continue to enact the reading pact and place these texts in conversation with one another.

AREAS FOR FURTHER EXPLORATION

In this monograph, we explored Jesus novels and their relationships with the canonical Gospels and so focused primarily on the texts themselves. By doing so, we explored only one small aspect of these novels. It is evident that the factors affecting the Christological portraits created and the overall worldview and shape of the novels' stories do not depend solely upon authors' relationships with the canonical Gospels or upon whether or not they ultimately wish to complement or compete with them. One of the other chief factors influencing a rewrite's composition is obviously its author's view of Christianity in general or of the institutional church in particular.

For example, Rice, who had recently returned to her Roman Catholic heritage at the time of writing her series, produces a Jesus character and a storyline that for the most part falls in line with Catholic teaching and tradition. Boyd, a former Catholic priest, also creates an orthodox Jesus character but one who constructively critiques certain problematic areas and practices of the church with the aim of ultimately reforming them. Ricci, who has transitioned from Catholicism to evangelism to no organized religion, says of Catholicism that it is "a particularly tempting corpse to dig my vulture claws into."[1] When we read Ricci's novel, we find that at the root of much of his subversion is a not too subtle grudge against Christianity, which he sees as based on myths, rumors, and misunderstandings, and at the church, which according to his depiction is populated with uneducated and gullible individuals. Saramago, an atheist, Communist, and political moralist, produces a novel that is most critical of religious violence and blind faith in an uncritical adherence to any system or deity that appears to dehumanize humanity. The role played by an author's own relations with Christianity and with Christian churches up until the time of his or her writing would be another area of exploration and would no doubt shed a great deal of light on the composition of fictional Jesuses.

In reflecting on the relationships of our four case study authors with Christianity, we notice that all of them came from Catholic backgrounds. Another potential area of study would be a comparative analysis of novels produced by authors of different faith traditions. Jesus novels have not only been written by Christians from various denominational backgrounds, but they have also been composed by Jewish and Muslim authors, for example.

---

1. Nino Ricci, no pages, cited 15 June 2010, http://ninoricci.com.

It would be informative to compare the fictional Jesuses that emerge from these religious influences.

Likewise, a comparative literature approach that analyzes Jesus novels from different cultures and countries would manifestly be profitable. In our own small sampling, we included Portuguese, Canadian, Irish, and American authors. Yet there are Jesus novelists from other parts of the world outside the Western world whose works would provide material for a rich comparative analysis.

Someone interested in the development of literary genres would be well suited to research the beginnings of the modern Jesus novel and to trace its evolution throughout recent decades. I suspect that such a survey would find that the fictional Jesus characters reflect the concerns and issues of the generation in which they were created, since one common technique used by novelists is the placing of their Jesuses in situations where they are faced with questions and issues that most perplex and fascinate society in the novelists' time period. Through fiction, authors are able to ask, "What would Jesus do?" in certain scenarios and then to offer narrative responses.

Another potential area for exploration could be a comparison of narration approaches. Most Jesus novelists choose to tell Jesus' story from the point of view of an omniscient, external narrator, as we saw in Saramago's *Gospel* and in Boyd's *Hidden Years*. Many others, however, use the point of view of a character or characters other than Jesus within the novel as in Ricci's *Testament* and in Fortney's *Thomas Jesus*. In most of these novels, Jesus himself is a participating character, but in some cases, Jesus rarely or never appears in scenes even though much of the plot revolves around discovering information about this elusive figure. Such was the narrative device used in Gerd Theissen's *Shadow of the Galilean*. A few bold or perhaps presumptuous authors, such as Rice and Norman Mailer, take on the challenge of narrating Jesus' life from his own first-person point of view. Other novels, such as Gabriel Meyer's *The Gospel of Joseph*, tell his story via an epistolary approach, in which ancient letters are uncovered that offer new information on Jesus' life. It would be interesting to investigate the ways in which these different narration styles affect the portrayal of Jesus in the novels.

One might finally offer comparisons between Jesus novels and Jesus novellas, between Jesus novels and Christ-figure novels, or between Jesus novels and the historical fiction genre in general. Of course, there is clearly room for more preposterous exegesis and examination between Gospel rewrites and their Gospel progenitors, so as we can see from some of the above suggestions, the potential avenues of investigation in this new area are many and varied.

SUMMATION

Although it points to a different kind of infinity to claim that the world could not contain the "many other things which Jesus did" were they to be written down, it might not be too fanciful to suggest in a parallel fashion that even the large and ever-growing corpus of Jesus novels cannot contain the diversity of opinion about this man from Galilee. That one man could inspire so many portraits, so varied in style and content, attests to the inexhaustible greatness of his character and the desire that so many feel to recreate him in a way that allows them to connect with him. That four Gospels could spawn over four hundred Gospel rewrites in the last century alone reminds us not only of their continued centrality within modern culture but also of the affective power of their stories. Recreations of Jesus and his stories are guaranteed an ongoing role in popular culture certainly for the foreseeable future, and for this we should be grateful because they continue to challenge us to reexamine that old, old story that many assume they know so well. So long as Jesus novels are produced, our quest for the fictional Jesus and for that elusive shadow of the Galilean standing behind him will continue. For now we see through the myriad of Jesus stories darkly, but perhaps one day we may see the reality face to face.

Works Consulted

Ackroyd, P. *Blake*. London: Sinclair-Stevenson, 1995.

Albright, W. F., and C. S. Mann. *Matthew*. Anchor Bible 26. Garden City, NY: Doubleday, 1971.

Alexander, Philip S. "Retelling the Old Testament." In *It Is Written: Scripture Citing Scripture: Essays in Honour of Barnabas Lindars, SSF*, edited by D. A. Carson, et al., 99–121. Cambridge, England: Cambridge University Press, 1988.

Allen, Willoughby C. *A Critical and Exegetical Commentary on the Gospel According to S. Matthew*. 3rd ed. International Critical Commentary 26. Edinburgh: T. & T. Clark, 1912.

Allison, Dale C. "Anticipating the Passion: The Literary Reach of Matthew 26:47— 27:56." *Catholic Biblical Quarterly* 56 (1994) 701–14.

———. *The End of the Ages Has Come: An Early Interpretation of the Passion and Resurrection of Jesus*. Edinburgh: T. & T. Clark, 1985.

———. *Jesus of Nazareth: Millenarian Prophet*. Minneapolis: Fortress, 1998.

———. "Matthew: Structure, Biographical Impulse and the *Imitatio Christi*." In *The Four Gospels*, edited by F. Van Segbroeck et al., 1203–21. Leuven, Belgium: Leuven University Press, 1992.

———. *The New Moses: A Matthean Typology*. Edinburgh: T. & T. Clark, 1993.

———. *Studies in Matthew: Interpretation Past and Present*. Grand Rapids, MI: Baker Academic, 2005.

Alter, Robert. *The Art of Biblical Narrative*. London: Allen & Unwin, 1982.

Alter, Robert, and Frank Kermode, eds. "General Introduction." In *The Literary Guide to the Bible*, 1–8. London: Collins, 1987.

Altieri, C. "Jean-Paul Sartre: The Engaged Imagination." In *The Quest for Imagination*, edited by O. B. Hardison, 167–89. Cleveland: Case Western Reserve, 1971.

Ambrose. *De excessu fratris sui Satyri*. Vol. 10, *The Nicene and Post-Nicene Fathers*. Series 2. 1886–1889. Reprint, Peabody, MA: Hendrickson, 1994.

Anderson, Graham. *Eros Sophistes: Ancient Novelists at Play*. Chico, CA: Scholars, 1982.

Angus, L., and J. McLeod, eds. *The Handbook of Narrative and Psychotherapy: Practice, Theory, and Research*. Thousand Oaks, CA: Sage, 2004.

Ankersmit, F. R. "Historical Representation." *History and Theory* 27 (1988) 205–28.

———. "History and Postmodernism." *History and Theory* 28 (1989) 137–53.

Aquinas, Thomas. *Catena Aurea: Gospel of Matthew*. Translated by William Whiston. London: J.G.F. and J. Rivington, 1842.

Archer, Jeffrey. *The Gospel According to Judas*. London: Macmillan, 2007.

Argyle, A. W. *The Gospel According to Matthew*. The Cambridge Bible Commentary on the New English Bible. Cambridge, England: Cambridge University Press, 1963.

Aristotle. *Poetics*. In vol. 23 of *Aristotle in Twenty-Three Volumes*. Cambridge, MA: Harvard University Press, 1932.

Asch, Sholem. *The Nazarene: A Novel Based on the Life of Christ*. New York: Carroll & Graf, 1984.

Ashton, Mark. "Luke 4:1–13: What Mattered to Jesus." *Evangel* 16, (1998) 4–7.

Athanasius. *Epistula ad episcopos Aegypti et Libyae*. Vol. 4, *The Nicene and Post-Nicene Fathers*. Series 2. 1886–1889. Reprint, Peabody, MA: Hendrickson, 1994.

————. *Orationes contra Arianos*. Vol. 4, of *The Nicene and Post-Nicene Fathers*. Series 2. 1886–1889. Reprint, Peabody, MA: Hendrickson, 1994.

Augustine. *De civitate Dei*. Vol. 2, *The Nicene and Post-Nicene Fathers*. Series 1. 1886–1889. Reprint, Peabody, MA: Hendrickson, 1994.

————. *De consensu evangelistarum*. Vol. 6, of *The Nicene and Post-Nicene Fathers*. Series 1. 1886–1889. Reprint, Peabody, MA: Hendrickson, 1994.

————. *Contra Faustum Manichaeum*. Vol. 4, of *The Nicene and Post-Nicene Fathers*. Series 1. 1886–1889. Reprint, Peabody, MA: Hendrickson, 1994.

————. *Contra Litteras Petiliani*. Vol. 4, *The Nicene and Post-Nicene Fathers*. Series 1. 1886–1889. Reprint, Peabody, MA: Hendrickson, 1994.

————. *De Correctione Donatistarum*. Vol. 4, of *The Nicene and Post-Nicene Fathers*. Series 1. 1886–1889. Reprint, Peabody, MA: Hendrickson, 1994.

————. *De doctrina christiana*. Vol. 2, *The Nicene and Post-Nicene Fathers*. Series 1. 1886–1889. Reprint, Peabody, MA: Hendrickson, 1994.

————. *Ennarationes in Psalmos*. Vol. 8, *The Nicene and Post-Nicene Fathers*. Series 1. 1886–1889. Reprint, Peabody, MA: Hendrickson, 1994.

————. *In epistulam Johannis ad Parthos tractatus*. Vol. 7, *The Nicene and Post-Nicene Fathers*. Series 1. 1886–1889. Reprint, Peabody, MA: Hendrickson, 1994.

————. *Sermones*. Vol. 6, *The Nicene and Post-Nicene Fathers*. Series 1. 1886–1889. Reprint, Peabody, MA: Hendrickson, 1994.

Aune, David E. "Greco-Roman Biography." In *Greco-Roman Literature and the New Testament: Selected Forms and Genre*, edited by David E. Aune, 107–26. Atlanta: Scholars, 1988.

————. *The New Testament in Its Literary Environment*. Edited by Wayne A. Meeks. Library of Early Christianity 8. Philadelphia: Westminster, 1987.

Avis, Paul. *God and the Creative Imagination: Metaphor, Symbol and Myth in Religion and Theology*. London: Routledge, 1999.

Baarda, Tjitze. "Diafwnia-Sumfwnia: Factors in the Harmonization of the Gospels, Especially in the Diatessaron of Tatian." In *Gospel Traditions in the Second Century: Origins, Recensions, Text and Transmission*, edited by William L. Petersen, 133–54. Notre Dame, IN: Notre Dame University Press, 1989.

Bailey, Steve. "Faith-Based Fare May Get Made-in-Mass. Tag: Producer Envisions $150m Studio, Jobs for 1,500." *The Boston Globe*, June 6, 2007, no pages. Online: http://www.boston.com/business/globe/articles/2007/06/06/faith_based_fare_may_get_made_in_mass_tag/?page=2.

Baillie, D. M. *God Was in Christ: An Essay on Incarnation and Atonement*. London: Faber and Faber, 1958.

Bakhtin, Mikhail. "Epic and Novel: Toward a Methodology for the Study of the Novel." In *Modern Genre Theory*, edited by David Duff, 68–81. Harlow, England: Longman, 2000.

Bakhtin, M. M., and P. M. Medvedev. *The Formal Method in Literary Scholarship.* Translated by Albert J. Wehrle. Cambridge, MA: Harvard University Press, 1985.

Bal, Mieke. *Loving Yusuf: Conceptual Travels from Present to Past.* Chicago: University of Chicago Press, 2008.

————. *Quoting Caravaggio: Contemporary Art, Preposterous History.* Chicago: University of Chicago Press, 1999.

Bale, John. *A Brefe Comedy of Enterlude Concernynge the Temptacyon of Our Lorde and Saver Jesus Christ, by Sathan in the Desart.* London, 1538.

Balmer, Kelly. "An Exposition of Matthew 4:1–11." *Interpretation* 29 (1975) 57–62.

Barclay, William. *The Gospel of Matthew.* 2 vols. Edinburgh: The Saint Andrews Press, 1975–1977.

————. *Jesus Christ for Today: Seven Studies in Luke's Gospel.* London: Methodist Home Mission, 1973.

————. *Jesus of Nazareth.* Glasgow: William Collins Sons & Co., 1977.

Barr, D. L. "The Drama of Matthew's Gospel: A Reconsideration of Its Structure and Purpose." *Theology Digest* 24 (1976) 349–59.

Barrett, C. K. *The Gospel According to St. John.* London: SPCK, 1955.

Barthes, Roland. *The Discourse of History.* Translated by Stephen Bann. Vol. 3. Cambridge, England: Cambridge University Press, 1981.

————. *Image, Music, Text.* Translated by Stephen Heath. New York: Hill and Wang, 1977.

Bauckham, Richard. "The Brothers and Sisters of Jesus: An Epiphanian Response to John P. Meier." *Catholic Biblical Quarterly* 56 (1994) 686–700.

————. "Gospels (Apocryphal)." In *Dictionary of Jesus and the Gospels*, edited by J. B. Green, et al., 286–91. Downers Grove, IL: InterVarsity, 1992.

————. *Jesus and the Eyewitnesses: The Gospels as Eyewitness Testimony.* Grand Rapids, MI: Eerdmans, 2006.

————. "The New Testament Apocrypha." In *Old Testament Pseudepigrapha course.* St. Mary's College, University of St. Andrews. St. Andrews: Fife, May 5, 1999.

————. "Reading Scripture as a Coherent Story." In *The Art of Reading Scripture*, edited by Richard B. Hays et al., 38–53. Grand Rapids, MI: Eerdmans, 2003.

————. "The Study of Gospel Traditions Outside the Canonical Gospels: Problems and Prospects." In *Gospel Perspectives: The Jesus Tradition Outside the Gospels*, edited by David Wenham, 369–403. Sheffield, England: JSOT Press, 1985.

Bauer, D. R. "Son of God." In *Dictionary of Jesus and the Gospels*, edited by J. B. Green, et al., 771–75. Downers Grove, IL: InterVarsity, 1992.

Beare, Francis Wright. *The Gospel According to Matthew: A Commentary.* Oxford: Basil Blackwell, 1981.

Ben-Porat, Ziva. "Introduction." *Journal of Romance Studies* 3 (2003) 1–7.

————. "The Poetics of Literary Allusion." *PTL: A Journal for Descriptive Poetics and Theory of Literature* 1 (1976) 105–28.

————. "Saramago's *Gospel* and the Poetics of Prototypical Rewriting." *Journal of Romance Studies* 3 (2003) 93–105.

Berger, Peter L., and Thomas Luckmann. *The Social Construction of Reality: A Treatise in the Sociology of Knowledge.* Baltimore: Penguin, 1966.

Beskow, Per. *Strange Tales About Jesus: A Survey of Unfamiliar Gospels*. Philadelphia: Fortress, 1983.

Best, Ernest. *The Temptation and the Passion: The Markan Soteriology*. Cambridge, England: Cambridge University Press, 1990.

Bien, P. A. "A Note on the Author and His Use of Language." In *The Last Temptation of Christ*, edited by Nikos Kazantzakis, 497–506. New York: Simon & Schuster, 1998.

Bishop, Jim. *The Day Christ Was Born*. New York: Pocket Books, 1960.

Bleich, David. "Epistemological Assumptions in the Study of Response." In *Reader-Response Criticism: From Formalism to Post-Structuralism*, edited by Jane P. Tompkins, 134–63. Baltimore: John Hopkins University Press, 1980.

Blomberg, Craig L. "Form Criticism." In *Dictionary of Jesus and the Gospels*, edited by J. B. Green, et al., 243–50. Downers Grove, IL: InterVarsity, 1992.

Bloom, Harold. "The One with the Beard Is God, the Other Is the Devil." *Portuguese Literary & Cultural Studies* 6 (2001) 155–66.

Booth, Wayne. *The Rhetoric of Fiction*. Chicago: University of Chicago Press, 1983.

Borg, Marcus. *Jesus, a New Vision: Spirit, Culture, and the Life of Discipleship*. San Francisco: Harper & Row, 1987.

———. *Meeting Jesus Again for the First Time: The Historical Jesus & the Heart of Contemporary Faith*. San Francisco: HarperSanFrancisco, 1994.

Borg, Marcus, and N. T. Wright. *The Meaning of Jesus: Two Visions*. London: SPCK, 1999.

Bornkamm, Günther, et al. *Tradition and Interpretation in Matthew*. Translated by Percy Scott, The New Testament Library. London: SCM, 1963.

Bowersock, G. W. *Fiction as History: Nero to Julian*. Berkeley, CA: University of California Press, 1994.

Boyd, Neil. *The Hidden Years: A Novel About Jesus*. London: Hodder & Stoughton, 1984.

Brandon, S. G. F. *The Trial of Jesus of Nazereth*. London: B. T. Batsford, 1968.

Brown, David. *Discipleship and Imagination: Christian Tradition and Truth*. Oxford: Oxford University Press, 2000.

———. *Tradition and Imagination: Revelation and Change*. Oxford: Oxford University Press, 1999.

Brown, Raymond E. *The Birth of the Messiah: A Commentary on the Infancy Narratives in the Gospels of Matthew and Luke*. New York: Doubleday, 1977.

———. *The Death of the Messiah: From Gethsemane to the Grave*. New York: Doubleday, 1994.

———. *The Gospel According to St. John*. Anchor Bible 29A. Garden City, NY: Doubleday, 1970.

———. "*The Gospel of Peter* and Canonical Gospel Priority." *New Testament Studies* 33 (1987) 321–43.

———. *An Introduction to the New Testament*. New York: Doubleday, 1997.

Bultmann, Rudolf. *The History of the Synoptic Tradition*. Translated by John Marsh. New York: Harper & Row, 1963.

Burdon, Christopher. "The Margin is the Message: Commentary's Displacement of Canon." *Journal of Literature and Theology* 13 (1999) 201–10.

Burridge, Richard A. *Four Gospels, One Jesus?* Grand Rapids, MI: Eerdmans, 1994.

———. *What are the Gospels? A Comparison with Graeco-Roman Biography*. 2nd ed. Grand Rapids, MI: Eerdmans, 1992.

Byrskog, Samuel. *Story as History—History as Story: The Gospel Tradition in the Context of Ancient Oral History*. Tübingen, Germany: Mohr, 2000.

Cairns, D. S. *The Faith That Rebels: A Re-Examination of the Miracles of Jesus*. 6th ed. London: SCM, 1954.

Calvin, John. *Commentary on a Harmony of the Evangelists, Matthew, Mark, and Luke*. Translated by William Pringle. 3 vols. Vol. 1. Grand Rapids, MI: Christian Classics Ethereal Library, 1999.

Cameron, Averil. *Christianity and the Rhetoric of Empire: The Development of Christian Discourse*, Sather Classical Lectures. Berkeley, CA: University of California Press, 1991.

Cameron, Ron. *The Other Gospels: Non-Canonical Gospel Texts*. Philadelphia: Westminster, 1982.

Canary, Robert H., and Henry Kozicki, eds. *The Writing of History: Literary Form and Historical Understanding*. Madison, WI: University of Wisconsin Press, 1978.

Carcopino, Jerome. *Daily Life in Ancient Rome: The People and the City at the Height of the Empire*. Translated by E. O. Lorimer. Edited by Henry T. Rowell. New Haven, CT: Yale University Press, 1968.

Carroll, John T., and Joel B. Green. *The Death of Jesus in Early Christianity*. Peabody, MA: Hendrickson, 1995.

Carson, D. A. *Matthew*. 2 vols. Expositor's Bible Commentary. Grand Rapids, MI: Zondervan, 1984.

Carter, Warren. *Matthew: Storyteller, Interpreter, Evangelist*. Peabody, MA: Hendrickson, 1996.

Champion, James. "The Parable as an Ancient and Modern Form." *Journal of Literature and Theology* 3 (1989) 16–39.

Chancey, Mark A. *Greco-Roman Culture and the Galilee of Jesus*. Cambridge: Cambridge University Press, 2005.

———. "How Jewish Was Jesus' Galilee." *Biblical Archaeological Review* 33.4 (2007) 42–50, 76.

———. *The Myth of a Gentile Galilee*. Cambridge, England: Cambridge University Press, 2002.

Charles, Ron. "What Shall I Do Then with Jesus?" *Christian Science Monitor*, May 13, 2003. No pages. Online: http://www.csmonitor.com/2003/0515/p18s02-bogn.html?related.

Charles, Robert H., ed. *The Apocrypha and Pseudepigrapha of the Old Testament in English*. Oxford, England: Clarendon, 1913.

Charlesworth, James H., ed. *The Old Testament Pseudepigrapha*. 2 vols. Garden City, NY: Doubleday, 1983–85.

Chatman, Seymour. *Story and Discourse: Narrative Structure in Fiction and Film*. Ithaca, NY: Cornell University Press, 1978.

Chilton, Bruce. *Galilean Rabbi and His Bible: Jesus' Use of the Interpreted Scripture of His Time*. Wilmington, DE: M. Glazier, 1984.

———. *Rabbi Jesus: An Intimate Biography*. London: Image, 2000.

Cipolla, Benedicta. "How Anne Rice Created Her Christ." *Beliefnet*, November 2005. No pages. Online: http://www.beliefnet.com/News/2005/11/How-Anne-Rice-Created-Her-Christ.aspx.

Clement of Alexandria. *Paedagogus*. Vol. 2, *The Ante-Nicene Fathers*. 1885–1887. Reprint, Peabody, MA.: Hedrickson, 1994.

Coady, C. A. J. *Testimony*. Oxford: Clarendon, 1992.

Cohn, Dorrit. *The Distinction of Fiction*. Baltimore: Johns Hopkins University Press, 1999.

Coles, Robert. *The Call of Stories: Teaching and the Moral Imagination*. Boston: Houghton Mifflin, 1989.

Colie, Rosalie. "Genre-Systems and the Functions of Literature." In *Modern Genre Theory*, edited by David Duff, 148–66. Harlow, England: Longman, 2000.

———. *The Resources of Kind: Genre-Theory*. New York: Routledge, 1973.

Collingwood, R. G. *The Idea of History*. Oxford: Oxford University Press, 1946.

———. *The Idea of Nature*. Oxford: Oxford University Press, 1945.

Combrink, H. J. B. "The Structure of the Gospel of Matthew as Narrative." *Tyndale Bulletin* 34 (1983) 61–90.

Condra, Ed. *Salvation for the Righteous Revealed: Jesus Amid Covenantal and Messianic Expectations in Second Temple Judaism*. Leiden, Netherlands: Brill, 2002.

Coulehan, Jack. "Empathy and Narrativity: A Commentary on Origins of Healing: An Evolutionary Perspective of the Healing Process." *Families, Systems & Health* 23 (2005) 261–65.

Cousland, J. Robert C. "José Saramago's *Kakaggelion*: The 'Badspel' According to Jesus Christ." In *Jesus in Twentieth-Century Literature, Art, and Movies*, edited by Paul C. Burns, 55–74. New York: Continuum, 2007.

Crace, Jim. *Quarantine*. London: Viking, 1997.

Croce, Benedetto. "Criticism of the Theory of Artistic and Literary Kinds." In *Modern Genre Theory*, edited by David Duff, 25–28. Harlow, England: Longman, 2000.

Crook, Zeba. "Fictionalizing Jesus: Story and History in Two Recent Jesus Novels." *Journal for the Study of the Historical Jesus* 5 (2007) 33–55.

Crosby, Cindy. "Interview with a Penitent." *Christianity Today*, December 1, 2005. No pages. Online: http://www.christianitytoday.com/ct/2005/december/11.50.html.

Crossan, John Dominic. *The Historical Jesus: The Life of a Mediterranean Jewish Peasant*. San Francisco: HarperSanFrancisco, 1991.

———. *Jesus: A Revolutionary Biography*. San Francisco: HarperSanFrancisco, 1994.

Cuddon, J. A. "Allegory." In *A Dictionary of Literary Terms*, 24–26. London: Penguin, 1979.

———. "Allusion." In *A Dictionary of Literary Terms*, 31. London: Penguin, 1979.

Culler, Jonathan. *Literary Theory: A Very Short Introduction*. Oxford: Oxford University Press, 1997.

———. *The Pursuit of Signs: Semiotics, Literature, Deconstruction*. Oxford: Oxford University Press, 1997.

Cullmann, Oscar. *The Early Church*. Edited by A. J. B. Higgins. London: SCM, 1956.

———. "Infancy Gospels." In *New Testament Apocrypha*, edited by Edgar Hennecke, et al., 363–417. London: SCM, 1973.

Culpepper, Alan. "Story and History in the Gospels." *Review and Expositor* 81 (1984) 467–77.

Cunningham, David S. *Reading Is Believing: The Christian Faith through Literature and Film*. Grand Rapids, MI: Brazos, 2002.

Cupitt, Don. *What Is a Story?* London: SCM, 1991.

Curtis, Arthur H. *The Vision and Mission of Jesus: A Literary and Critical Investigation*. Edinburgh: T. & T. Clark, 1954.

Danker, Frederick William, et al., eds. *Greek-English Lexicon of the New Testament and Other Early Christian Literature*. Chicago: University of Chicago Press, 2000.

Danto, A. C. *Analytic Philosophy of History*. New York: Cambridge University Press, 1965.

————. *The Transfiguration of the Commonplace*. Cambridge, MA: Harvard University Press, 1983.

Davies, W. D., and Dale C. Allison. *A Critical and Exegetical Commentary on the Gospel According to Saint Matthew*. 3 vols. International Critical Commentary. Edinburgh: T. & T. Clark, 1987–1983.

de Diétrich, Suzanne. *Saint Matthew*. Layman's Bible Commentary 16. London: SCM, 1961.

de Voragine, Jacobus. *The Golden Legend: Readings on the Saints*. Translated by William Granger Ryan. Princeton, NJ: Princeton University Press, 1993.

de Wohl, Lloyd. *The Spear: A Novel of the Crucifixion*. San Francisco: Ignatius, 1955.

Derrida, Jacques. "The Law of Genre." In *Modern Genre Theory*, edited by David Duff, 219–31. Harlow, England: Longman, 2000.

Detweiler, Robert, and David Jasper, eds. *Religion and Literature: A Reader*. Louisville, KY: Westminster John Knox, 2000.

Dibelius, Martin. *From Tradition to Gospel*. Translated by Bertram Lee Woolf. London: Ivor Nicholson and Watson Limited, 1934.

Dillistone, F. W. *The Novelist and the Passion Story*. London: Collins, 1960.

————. *The Power of Symbols*. London: SCM, 1986.

Dodd, C. H. *The Interpretation of the Fourth Gospel*. Cambridge, England: Cambridge University Press, 1953.

Dolezel, Lubomír. "Fictional and Historical Narrative: Meeting the Postmodern Challenge." In *Narratologies*, edited by David Herman, 247–73. Columbus: Ohio State University Press, 1999.

Donaldson, Terence L. *Jesus on the Mountain: A Study in Matthean Theology*. Sheffield, England: JSOT Press, 1985.

————. "The Mockers and the Son of God (Matthew 27:37–44) Two Characters in Matthew's Story of Jesus." *Journal for the Study of the New Testament* 41 (1991) 3–18.

Dormandy, Richard. "Jesus' Temptations in Mark's Gospel: Mark 1:12–13." *Expository Times* 114 (2003) 183–87.

Dostoevsky, Fyodor. *The Brothers Karamazov*. Translated by Andrew R. MacAndrew. New York: Bantam Classics, 1970.

————. *Fyodor Doestoevsky Complete Letters*. Translated by David A. Lowe. Edited by David A. Lowe. Vol. 4. 1872–1877. Ann Arbor, MI: Ardis, 1988–1991.

Dowd, Sharyn. *Reading Mark: A Literary and Theological Commentary on the Second Gospel*. Reading the New Testament Series. Macon, GA: Smyth & Helwys, 2000.

Drury, John. "Mark." In *The Literary Guide to the Bible*, edited by Robert Alter, et al., 402–17. London Collins, 1987.

————. "Luke." In *The Literary Guide to the Bible*, edited by Robert Alter, et al., 418–39. London: Collins, 1987.

Duarte, J. F. "What Is It That Saramago Is Doing in *the Gospel According to Jesus Christ*? Rewriting the Gospels into Genre." Paper presented at the Proceedings of the 17th Triennial Congress of the International Comparative Literature Association, Hong Kong, August 8–15, 2004.

Duensing, H. "Epistula Apostolorum." In *New Testament Apocrypha*, edited by Edgar Hennecke, et al., 189–226. London: SCM, 1973.

Duff, David, ed. *Modern Genre Theory*. Harlow, England: Longman, 2000.

Dunn, James D. G. *Jesus Remembered: Christianity in the Making*. Vol. 1. Grand Rapids, MI: Eerdmans, 2003.

Edwards, Richard A. *Matthew's Story of Jesus*. Philadelphia: Fortress, 1985.

———. "Reading Matthew." *Listening* 24 (1989) 251–61.

Ehrman, Bart D. *Lost Christianities: The Battles for Scripture and the Faiths We Never Knew*. Oxford: Oxford University Press, 2003.

Ellingsen, Mark. *Integrity of Biblical Narrative: Story in Theology and Proclamation*. Minneapolis: Fortress, 1990.

Elliott, John H. "'Jesus the Israelite Was Neither a 'Jew' nor a 'Christian': On Correcting Misleading Nomenclature." *Journal for the Study of the Historical Jesus* 5, no. 2 (2007) 119–54.

Elliott, J. K. "Manuscripts, the Codex and the Canon." *Journal for the Study of the New Testament* 63 (1996) 105–23.

———. *A Synopsis of the Apocryphal Nativity and Infancy Narratives*. New Testament Tools and Studies 34. Boston: Brill, 2006.

Elliott, John R., and Graham A. Runnalls, eds. *The Baptism and Temptation of Christ: The First Day of a Medieval Passion Play*. New Haven, CT: Yale University Press, 1978.

Epiphanius. *The Panarion of Epiphanius of Salamis*. Translated by Frank Williams. Leiden, Netherlands: E. J. Brill, 1987.

Eusebius. *Ecclesiastical History*. In vol. 1 of *The Nicene and Post-Nicene Fathers*. Series 2. 1886–1889. 14 vols. Reprint, Peabody, MA: Hendrickson, 1994.

Evans, Craig A. *Fabricating Jesus: How Modern Scholars Distort the Gospels*. Downers Grove, IL: IVP, 2006.

———. "Images of Christ in the Canonical and Apocryphal Gospels." In *Images of Christ: Ancient and Modern*, edited by Stanley E. Porter, et al., 34–72. Sheffield, England: Sheffield Academic, 1997.

Evans, C. F. *Saint Luke*. TPI New Testament Commentaries. London: SCM, 1990.

Falk, Harvey. *Jesus the Pharisee: A New Look at the Jewishness of Jesus*. New York: Paulist, 1985.

Fenton, J. C. *Saint Matthew*. The Pelican New Testament Commentaries. Middlesex, England: Penguin, 1963.

Feuerbach, Ludwig. *The Essence of Christianity*. Translated by George Eliot. New York: Harper & Row, 1957.

Filson, Floyd V. *A Commentary on the Gospel According to St. Matthew*. London: Adams & Charles Black, 1960.

Fishbane, Michael. *Biblical Interpretation and Ancient Israel*. Oxford: Clarendon, 1985.

Fleming, Michael. "Rice Will Trace Faith: Good News Holdings Picks up Christian Bestseller." *Variety*, June 28, 2006. No pages. Online: http://www.variety.com/article/VR1117946109.

Fortney, Steven. *The Thomas Jesus*. Oregon, WI: Waubesa, 2000.

Fossum, Jarl. "Son of God." In *The Anchor Bible Dictionary*, edited by David Noel Freedman, 6:128–37. New York: Doubleday, 1992.

France, R. T. *The Gospel According to Matthew*. Tyndale New Testament Commentaries. Leicester, England: InterVarsity, 1985.

————. *The Gospel of Matthew*. New International Commentary on the New Testament. Grand Rapids, MI: Eerdmans, 2007.

Freedman, Jill, and Gene Combs. *Narrative Therapy: The Social Construction of Preferred Realities*. New York: Norton, 1996.

Frei, Hans. *The Eclipse of Biblical Narrative: A Study in Eighteenth and Nineteenth Century Hermeneutics*. New Haven, CT: Yale University Press, 1974.

————. *The Identity of Jesus Christ: The Hermeneutical Bases of Dogmatic Theology*. Philadelphia: Fortress, 1975.

Frier, David G. "José Saramago's 'O Evangelho Segundo Jesus Cristo': Outline of a Newer Testament." *The Modern Language Review* 100.2 (2005) 367–82.

Frow, John. *Genre*. London: Routledge, 2006.

Frye, Northrop. *Anatomy of Criticism: Four Essays*. Princeton, NJ: Princeton University Press, 1957.

Funk, Robert W. "The Issue of Jesus." *Forum* 1, no. 1 (1985) 7–12.

Funk, Robert W., and Roy W. Hoover. *The Five Gospels: The Search for the Authentic Words of Jesus*. New York: Macmillan, 1993.

Gallie, W. B. *Philosophy and the Historical Understanding*. New York: Schocken, 1968.

Gamble, Harry Y. *The New Testament Canon: Its Making and Meaning*. Philadelphia: Fortress, 1985.

Garland, David E. *Reading Matthew: A Literary and Theological Commentary*. Reading the New Testament Series. Macon, GA: Smyth & Helwys, 2001.

Gates, David. "The Gospel According to Anne." *Newsweek*, October 30, 2005. No pages. Online: http://www.thedailybeast.com/newsweek/2005/10/30/the-gospel-according-to-anne.html

Genette, Gérard. "The Architext." In *Modern Genre Theory*, edited by David Duff, 210–18. Harlow, England: Longman, 2000.

————. *Narrative Discourse*. Translated by Jane E. Lewin. Oxford: Basil Blackwell, 1980.

Gerhardsson, Birger. "Du Judéo-Christianisme a Jésus Par La Shema " *Recherches de Science Religieuse* 60 (1972) 23–36.

————. "Gottes Sohn Als Diener Gottes." *Studia Theologica* 27 (1973) 73–106.

————. *The Mighty Acts of Jesus According to Matthew*. Lund, Sweden: CWK Gleerup, 1979.

————. *The Testing of God's Son (Matt 4:1–11 & Par) An Analysis of an Early Christian Midrash*. Translated by John Toy. Lund, Sweden: CWK Gleerup, 1966.

Gibson, Jeffrey. "Jesus' Wilderness Temptation According to Mark." *Journal for the Study of the New Testament* 53 (1994) 3–34.

————. *The Temptations of Jesus in Early Christianity*, Journal for the Study of the New Testament: Supplement Series 112. Sheffield, England: Sheffield Academic, 1995.

————. "A Turning on Turning Stones to Bread: A New Understanding of the Devil's Intention in Q 4:3." *Biblical Research* 41 (1996) 37–57.

Gibson, John Monro. *The Gospel of St. Matthew*. London: Hodder & Stoughton, 1892.

Gibson, Walker. "Authors, Speakers, Readers, and Mock Readers." In *Reader-Response Criticism: From Formalism to Post-Structuralism*, edited by Jane P. Tompkins, 1–6. Baltimore: John Hopkins University Press, 1980.

Girzone, J. F. *Joshua: A Parable for Today*. Garden City, NY: Doubleday, 1994.

Gomez, Felipe. "Review of *the Hidden Years: A Novel About Jesus*." (1987). No pages. Cited May 11, 2009. Online: http://www.donghanh.org/main/diemsach/diemsach_06.htm.

Gompertz, Rolf. *My Jewish Brother Jesus: A Different Biblical Novel*. North Hollywood, CA: WorDoctor, 1977.

Gorbunov, Andrey N. "Christ's Temptation in the Wilderness (Milton and Dostoyevsky)." *Journal of Literature and Theology* 20 (2006) 46–62.

Goulder, M. D. *Midrash and Lection in Matthew*. London: SPCK, 1974.

Graham, David J. "Christ Imagery in Recent Film: A Savior from Celluloid?" In *Images of Christ: Ancient and Modern*, edited by Stanley E. Porter, et al., 305–14. Sheffield, England: Sheffield Academic, 1997.

Graham, Susan Lochrie. "A Strange Salvation: Intertextual Allusion in Mt 27,39–44." In *The Scriptures in the Gospels*, edited by C. M. Tuckett, 501–11. Leuven, Belgium: Leuven University Press, 1997.

Green, F. W. *The Gospel According to Saint Matthew*. Clarendon Bible. Oxford, England: Clarendon, 1936.

Green, Garrett. *Imagining God: Theology and the Religious Imagination*. Grand Rapids, MI: Eerdmans, 1989.

———. *Theology, Hermeneutics, and Imagination: The Crisis of Interpretation at the End of Modernity*. Cambridge, England: Cambridge University Press, 2000.

Green, H. Benedict. *The Gospel According to Matthew: In the Revised Standard Version*. New Clarendon Bible. Oxford, England: Oxford University Press, 1975.

Green, Joel B. *The Death of Jesus: Tradition and Interpretation in the Passion Narrative*. Tübingen, Germany: Mohr, 1988.

———. "The Gospel of Peter: Source for a Pre-Canonical Passion Narrative?" *Zeitschrift für die neutestamentliche Wissenschaft und die Kunde der* älteren *Kirche* 78.3–4 (1987) 293–301.

Green, William Scott. "Introduction: Messiah in Judaism: Rethinking the Question." In *Judaisms and Their Messiahs at the Turn of the Christian Era*, edited by Jacob Neusner, 1–13. Cambridge, England: Cambridge University Press, 1987.

Greene, Graham. *The Power and the Glory*. New York: Viking, 1940.

Gribben, Crawford. "Rapture Fictions and the Changing Evangelical Condition." *Journal of Literature and Theology* 18 (2004) 77–94.

Grimwood, Steven. "Iconography and Postmodernity." *Journal of Literature and Theology* 17 (2003) 76–97.

Grossman, Lev. "Junior Jesus: Anne Rice Fills in Some Gaps in the Gospels." *Time*, October 23, 2005. No pages. Online: http://www.time.com/time/magazine/article/0,9171,1122006,00.html.

Gundry, Robert H. *Matthew: A Commentary on His Literary and Theological Art*. Grand Rapids, MI: Eerdmans, 1982.

Gundry, Stanley N., ed. *Show Them No Mercy: 4 Views on God and Canaanite Genocide*. Grand Rapids, MI: Zondervan, 2003.

Gurbunov, Andrey N. "Christ's Temptations in the Wilderness." *Journal of Literature and Theology* 20 (2006) 46–62.

Hägg, Thomas. *The Novel in Antiquity*. Translated by Thomas Hägg. Worcester, MA: Basil Blackwell, 1983.

Hagner, Donald A. *Matthew*. 2 vols. Word Biblical Commentary 33. Dallas, TX: Word Books, 1993.

Harrington, Daniel J. *The Gospel of Matthew*. Sacra Pagina Series 1. Collegeville, MN: Liturgical, 1991.

Harshaw, Benjamin. "Fictionality and Fields of Reference." *Poetics Today* 5 (1984) 227–51.

Hart, R. L. *Unfinished Man and the Imagination*. New York: Seabury, 1979.

Hart, Trevor. "Imagination for the Kingdom of God?" In *God Will Be All in All: The Eschatology of Jürgen Moltmann*, edited by Richard Bauckham, 49–76. Minneapolis: Fortress, 1999.

———. *Regarding Karl Barth: Essays toward a Reading of His Theology*. Carlisle, England: Paternoster, 1999.

Hawking, Stephen. *Black Holes and Baby Universes and Other Essays*. New York: Bantam, 1993.

Hays, Richard. "Can Narrative Criticism Recover the Theological Unity of Scripture." *Journal for Theological Interpretation* 2.2 (2008) 193–211.

———. *The Conversion of the Imagination: Paul as Interpreter of Israel's Scripture*. Grand Rapids, MI: Eerdmans, 2005.

Hecht, Richard D. "Philo and Messiah." In *Judaisms and Their Messiahs at the Turn of the Christian Era*, edited by Jacob Neusner, 139–68. Cambridge, England: Cambridge University Press, 1987.

Hegesippus. *Concerning the Martyrdom of James, the Brother of the Lord*. Vol. 8, *The Ante-Nicene Fathers*. 1885–1887. Reprint, Peabody, MA.: Hedrickson, 1994.

———. *Concerning the Relatives of Our Saviour*. Vol. 8, *The Ante-Nicene Fathers*. 1885–1887. Reprint, Peabody, MA.: Hedrickson, 1994.

Heil, John Paul. *The Death and Resurrection of Jesus: A Narrative-Critical Reading of Matthew 26–28*. Minneapolis: Fortress, 1991.

Hendra, Tony. *The Messiah of Morris Avenue: A Novel*. New York: Henry Holt, 2006.

Hengel, Martin. *Crucifixion: In the Ancient World and the Folly of the Message of the Cross*. London: SCM, 1977.

———. *The Four Gospels and the One Gospel of Jesus Christ*. Translated by John Bowden. London: SCM, 2000.

Hester, David C. "Luke 4:1–13." *Interpretation* 31 (1997) 53–59.

Hill, David, ed. *The Gospel of Matthew*. New Century Bible. London: Oliphants, 1978.

Hoad, T. F., ed. *The Concise Oxford Dictionary of English Etymology*. Oxford, England: Clarendon, 1986.

Hock, Ronald F. "The Greek Novel." In *Greco-Roman Literature and the New Testament: Selected Forms and Genres*, edited by David E. Aune, 127–46. Atlanta: Scholars, 1988.

———. *The Infancy Gospels of James and Thomas: With Introduction, Notes, and Original Text Featuring the New Scholars Version Translation*. Santa Rosa, CA: Polebridge, 1995.

Hoffmann, R. Joseph, ed. *The Secret Gospels: A Harmony of Apocryphal Jesus Traditions*. Amherst, NY: Prometheus, 1996.

Holmes, Marjorie. *The Messiah*. New York: Guideposts, 1987.

———. *Three from Galilee: The Young Man from Nazareth*. New York: Harper & Row, 1985.

———. *Two from Galilee: The Story of Mary and Joseph*. New York: Bantam, 1972.

Hoshmand, Lisa Tsoi. "Narratology, Cultural Psychology, and Counseling Research." *Journal of Counseling Psychology* 52 (2005) 178–86.

Howell, D.B. *Matthew's Inclusive Story: A Study in the Narrative Rhetoric of the First Gospel*. Sheffield, England: JSOT Press, 1990.

Hughes, Barbara. "Review of *Christ the Lord: Out of Egypt* and *Christ the Lord: The Road to Cana.*" *Anglican Theological Review* 90.4 (2008) 833–34.

Hultgren, Stephen. *Narrative Elements in the Double Tradition*. Vol. 113. Berlin: Walter de Gruyter, 2002.

Humphrey, H. M. *The Relationship of Structure and Christology in the Gospel of Matthew*. New York: Fordham, 1977.

Humphrey, Richard. *The Historical Novel as Philosophy of History: Three German Contributions: Alexis, Fontane, Döblin*. Leeds, England: W. S. Maney & Son, 1986.

Hutton, Francis H. *A Series of Discourses on Christ's Temptation in the Wilderness: Delivered During the Season of Lent, 1833, in Trinity Church, St. Mary-Le-Bone: With Other Sermons*. London: Bowdery and Kerby, 1883.

Ignatius. *To the Philippians*. Vol. 1, *The Ante-Nicene Fathers*. 1885–1887. Reprint, Peabody, MA.: Hedrickson, 1994.

Ignelzi, Lenny. "Rice Takes Leap of Faith from Vampires to 'Christ.'" *USA Today*, November 2, 2005. No pages. Online: http://www.usatoday.com/life/books/reviews/2005-11-02-anne-rice_x.htm.

Infancy Gospel of Thomas. Translated by R. Mcl. Wilson. Edited by Edgar Hennecke, et al. 2nd ed. 2 vols. Vol. 1, *New Testament Apocrypha: Gospels and Related Writings*. London: SCM, 1973.

Irenaeus. *Adversus haereses*. Vol. 1, *The Ante-Nicene Fathers*. 1886–1889. Reprint, Peabody, MA: Hendrickson, 1994.

Iser, Wolfgang. *The Act of Reading: A Theory of Aesthetic Response*. London: Routledge & Kegan Paul, 1976.

James, Montague Rhodes. *The Apocryphal New Testament: Being the Apocryphal Gospels, Acts, Epistles, and Apocalypses*. Oxford, England: Clarendon, 1924.

Jasper, David. *The New Testament and the Literary Imagination*. Basingstoke, England: Macmillan, 1987.

———. *A Short Introduction to Hermeneutics*. Louisville, KY: Westminster John Knox, 2004.

Jasper, David, and Stephen Prickett. *The Bible and Literature: A Reader*. Oxford, England: Blackwell, 1998.

Jauhiainen, Marko. *The Use of Zechariah in Revelation*. Wissenschaftliche Untersuchungen zum Neuen Testament 2. Reihe 199. Tübingen, Germany: Mohr Siebeck, 2005.

Jenkins, Keith. *Re-Thinking History*. London: Routledge, 1991.

Jeremias, Joachim. *The Eucharistic Words of Jesus*. London: SCM, 1966.

———. *Jerusalem in the Time of Jesus: An Investigation into Economic and Social Conditions During the New Testament Period*. Translated by F. H. and C. H. Cave. London: SCM, 1962.

Jerome. *Epistulae*. Vol. 6, *The Nicene and Post-Nicene Fathers*. Series 2. 1886–1889. Reprint, Peabody, MA: Hendrickson, 1994.

John Cassian. *The Conferences of John Cassian*. Vol. 11, *The Nicene and Post-Nicene Fathers*. Series 2. 1886–1889. Reprint, Peabody, MA: Hendrickson, 1994.

———. *The Seven Books of John Cassian on the Incarnation of the Lord, Against Nestorius*. Vol. 11, *The Nicene and Post-Nicene Fathers*. Series 2. 1886–1889. Reprint, Peabody, MA: Hendrickson, 1994.

John Chrysostom. *Homiliae in epistualm ad Hebraeos*. Vol. 14, *The Nicene and Post-Nicene Fathers*. Series 1. 1886–1889. Reprint, Peabody, MA: Hendrickson, 1994.

———. *Homiliae in Matthaeum*. Vol. 10, *The Nicene and Post-Nicene Fathers*. Series 1. 1886–1889. Reprint, Peabody, MA: Hendrickson, 1994.

John of Damascus. *De Fide Orthodoxa*. Vol. 9, *The Nicene and Post-Nicene Fathers*. Series 2. 1886–1889. Reprint, Peabody, MA: Hendrickson, 1994.

Johnson, B. W. *People's NT*. No pages. Grand Rapids, MI: Christian Classics Ethereal Library, 2000. Online: http://www.ccel.org/ccel/johnson_bw/pnt.html.

Johnson, Luke Timothy. *The Real Jesus: The Misguided Quest for the Historical Jesus and the Truth of the Traditional Gospels*. San Francisco: HarperSanFrancisco, 1996.

———. *The Writings of the New Testament*. Philadelphia: SCM, 1986.

Johnson, Mark. *The Body in the Mind: The Bodily Basis of Meaning, Imagination, and Reason*. Chicago: University of Chicago Press, 1987.

Jones, Ivor H. *The Gospel of Matthew*. Epworth Commentaries. London: Epworth, 1994.

Josephus. Translated by H. St. J. Thackeray et. al. 10 vols. Loeb Classical Library. Cambridge, MA: Harvard University Press, 1926–65.

Josselson, Ruthellen, Amia Lieblich, and Dan P. McAdams. *Up Close and Personal: The Teaching and Learning of Narrative Research*. Washington, DC: American Psychological Association, 2003.

Justin Martyr. *Dialogus cum Tryphone*. Vol. 1, *The Ante-Nicene Fathers*. 1885–1887. Reprint, Peabody, MA.: Hedrickson, 1994.

Kähler, Martin. *The So-Called Historical Jesus and the Historic Biblical Christ*. Translated by Carl E. Braaten. Philadelphia: Fortress, 1964.

Kammler, Hans Christian. "Sohn Gottes Und Kreuz: Die Versuchungs-Geschichte Mt. 4,1–11 Im Kontext Des Matthäusevangeliums." *Zeitschrift für Theologie und Kirche* 100 (2003) 163–86.

Kaneshiro, Vanessa. "10 Questions for Anne Rice" *Time*, May 27, 2009. Online: http://www.time.com/time/video/player/0,32068,1446813083_1722024,00.html.

Kant, Immanuel. *Critique of Pure Reason*. Translated by Norman Kemp Smith. New York: St Martin's, 1968.

Kazantzakis, Nikos. *The Last Temptation of Christ*. Translated by P. A. Bien. New York: Simon & Schuster, 1998.

Kearney, R. *The Wake of the Imagination*. London: Routledge, 1994.

Keck, L. E. *A Future for the Historical Jesus*. Philadelphia: Fortress, 1981.

Keen, Suzanne. *Narrative Form*. New York: Palgrave Macmillan, 2003.

Keener, Craig S. *A Commentary on the Gospel of Matthew*. Grand Rapids, MI: Eerdmans, 1999.

Kelly, Balmer H. "Exposition of Matthew 4:1–11." *Interpretation* 29 (1975) 57–62.

Kelly, H. A. "The Devil in the Desert." *Catholic Biblical Quarterly* 26 (1964) 190–220.

Kermode, Frank. "Introduction to the New Testament." In *The Literary Guide to the Bible*, edited by Robert Alter and Frank Kermode, 375–86. London: Collins, 1987.

———. "John." In *The Literary Guide to the Bible*, edited by Robert Alter, et al., 440–66. London: Collins, 1987.

———. "Matthew." In *The Literary Guide to the Bible*, edited by Robert Alter et al., 387–401. London: Collins, 1987.

Kingsbury, Jack Dean. *Conflict in Luke: Jesus, Authorities, Disciples*. Minneapolis: Fortress, 1991.

———. "The Gospel in Four Editions." *Interpretation* 33.4 (1979) 363–75.

————. *Matthew: A Commentary for Preachers and Others*. Proclamation commentaries. London: SPCK, 1978.

————. *Matthew as Story*. 2nd ed. Philadelphia: Fortress, 1988.

————. *Matthew: Structure, Christology, Kingdom*. London: SPCK, 1975.

————. "The Plot of Matthew's Story." *Interpretation* 46 (1992) 347–56.

Kirk, J. Andrew. "The Messianic Role of Jesus and the Temptation Narrative: A Contemporary Perspective." *Evangelical Quarterly* 44 (1972) 11–29.

Kittel, G., and G. Friedrich, eds. *Theological Dictionary of the New Testament*. 10 vols. Grand Rapids, MI: Eerdmans, 1964–1976.

Klauck, Hans-Josef. *Apocryphal Gospels: An Introduction*. London: T. & T. Clark, 2003.

Klobucka, Anna. "Bibliography of José Saramago." *Portuguese Literary & Cultural Studies* (2001) 271–77.

————. "An Interview with Nobel Prize-Winning Portuguese Novelist José Saramago." *Mass Humanities*, Spring (2002). No pages. Online: http://www.masshumanities. org/s02_wp.

————. "Introduction: Saramago's World." *Portuguese Literary & Cultural Studies* (2001) xi–xxii.

Knight, Henry Joseph Corbett. *The Temptation of Our Lord: Considered as Related to the Ministry and as a Revelation of His Person: The Hulsean Lectures 1905–6*. London: Longmans, Green, 1907.

Koester, Helmut. *Ancient Christian Gospels: Their History and Development*. London: SCM, 1990.

Kort, Wesley A. "Narrative and Theology." *Journal of Literature and Theology* 1 (1987) 27–38.

————. *Narrative Elements and Religious Meanings*. Philadelphia: Fortress, 1982.

————. "'Religion and Literature' in Postmodernist Contexts." *Journal of the American Academy of Religion* 58 (1990) 575–88.

————. *Shriven Selves: Religious Problems in Recent American Fiction*. Philadelphia: Fortress, 1972.

————. *Story, Text, and Scripture: Literary Interests in Biblical Narrative*. University Park, PA: Pennsylvania State University Press, 1988.

————. *"Take, Read": Scripture, Textuality, and Cultural Practice*. University Park, PA: Pennsylvania State University Press, 1996.

Kreitzer, Larry J. *The New Testament in Fiction and Film: On Reversing the Hermeneutical Flow*. Sheffield, England: JSOT Press, 1993.

Kugel, James L. *In Potiphar's House: The Interpretive Life of Biblical Texts*. Cambridge. MA: Harvard University Press, 1994.

Kuhn, Thomas. *The Structure of Scientific Revolutions*. Chicago: University of Chicago Press, 1970.

Kumai, Hidenori (Script Writer), Kozumi Shinozawa (Artist), Atsuko Ogawa (Assistant Artist), Chihaya Tsutsum (Art Director), Kenichi Nakagawa (Supervisor), and Toshikazu Iwaoka (Coordinator). *Manga Messiah*. Wheaton, IL: Tyndale House, 2006.

Kuo, David. "Jesus: The Ultimate Supernatural Hero." *Beliefnet*, November 2005. No pages. Online: http://www.beliefnet.com/Faiths/Christianity/2005/11/Jesus-The-Ultimate-Supernatural-Hero.aspx.

Langenhorst, George. "The Rediscovery of Jesus as a Literary Figure." *Journal of Literature and Theology* 9 (1995) 85–98.

Lapham, Fred. *An Introduction to the New Testament Apocrypha*. London: T. & T. Clark, 2003.

Lawrence, D. H. *The Man Who Died*. Middlesex, England: Penguin, 1979.

Leo the Great. *Sermons*. Vol. 12, *The Nicene and Post-Nicene Fathers*. Series 2. 1886–1889. Reprint, Peabody, MA: Hendrickson, 1994.

Lepakhin, Valerii. "Basic Types of Correlation between Text and Icon, between Verbal and Visual Icons." *Journal of Literature and Theology* 20 (2006) 20–30.

Levi, A. H. T. "The Relationship between Literature and Theology: An Historical Reflection." *Journal of Literature and Theology* 1 (1987) 11–18.

Lewis, C. S. *The Allegory of Love: A Study in Medieval Tradition*. Oxford, England: Oxford University Press, 1936.

———. *The Chronicles of Narnia*. New York: HarperCollins, 2001.

———. *The Collected Letters of C. S. Lewis*. Vol. 2. Edited by Walter Hooper. San Francisco: HarperSanFrancisco, 2004.

Liddell, Henry George, and Robert Scott, eds. *A Greek-English Lexicon*. Oxford: Clarendon, 1996.

Lightfoot, John. "From the Talmud and Hebraica." Grand Rapids, MI: Christian Classics Ethereal Library, 2003.

Little, William, H., Wh. Fowler, and Jessie Coulson, eds. *The Shorter Oxford English Dictionary: On Historical Principles*. 3rd ed. Vol. 3. Oxford, England: Clarendon, 1973.

Loader, William. *The New Testament with Imagination: A Fresh Approach to Its Writings and Themes*. Grand Rapids, MI: Eerdmans, 2007.

Lohr, C. H. "Oral Techniques in the Gospel of Matthew." *Catholic Biblical Quarterly* 23 (1961) 403–35.

Longenecker, Bruce W. "Evil at Odds with Itself (Matthew 12:22–29) Demonising Rhetorics and Deconstructive Potential in the Matthean Narrative." *Biblical Interpretation* 11 (2003) 503–14.

———. "'What God Wants, God Gets, God Help Us All': The 'Hopeless' God of Saramago's *the Gospel According to Jesus Christ*." In *Patterns of Promise: Art, Imagination and Christian Hope*. St. Andrews: 2006.

Longfellow, Henry Wadsworth. *Christus: A Mystery*. No pages. Online: http://www.everypoet.com/archive//poetry/Henry_Wadsworth_Longfellow/longfellow_christus_1_2_mount_quarantania.htm.

Lövestam, Evald. *Son and Saviour: A Study of Acts 13, 32–37. With an Appendix: 'Son of God' in the Synoptic Gospels*. Lund and Copenhagen: C.W.K. Gleerup, 1961.

Lust, J., E. Eynikel, and K. Hauspie, eds. *A Greek-English Lexicon of the Septuagint*. Stuttgart, Germany: Deutsche Bibelgesellschaft, 1996.

Luz, Ulrich. *Matthew 1–7: A Commentary*. Translated by Wilhelm C. Linss. Hermeneia: A Critical and Historical Commentary on the Bible. Edinburgh: T. & T. Clark, 1989.

———. *Matthew 21–28: A Commentary*. Translated by James E. Crouch. Hermeneia: A Critical and Historical Commentary on the Bible. Minneapolis: Fortress, 2005.

———. *Studies in Matthew*. Grand Rapids, MI: Eerdmans, 2005.

———. *The Theology of the Gospel of Matthew*. Translated by J. Bradford Robinson. Cambridge: Cambridge University Press, 1995.

MacDonald, George. *Dish of Orts, Chiefly Papers on the Imagination, and on Shakespeare*. London: Sampson Low Marston, 1893.

————. "The Temptation in the Wilderness." In *Unspoken Sermons*. Grand Rapids, MI: Christian Classics Ethereal Library, 2003.

MacDonald, John, and A. J. B. Higgins. "The Beginnings of Christianity According to the Samaritans." *New Testament Studies* 18 (1971) 54–80.

Mack, Burton L. "Wisdom Makes a Difference: Alternatives to 'Messianic' Configurations." In *Judaisms and Their Messiahs at the Turn of the Christian Era*, edited by Jacob Neusner, 15–48. Cambridge, England: Cambridge University Press, 1987.

MacLeod, Norman. *The Temptation of Our Lord*. London: Strahan, 1873.

Mailer, Norman. *The Gospel According to the Son*. London: Little, Brown, 1997.

Malina, Bruce J. "Honor and Shame: Pivotal Values of the First-Century Mediterranean World." In *The New Testament World: Insights from Cultural Anthropology.*, 27–56. Louisville, KY: Westminister John Knox, 2001.

Malina, Bruce, and Richard L. Rohrbaugh. *Social Science Commentary on the Synoptic Gospels*. Minneapolis: Fortress, 1992.

Margolin, Uri. "Reference, Coreference, Referring, and the Dual Structure of Literary Narrative." *Poetics Today* 12 (1991) 517–42.

Marrou, Henri I. *The Meaning of History*. Translated by Robert J. Olson. Baltimore: Helicon, 1954.

Marshall, I. Howard. *Biblical Inspiration*. Grand Rapids, MI: Eerdmans, 1982.

————. *The Gospel of Luke: A Commentary on the Greek Text*. The New International Greek Testament Commentary. Exeter, England: Paternoster, 1978.

Marx, Karl. *Critique of Hegel's 'Philosophy of Right'*. Translated by Annette Jolin and Joseph O'Malley. Cambridge, England: Cambridge University Press, 1970.

Maslin, Janet. "A Boy Tells of Angels, Bethlehem and Family." *New York Times*, November 3, 2005. No pages. Online: http://www.nytimes.com/2005/11/03/books/03masl.html?ex=1160798400&en=bc082e73c0305687&ei=5070.

Maslow, Abraham H. *Motivation and Personality*. 3rd ed. New York: Harper & Row, 1987.

Maurer, Christian. "The Gospel of Peter." In *New Testament Apocrypha*, edited by Edgar Hennecke, et al., 179–87. London: SCM, 1973.

Mauser, Ulrich. *Christ in the Wilderness: The Wilderness Theme in the Second Gospel and Its Basis in the Biblical Tradition*. London: SCM, 1963.

May, John R. *Nourishing Faith through Fiction: Reflections of the Apostles' Creed in Literature and Film*. Franklin, WI: Sheed & Ward, 2001.

McCant, Jerry W. "The Gospel of Peter: The Docetic Question Re-Examined." PhD diss., Emory University, 1978.

McGarvey, J. W. and Philip Y. Pendleton "Jesus Tempted in the Wilderness: Matt. IV.1–11; Mark I.12, 13; Luke IV.1–13." In *The Four-Fold Gospel*. No pages. Grand Rapids, MI: Christian Classics Ethereal Library, 2003. Online: http://www.ccel.org/m/mcgarvey/ffg/FFG019.HTM.

McIntyre, John. *Faith, Theology and Imagination*. Edinburgh: Handsel, 1987.

McVann, Mark. "One of the Prophets: Matthew's Testing Narrative as a Rite of Passage." *Biblical Theology Bulletin* 23 (1993) 14–20.

Mealand, David L. *Poverty and Expectations in the Gospels*. London: SPCK, 1980.

Meier, John P. *A Marginal Jew: Rethinking the Historical Jesus*. Vol. 1. New York: Doubleday, 1991.

———. "On Retrojecting Later Questions from Later Texts: A Reply to Richard Bauckham." *Catholic Biblical Quarterly* 59 (1997) 511–27.

Merenlahti, Petri. "Reading as a Little Child: On the Model Reader of the Gospels." *Journal of Literature and Theology* 18 (2004) 139–52.

Metzger, Bruce M. *The Canon of the New Testament: Its Origin, Development, and Significance*. Oxford, England: Clarendon, 1987.

———. "Names for the Nameless in the New Testament: A Study in the Growth of Christian Tradition." In *Kyriakon: Festschrift Johanees Quasten*, edited by Patrick Granfield and Josef A. Jungmann, 79–99. Münster, Germany: Verlag Aschendorff, 1970.

Meyer, Gabriel. *In the Shade of the Terebinth: Tales of a Night Journey*. Leavenworth, KS: Forest of Peace, 1994.

———. "Rice Weaves Rich Tale of a Young Jesus." *JewishJournal.com*, November 24, 2005. No pages. Online: http://www.jewishjournal.com/arts/article/rice_weaves_rich_tale_of_a_young_jesus_20051125/.

Meyer, Marvin. *The Gnostic Discoveries: The Impact of the Nag Hammadi Library*. San Francisco: HarperSanFrancisco, 2005.

Miller, George. *The Temptations of Jesus Christ in the Wilderness Explained as Symbolically Representing the Trials of the Christian Church*. London: C. and J. Rivington, 1826.

Minear, Paul S. *Matthew: The Teacher's Gospel*. London: Darton, Longman & Todd, 1982.

Moberly, R. W. L. "Did the Serpent Get It Right?" *Journal of Theological Studies* 39 (1988) 1–27.

———. *From Eden to Golgotha: Essays in Biblical Theology*. Atlanta: Scholars, 1992.

Moo, Douglas J. *The Old Testament in the Gospel Passion Narratives*. Sheffield, England: Almond, 1983.

Moore, Christopher. *Lamb: The Gospel According to Biff, Christ's Childhood Pal*. New York: Perennial, 2002.

Moore, Stephen. *Literary Criticism and the Gospels: The Theoretical Challenge*. New Haven, CT: Yale University Press, 1989.

Morgan, J. R. "Make-Believe and Make Believe: The Fictionality of the Greek Novels." In *Lies and Fiction in the Ancient World*, edited by Christopher Gill et al., 175–229. Exeter, England: University of Exeter Press, 1993.

Morgan, Robert. "The Hermeneutical Significance of Four Gospels." *Interpretation* 33 (1979) 376–88.

Moring, Mark. "Out of Egypt Scrapped." *Christianity Today*, August 28, 2007. No pages. Online: http://www.christianitytoday.com/movies/news/christthelord.html.

Morris, Leon. *The Gospel According to Matthew*. Pillar New Testament Commentary. Grand Rapids, MI: Eerdmans, 1992.

Murphy-O'Connor, Jerome. "Triumph over Temptation." *Bible Review* 15 (1999) 34–43.

Nelson-Pallmeyer, Jack. *Jesus Against Christianity: Reclaiming the Missing Jesus*. Harrisburg, PA: Trinity, 2001.

Neufeld, Dietmar. "Imagining Jesus Then and Now: Nino Ricci's *Testament*." In *Jesus in Twentieth-Century Literature, Art, and Movies*, edited by Paul C. Burns, 19–35. New York: Continuum, 2007.

Nichols, Stephen G. "Foreword." In *Fictional Truth*, edited by Michael Riffaterre, vi–x. Baltimore: John Hopkins University Press, 1990.

Nickelsburg, George W. E. "The Genre and Function of the Markan Passion Narrative." *Harvard Theological Review* 73 (1980) 153–84.

———. "Salvation Without and With a Messiah: Developing Beliefs in Writings Ascribed to Enoch." In *Judaisms and Their Messiahs at the Turn of the Christian Era*, edited by Jacob Neusner, 49–68. Cambridge, England: Cambridge University Press, 1987.

Nolan, Steve. "The Books of the Films: Trends in Religious Film-Analysis." *Journal of Literature and Theology* 12 (1998) 1–15.

Nolland, John. *The Gospel of Matthew: A Commentary on the Greek Text*, The New International Greek Testament Commentary. Grand Rapids, MI: Eerdmans, 2005.

Nussbaum, Martha C. *Love's Knowledge*. New York: Oxford University Press, 1990.

Oegema, Gerbern S. *The Anointed and His People: Messianic Expectations from the Maccabees to Bar Kochba*. Sheffield, England: Sheffield Academic, 1998.

Origen. *Commentarii in evangelium Joannis*. Vol. 9, *The Ante-Nicene Fathers*. 1885–1887. Reprint, Peabody, MA.: Hedrickson, 1994.

———. *Commentarii in evangelium Matthaei*. Vol. 9, *The Ante-Nicene Fathers*. 1885–1887. Reprint, Peabody, MA.: Hedrickson, 1994.

———. *Contra Celsum*. Vol. 4, *The Ante-Nicene Fathers*. 1885–1887. Reprint, Peabody, MA.: Hedrickson, 1994.

The Oxford Dictionary of Quotations. 3rd ed. Oxford: Oxford University Press, 1979.

Pattison, George. "Idol or Icon? Some Principles of an Aesthetic Christology." *Journal of Literature and Theology* 3 (1989) 1–15.

Pearsall, Judy, ed. *The New Oxford Dictionary of English*. Oxford: Clarendon, 1998.

Perrin, Norman. *Rediscovering the Teaching of Jesus*. London: SCM, 1967.

Perry, M. "Literary Dynamics: How the Order of a Text Creates Its Meaning." *Poetics Today* 1 (1979–1980) 35–64, 311–64.

Petersen, William L. "Textual Evidence of Tatian's Dependence Upon Justin's Apomnhmoneumata." *New Testament Studies* 36 (1990) 512–34.

———, ed. *Gospel Traditions in the Second Century: Origins, Recensions, Text, and Transmission*. Notre Dame, IN: University of Notre Dame Press, 1989.

Pfefferman, Naomi. "Revelation Led Rice to Pen Jesus Novel." *Jewish Journal*, November 24, 2005. No pages. Online: http://www.jewishjournal.com/arts/article/revelation_led_rice_to_pen_jesus_novel_20051125/.

Plate, S. Brent. "Religion/Literature/Film: Toward a Religious Visuality of Film Literature and Theology." *Journal of Literature and Theology* 12 (1998) 16–38.

Poovey, W. A. *The Power of the Kingdom: Meditations on Matthew*. Minneapolis: Augsburg, 1974.

Poulet, Georges. "Criticism and the Experience of Interiority." In *Reader-Response Criticism: From Formalism to Post-Structuralism*, edited by Jane P. Tompkins, 41–49. Baltimore: John Hopkins University Press, 1980.

Powell, Mark A. "Narrative Criticism." In *Hearing the New Testament*, edited by Joel B. Green, 239–55. Grand Rapids, MI: Eerdmans, 1995.

———. "Toward a Narrative-Critical Understanding of Matthew." *Interpretation* 46 (1992) 341–46.

———. *What Is Narrative Criticism?* London: SPCK, 1993.

Protoevangelium of James. Vol. 1, *New Testament Apocrypha: Gospels and Related Writings*. Translated by R. Mcl. Wilson. Edited by Edgar Hennecke, et al. 2nd ed. London: SCM, 1973.

Pseudo-Clementine. *The Clementine Homilies*. Vol. 8, *The Ante-Nicene Fathers*. 1885–1887. Reprint, Peabody, MA.: Hedrickson, 1994.

―――. *The Recognitions of Clement*. Vol. 8, *The Ante-Nicene Fathers*. 1885–1887. Reprint, Peabody, MA.: Hedrickson, 1994.

Puech, Henri-Charles. "Gnostic Gospels and Related Documents." In *New Testament Apocrypha*, edited by Edgar Hennecke, et al., 231–362. London: SCM, 1973.

Pullman, Philip. *The Good Man Jesus and the Scoundrel Christ*. Edinburgh: Canongate, 2010.

Pyper, Hugh S. "Modern Gospels of Judas: Canon and Betrayal." *Journal of Literature and Theology* 15 (2001) 111–22.

Querdray, Georges. "La Tentation De Jésus Au Désert: Prélude De La Passion." *Esprit et Vie* 90 (1980) 184–89.

Rae, Murray. *History and Hermeneutics*. London: T. & T. Clark, 2005.

Ranke, Leopold von. *The Theory and Practice of History*. Translated by Wilma A. Iggers and Konrad von Moltke. Edited by Georg G. Iggers and Konrad von Moltke. New York: Irvington, 1983.

Reinhartz, Adele. "'Rewritten Gospel': The Case of Caiaphas the High Priest." *New Testament Studies* 55 (2009) 160–78.

Reynolds, David S. *Faith in Fiction: The Emergence of Religious Literature in America*. Cambridge, MA: Harvard University Press, 1981.

Ricci, Nino. "Nino Ricci's official website." No pages. Online: http://ninoricci.com.

―――. "An Interview with Nino Ricci." *Houghton Mifflin Harcourt*. Online: http://www.houghtonmifflinbooks.com/readers_guides/ricci_testament.shtml.

―――. *Testament*. New York: Houghton Mifflin, 2002.

Rice, Anne. *Christ the Lord: Out of Egypt: A Novel*. New York: Alfred A. Knopf, 2005.

―――. *Christ the Lord: The Road to Cana: A Novel*. London: Chatto & Windus, 2008.

―――. "A Conversation with Anne Rice." *Random House, Inc.*, 2008. Online: http://www.randomhouse.com/catalog/display.pperl?isbn=9780375412011&view=auqa.

―――. "Note to the Paperback Edition." In *Christ the Lord: Out of Egypt: A Novel*. New York: Ballantine, 2006.

Ricoeur, Paul. *Figuring the Sacred: Religion, Narrative, and Imagination*. Translated by David Pellauer. Edited by Mark I. Wallace. Minneapolis: Fortress, 1995.

―――. *Memory, History, Forgetting*. Translated by Kathleen Blamey and David Pellauer. Chicago: University of Chicago Press, 2004.

―――. "Narrative Time." *Critical Inquiry* 7 (1980) 169–90.

―――. *Time and Narrative*. Translated by Kathleen McLaughlin and David Pellauer. 2 vols. Chicago: University of Chicago Press, 1983–85.

Riddle, M.B. "Introductory Notice to Apocrypha of the New Testament." Vol. 8 of *The Ante-Nicene Fathers*. 1885–1887. 10 vols. Reprint, Peabody, MA.: Hedrickson, 1994.

Riffaterre, Michael. *Fictional Truth*. Baltimore: John Hopkins University Press, 1990.

Robinson, J. A. T. *The Priority of John*. Oak Park, IL: Meyer-Stone, 1985.

Robinson, Theodore H. *The Gospel of Matthew*. Moffat New Testament Commentary 1. London: Hodder & Stoughton, 1928.

Ronen, Ruth. *Possible Worlds in Literary Theory*. Cambridge, England: Cambridge University Press, 1994.

Runia, David T. "Philo, Alexandrian and Jew." In *Exegesis and Philosophy: Studies on Philo of Alexandria*, 1–18. Aldershot, UK: Variorum, 1990.

Sanders, E. P. *The Historical Figure of Jesus*. London: Penguin, 1993.

———. *Jesus and Judaism*. Philadelphia: Fortress, 1985.

———. *The Tendencies of the Synoptic Tradition*. Cambridge, England: Cambridge University Press, 1969.

Saramago, José. *The Gospel According to Jesus Christ*. San Diego: Harcourt Brace & Co., 1991.

———. "Is It Time to Return to the Author? Between Omniscient Narrator and Interior Monologue." *CLCWeb: Comparative Literature and Culture: A WWWeb Journal* (2000). Online: http://docs.lib.purdue.edu/clcweb/vol2/iss3/1/.

———. "The 1998 Nobel Lecture." *World Literature Today* 73, no. 1 (1999) 5.

Sauter, Gerhard, and John Barton, eds. *Revelation and Story: Narrative Theology and the Centrality of Story*. Aldershot, UK: Ashgate, 2000.

Sayers, Dorothy. *The Devil to Pay (a Faustian Drama)*. Noroton, CT: Vineyard, 1977.

———. *The Man Born to Be King*. London: Victor Gollancz, 1946.

Schneemelcher, Wilhelm. "General Introduction." In *New Testament Apocrypha*, edited by Edgar Hennecke, et al., 19–68. London: SCM, 1973.

———. "The Gospel of the Egyptians." In *New Testament Apocrypha*, edited by Edgar Hennecke, et al., 166–78. London: SCM, 1973.

———. "Gospels: Non-Biblical Material About Jesus." In *New Testament Apocrypha*, edited by Edgar Hennecke, et al., 69–84. London: SCM, 1973.

Scholes, Robert. *Semiotics and Interpretation*. New Haven, CT: Yale University Press, 1982.

———. *Textual Power: Literary Theory and the Teaching of English*. New Haven, CT: Yale University Press, 1985.

Schweitzer, Albert. *The Quest of the Historical Jesus: A Critical Study of Its Progress from Reimarus to Wrede*. Translated by W. Montgomery. London: Adam & Charles Black, 1910.

Schweizer, Eduard. *The Good News According to Matthew*. Translated by David E. Green. London: SPCK, 1982.

Searle, John. "The Logical Status of Fictional Discourse." *New Literary History* 6 (1975) 319–32.

Seibert, Eric A. *Disturbing Divine Behavior: Troubling Old Testament Images of God*. Minneapolis: Fortress, 2009.

Senior, Donald. *The Gospel of Matthew*, Interpreting Biblical Texts. Nashville, TN: Abingdon, 1997.

———. *The Passion Narrative According to Matthew: A Redactional Study*. Louvain, Belgium: Leuven University Press, 1975.

———. *The Passion of Jesus in the Gospel of Matthew*. Wilmington, DE: Michael Glazier, 1985.

Shelton, Jo-Ann. *As the Romans Did: A Sourcebook in Roman Social History*. 2nd ed. Oxford, England: Oxford University Press, 1998.

Smith, James K. A. "Staging the Incarnation: Revisioning Augustine's Critique of Theatre." *Journal of Literature and Theology* 15 (2001) 123–29.

Smith, Morton. *Jesus the Magician*. San Francisco: Harper & Row, 1978.

Stanford, Michael. *An Introduction to the Philosophy of History*. Oxford: Blackwell, 1998.

Stanton, Graham N. *A Gospel for a New People: Studies in Matthew*. Edinburgh: T. & T. Clark, 1992.

———. *The Gospels and Jesus*. Oxford, England: Oxford University Press, 2002.

———. *Jesus and the Gospel*. Cambridge, England: Cambridge University Press, 2004.

Stanzel, F. K. *A Theory of Narrative*. Translated by Charlotte Goedsche. Cambridge, England: Cambridge University Press, 1984.

Stegemann, Ekkehard W., and Wolfgang Stegemann. *The Jesus Movement: A Social History of Its First Century*. Translated by O. C. Dean, Jr. Minneapolis: Fortress, 1999.

Stegner, William Richard. *Narrative Theology in Early Jewish Christianity*. Louisville, KY: Westminister John Knox, 1989.

———. "The Temptation Narrative: A Study in the Use of Scripture by Early Jewish Christians." *Biblical Research* 35 (1989) 5–17.

Sternberg, Meir. *The Poetics of Biblical Narrative: Ideological Literature and the Drama of Reading*. Bloomington, IN: Indiana University Press, 1985.

Strange, James F. "First Century Galilee from Archaeology and from the Texts." In *Archaeology and the Galilee*, edited by Douglas R. Edwards and C. Thomas McCollough, 39–48. Atlanta: Scholars, 1997.

Strauss, David Friedrich. *The Life of Jesus Critically Examined*. Translated by George Eliot. London: SCM, (1835) 1973.

Struever, Nancy S. "Topics in History." *History and Theory* 19 (1980) 66–79.

Sykes, S. W. "The Role of Story in the Christian Religion: An Hypothesis." *Journal of Literature and Theology* 1 (1987) 19–26.

Talbert, Charles H. "The Gospel and the Gospels." *Interpretation* 33 (1979) 351–62.

———. "Once Again: Gospel Genre." *Semia* 43 (1988) 53–73.

———. *What Is a Gospel? The Genre of the Canonical Gospels*. Philadelphia: Fortress, 1977.

———, ed. *Reimarus: Fragments*. Philadelphia: Fortress, 1970.

Talmon, Shemaryahu. "Waiting for the Messiah: The Spiritual Universe of the Qumran Covenanters." In *Judaisms and Their Messiahs at the Turn of the Christian Era*, edited by Jacob Neusner, 111–37. Cambridge, England: Cambridge University Press, 1987.

Tannehill, Robert C. "Narrative Criticism." In *A Dictionary of Biblical Interpretation*, edited by R. J. Coggins and J. L. Houlden, 488–89. London: SCM, 1990.

Tatian. *Diatessaron*. Vol. 9, *The Ante-Nicene Fathers*. 1885–1887. Reprint, Peabody, MA: Hedrickson, 1994.

Taylor, N. H. "The Temptation of Jesus on the Mountain: A Palestinian Christian Polemic against Agrippa I." *Journal for the Study of the New Testament* 83 (2001) 27–49.

Telford, W. R. "The New Testament in Fiction and Film: A Biblical Scholar's Perspective." In *Words Remembered, Texts Renewed*, edited by Jon Davies, et al., 360–94. Sheffield, England: Sheffield Academic Press, 1995.

Tertullian. *Adversus Praxean*. Vol. 3, *The Ante-Nicene Fathers*. 1885–1887. Reprint, Peabody, MA.: Hedrickson, 1994.

———. *De baptismo*. Vol. 3, *The Ante-Nicene Fathers*. 1885–1887. Reprint,Peabody, MA.: Hedrickson, 1994.

———. *De resurrectione carnis*. Vol. 3, *The Ante-Nicene Fathers*. 1885–1887. Reprint, Peabody, MA.: Hedrickson, 1994.

———. *Scorpiace*. Vol. 3, *The Ante-Nicene Fathers*. 1885–1887. Reprint, Peabody, MA.: Hedrickson, 1994.

Tesser, Carmen Chaves. "A Tribute to Jose Saramago, 1998 Nobel Literature Laureate." *Hispania* 82, no. 1 (1999) 1–28.

Theissen, Gerd. *The Gospels in Context: Social and Political History in the Synoptic Tradition*. Translated by Linda M. Maloney. Minneapolis: Fortress, 1991.

———. *The Shadow of the Galilean: The Quest of the Historical Jesus in Narrative Form*. Translated by John Bowden. Philadelphia: Fortress, 1987.

Thiselton, Anthony C. *New Horizons and Hermeneutics*. London: HarperCollins, 1992.

———. *The Two Horizons: New Testament Hermeneutics and Philosophical Description with Special Reference to Heidegger, Bultmann, Gadamar, and Wittgenstein*. Grand Rapids, MI: Eerdmans, 1980.

Thoene, Bodie, and Brock Thoene. *The Jerusalem Scrolls*. New York: Penguin, 2001.

———. *Jerusalem's Hope*. New York: Penguin, 2002.

———. *The Stones of Jerusalem*. New York: Penguin, 2002.

Thomas, Kazen. "Sectarian Gospels for Some Christians? Intention and Mirror Reading in the Light of Extra-Canonical Texts." *New Testament Studies* 51 (2005) 561–78.

Thompson, Michael B. *Clothed with Christ: The Example and Teaching of Jesus in Romans 12.1–15.13*. Sheffield, England: Sheffield Academic, 1991.

Tierney, Robert J., Patricia L. Anders, and Judy Nichols Mitchell. *Understanding Readers' Understanding: Theory and Practice*. Hillsdale, NJ: L. Erlbaum Associates, 1987.

Tillich, Paul. *Systematic Theology*. 3 vols. Welwyn, England: Nisbet, 1968.

Tippens, Darryl. "'The Passionate Pursuit of the Real': Christianity and Literature in Our Time." *Christianity and Literature* 54 (2004).

Todorov, Tzvetan. "The Origin of Genres." In *Modern Genre Theory*, edited by David Duff, 193–209. Harlow, England: Longman, 2000.

Tolkien, J. R. R. *Tree and Leaf*. London: Grafton, 1988.

Tompkins, Jane P. "An Introduction to Reader-Response Criticism." In *Reader-Response Criticism: From Formalism to Post-Structuralism*, edited by Jane P. Tompkins, ix–xxvi. Baltimore: John Hopkins University Press, 1980.

———. "The Reader in History: The Changing Shape of Literary Response." In *Reader-Response Criticism: From Formalism to Post-Structuralism*, edited by Jane P. Tompkins, 201–32. Baltimore: John Hopkins University Press, 1980.

Trevor-Roper, H. R. "History and Imagination." In *History and Imagination: Essays in Honour of H. R. Trevor-Roper*, edited by Hugh Lloyd-Jones, et al., 356–69. London: Duckworth, 1981.

Trilling, Wolfgang. *The Gospel According to St. Matthew*. Vol. 1, New Testament for Spiritual Reading. London: Burns & Oates, 1969.

Tuckett, Christopher M. *Nag Hammadi and the Gospel Tradition*. Edinburgh: Clark, 1986.

Tupper, Frank. *A Scandalous Providence: The Jesus Story of the Compassion of God*. Macon, GA: Mercer University Press, 1995.

Twain, Mark. *Extracts from Adam's Diary*. New York: Harper & Brothers, 1904.

Twelftree, G. H. "Temptation of Jesus." In *Dictionary of Jesus and the Gospels*, edited by J. B. Green et al., 821–27. Downers Grove, IL: InterVarsity, 1992.

Tynyanov, Yury. "The Literary Fact." In *Modern Genre Theory*, edited by David Duff, 29–49. Harlow, England: Longman, 2000.

Vaganay, Léon. *L'évangile De Pierre*. Paris: Gabalda, 1930.

van Dyke, Henry. *The Story of the Other Wise Man*. London: Harper & Brothers, 1931.

van Henten, Jan Willem. "The First Testing of Jesus: A Rereading of Mark 1:12–13." *New Testament Studies* 45 (1999) 349–66.

Van Wolde, E. "Trendy Intertexutality?" In *Intertextuality in Biblical Writings*, edited by S. Draisma, 43–50. Kampen, Netherlands: FS B. van Iersel, 1989.

Vanhoozer, Kevin J. *The Drama of Doctrine: A Canonical-Linguistic Approach to Christian Theology*. Louisville, KY: Westminster John Knox, 2005.

———. *Is There a Meaning in This Text? The Bible, the Reader, and the Morality of Literary Knowledge*. Grand Rapids, MI: Zondervan, 1998.

Vermès, Géza. *Jesus and the World of Judaism*. Philadelphia: Fortress, 1984.

———. *Jesus the Jew: A Historian's Reading of the Gospels*. Philadelphia: Fortress Press, 1981.

———. *Scripture and Tradition in Judaism*. Leiden, Netherlands: Brill, 1973.

Vidal, Gore. *Live from Golgotha*. London: Abacus, 1993.

Vielhauer, P. "Jewish-Christian Gospels." In *New Testament Apocrypha*, edited by Edgar Hennecke, et al. 117–65. London: SCM, 1973.

Volkova, Elena. "Literature as Icon: Introduction." *Journal of Literature and Theology* 20 (2006) 1–6.

Waldman, Steven. "Beliefwatch: Good Word." *Newsweek*, May 22, 2006. No pages. Online: http://findarticles.com/p/articles/mi_kmnew/is_200605/ai_n16422167/.

Wallace, Lew. *Ben Hur: A Tale of the Christ*. Hertfordshire, England: Wordsworth Classics, 1996.

Wallace, Mark I. "Introduction." In *Figuring the Sacred: Religion, Narrative, and Imagination*, 1–32. Minneapolis: Fortress, 1995.

Walsh, Richard G. *Reading the Gospels in the Dark: Portrayals of Jesus in Film*. Harrisburg, PA: Trinity, 2003.

Wangerin, Walter. *Jesus: A Novel*. Grand Rapids: Zondervan, 2005.

Wardman, A. *Plutarch's Lives*. London: Elk, 1974.

Warnock, Mary. *Imagination*. London: Faber and Faber, 1976.

Waters, Jen. "Leaving the Dark Side." *The Washington Times*, December 5, 2005. No pages. Online: http://washingtontimes.com/culture/20051205–110548-3523r.htm.

Weaver, Dorothy Jean. "Power and Powerlessness: Matthew's Use of Irony in the Portrayal of Political Leaders." In *Treasures New and Old: Contributions to Matthean Studies*, edited by David R. Bauer and Mark A. Powell, 179–96. Atlanta: Scholars, 1996.

Webster, John B., ed. *Eberhard Jüngel: Theological Essays*. Edinburgh: T. & T. Clark, 1989.

Welch, J. W. "Foreward." In *The Man Born To Be King: A Play-Cycle on the Life of our Lord and Saviour Jesus Christ*, edited by Dorothy Sayers. London: Victor Gollancz, 1946.

Wesley, John. "John Wesley's Notes on the Whole Bible." Grand Rapids, MI: Christian Classics Ethereal Library, 2003.

White, Hayden. *The Content of the Form: Narrative Discourse and Historical Representation*. Baltimore: John Hopkins University Press, 1990.

———. *Metahistory: The Historical Imagination in Nineteenth-Century Europe*. Baltimore: John Hopkins University Press, 1973.

———. *Tropics of Discourse*. Baltimore: John Hopkins University Press, 1978.

———. "The Value of Narrativity in the Representation of Reality." *Critical Inquiry* 7 (1980) 5–27.

White, Michael. *Narrative Means to Therapeutic Ends*. New York: Norton, 1990.

Works Consulted

Wiedemann, Lyris. "Review of *O Evangelho Segundo Jesus Cristo.*" *Hispania* 82.1 (1999) 23–35.

Wiedemann, Thomas. *Adults and Children in the Roman Empire.* London: Routledge, 1989.

Wiggins, James B., and Stephen Crites. *Religion as Story.* New York: Harper & Row, 1975.

Williamson, Lamar. "Matthew 4:1–11." *Interpretation* 38 (1984) 51–55.

Wills, Lawrence M. *The Jewish Novel in the Ancient World.* Ithaca, NY: Cornell University Press, 1995.

Wink, Walter. "Matthew 4:1–11." *Interpretation* 37 (1983) 392–97.

Wisse, Frederick. "The Use of Early Christian Literature as Evidence for Inner Diversity and Conflict." In *Nag Hammadi, Gnosticism, and Early Christianity,* edited by Charles W. Hedrick and Jr. Robert Hodgson, 177–92. Peabody, MA: Hendrickson, 1986.

Witherington III, Ben. *The Living Word of God: Rethinking the Theology of the Bible.* Waco, TX: Baylor University Press, 2007.

Wolfgang, Iser. "The Reading Process: A Phenomenological Approach." In *Reader-Response Criticism: From Formalism to Post-Structuralism,* edited by Jane P. Tompkins, 50–69. Baltimore: John Hopkins University Press, 1980.

Wolterstorff, Nicholas. *Art in Action.* Grand Rapids, MI: Eerdmans, 1980.

Wrede, William. *The Messianic Secret.* Translated by J. C. G. Greig. Cambridge, England: James Clarke, 1971.

Wright, N. T. *Jesus and the Victory of God.* Minneapolis: Fortress, 1996.

———. *The New Testament and the People of God.* Minneapolis: Fortress, 1992.

———. *The Original Jesus: The Life and Vision of a Revolutionary.* Grand Rapids, MI: Eerdmans, 1996.

———. *Who Was Jesus.* Grand Rapids, MI: Eerdmans, 1993.

Wright, N. T., and Anne Rice. "N.T. Wright and Anne Rice: Writing Our Way to God." May 14, 2006. Online: http://www.learnoutloud.com/Free-Audio-Video/Education-and-Professional/Writing/Writing-Our-Way-to-God/22047.

Wright, Terence R. *D. H. Lawrence and the Bible.* Cambridge, England: Cambridge University Press, 2000.

Zagorin, Perez. "Historiography and Postmodernism: Reconsiderations." *History and Theory* 29 (1990) 263–74.

Ziolkowski, Theodore. *Fictional Transfigurations of Jesus.* Princeton, NJ: Princeton University Press, 1972.